COMMUNICATIONS
AND
INEQUALITY

For Jen

COMMUNICATIONS
AND
INEQUALITY

PETER GOLDING

S Sage

S Sage

1 Oliver's Yard
55 City Road
London EC1Y 1SP

2455 Teller Road
Thousand Oaks
California 91320

Unit No 323-333, Third Floor, F-Block
International Trade Tower
Nehru Place, New Delhi 110 019

8 Marina View Suite 43-053
Asia Square Tower 1
Singapore 018960

Library of Congress Control Number: 2024944565

British Library Cataloguing in Publication data

A catalogue record for this book is available from the British Library

Editor: Rhoda Toweh
Editorial assistant: Sarah Moorhouse
Production editor: Nicola Marshall
Copyeditor: Ritika Sharma
Indexer: TNQ Tech Pvt. Ltd.
Marketing manager: Susheel Gokarakonda
Cover design: Victoria Bridal
Typeset by: TNQ Tech Pvt. Ltd.

ISBN 978-1-4739-6688-8
ISBN 978-1-4739-6689-5 (pbk)

Contents

List of tables

Acknowledgements

This book has been a long time in gestation. In truth it derives from pretty much all the work I have undertaken over many years in trying to understand the social ramifications of media and communications, and I have no doubt elements of its arguments appear in much I have written in that time. In practice, however, I can trace its roots to the forceful assertions that I ought to write something along these lines in talking with my former colleague Natalie Fenton, and with Mila Steele, then of Sage, at an ICA conference some years ago. It is certainly not their responsibility that so much time has elapsed between those initial conversations and the work's realisation.

My conviction about the links between inequality and communications has been driven from two directions. Many years as a member of the Child Poverty Action Group's Executive Committee, and as an active member of a local Child Poverty Action Group (CPAG) branch, made me very aware of the practicalities and powerful consequences of poverty for people's civic lives as well as for more mundane features of their obstructed search for the basics of food and shelter. The work of Ruth Lister as Director of CPAG and subsequently as a colleague at Loughborough, and of Fran Bennett, Ruth's successor at CPAG, has been invaluable. Academically, I owe a continuing and profound debt to Graham Murdock, whose collegiality I have enjoyed over several decades. Graham and I have frequently written joint articles, and I have no doubt my thinking reflects the rich and perceptive insights he brings to bear on so much of the interests we share. It is no fault of his that our shared work sometimes results in confused identities. More than once we have been muddled for one another at international conferences, and we still treasure receipt of a missive addressed to the 'Golding P. Murdock Research Centre'. More particularly I wish to acknowledge the help and support of John Downey, a former colleague at Loughborough, and of Karen Williamson, former student and colleague at Northumbria University, each of whom was critically involved in work which features centrally in chapter five. I stress they bear no blame for the context and extrapolation of that work in the chapter.

As the book began, painfully and slowly, to be written, I received recurrent and patient encouragement from my editor until very recently at Sage, Michael Ainsley. Michael was endlessly helpful and supportive, and his move very shortly before the book was delivered was, I hope, unrelated to its dilatoriness. Since his departure I have been grateful for the help and support received from Pippa Wills and Rhoda Toweh, and also for final production chaperoning by Vijayakumar and Nicola Marshall.

Most importantly I wish to acknowledge the extraordinary support and encouragement of my wife, Jen. She has read carefully and critically every word, offered innumerable helpful suggestions and amendments, endured indefensible procrastination and made possible what often seemed unlikely. She is, in the fullest sense possible, the book's dedicatee.

Peter Golding

July 2024

Author biography

Peter Golding is an Emeritus Professor at Northumbria University, UK. Until July 2015 he was Pro Vice-Chancellor at Northumbria University, and previously Pro Vice-Chancellor (Research) at Loughborough University, where he was Head of Social Sciences from 1991 to 2006. He is Hon. President of the Media Research Network of the European Sociological Association, editor of the *European Journal of Communication*, and Hon. Sec. of the subject association for the field in the United Kingdom (MeCCSA). He chaired the Research Assessment Exercise for the field in the United Kingdom in 2008 and 2014. He has published widely on media sociology, the political economy of the media and on communications and social policy.

1
Introduction

Many people living in diverse parts of the globe in the twenty-first century must have noticed their world changing in two fundamental respects: communications and inequality. Walk along any street in major urban centres, east or west, and you will be dodging people apparently in deep conversation with invisible friends, or staring at a waist-high held device as though forward motion was impossible without reading instructions from a small portable screen. 'Just Google it' has become, for many, an instant and instinctive response to any uncertainty or question, while postal services everywhere are crumbling, as quaint systems derived from pen, paper, stamp and post give way to electronic mail.

At the same time, the luxurious lifestyles on show in what was once the fanciful but popular world of 'greed and grope' television series have become a reality for a slim sliver of humanity atop, in most countries, an extending stretch from top to bottom of the inequality tables. Behind the complex data of Gini coefficients and income decile bar charts lie extremes of resources and circumstances at top and bottom whose divergence is largely unprecedented.

In the United Kingdom, the number of 'food banks' has massively multiplied in recent years; by 2023, the Trussell Trust, the country's largest provider of such havens of last resort for those desperate enough to obtain a referral to them, was providing over 1,300 such banks, and in six months of 2023 alone distributed 1.3 million emergency food parcels (https://www.trussell-trust.org/). In the same year, NHS figures revealed that more than 800,000 people had been admitted to UK hospitals with malnutrition caused by their inability through poverty to meet the rapidly rising cost of basic foodstuffs (Devlin, 2023). In 2023, figures on rough sleeping showed that the numbers forced onto the street had more than doubled since 2010, following the largest annual increase since 2015. At the same time, the safety net intended to ensure such extremes of poverty were avoided had become tattered and inadequate. A combination of diminishing welfare benefits, administratively complex and often punitive regulations, and benefit rates detached from the evidence of need, had 'become so pervasive that benefits are . . . woefully and systematically short of protecting citizens against hard times' (Hirsch, 2024). Overall, by 2024 in the United Kingdom, 12 million people were in absolute poverty – equivalent to 18% of the population, including 3.6 million children (DWP, 2024).

In almost obscene contrast, sales of luxury cars have soared. Porsche car purchases were at a record high in 2022, while the trade journal in the field recorded that business jets flew 3.3 million flights in 2021, the most ever recorded in a single year, figures driven significantly by activity in north America (Lynch, 2022). At an even more luxurious and sumptuous level, the seas and harbours of the world saw an influx of 'super-yachts', a record 887, nearly 80%

higher than the previous year, being sold in 2021 (Tan, 2022). More routinely, analysis of salaries at the leading UK companies found the ratio of payments to Chief Executive Officers to those of median employees to be 80:1 in 2022; in 2023, the lucky CEO would have to wait no longer than January 3 for their aggregate annual income to exceed that of the median employee (High Pay Centre, 2024).

The data behind and significance of these extremes are examined in Chapter 2. But they are certainly not restricted to the uncomfortably changing circumstances of the United Kingdom. The problem is of course international. US Census Bureau figures show that in 2022 the poorest quintile of Americans shared 2.9% of aggregate income, while the richest quintile got by with 52.7% (and the top 5% with 23.5%) (US Census Bureau, 2023). As an Oxfam briefing paper succinctly, but tellingly, summarised it in 2024, 'Since 2020, the richest five men in the world have doubled their fortunes. During the same period, almost five billion people globally have become poorer' (Oxfam, 2024: 3). The political implications were not lost on international figures, and it was no surprise that the head of the International Monetary Fund, reviewing these trends in a keynote speech at Cambridge University later in the year, concluded that 'We have an obligation to correct what has been most seriously wrong over the last 100 years – the persistence of high economic inequality…economic inequality remains too high, within and between countries' (Georgieva, 2024).

These startling, and manifestly grotesque trends, are but the more dramatic symbols of a structural feature of 'advanced' industrial societies. The processes and social structures behind them are discussed more fully in Chapter 2. Their importance to the theme of this book, however, is that inequality determines the very differentiated capacity both to seek and to obtain the information necessary for active and informed citizenship, while also driving variances in potential and opportunity to formulate and disseminate demands – to exert what is later in the book labelled 'voice' – between different groups and sub-sets of the population. The link between inequality and citizenship via communications is thus pivotal. In a simple diagnosis, communications inequality truncates citizenship. Truncated citizenship dilutes or even invalidates democracy.

The scale and substance of inequality may be alarming and new but are not in themselves unexpected or wholly novel. However, to this unappetising portrayal of life in the 21st century, has been added a new dimension, digital inequity. Inequitable distribution of literacy, closely mirroring that of material resources, is an almost universal feature of the path to modernity in industrial societies. Access to books, newspapers or the capacity to produce and distribute seditious literature or merely encouraging tracts have always paralleled the availability of the means to purchase the goods concerned or to manufacture and disseminate them, as well as (until relatively recently) to buy the education essential for their use. The link between material inequality, citizenship and communications is thus, in this sense, not itself unprecedented – indeed, it is a 'normal' relationship. But the scale and importance of communications goods and forms in the 21st century propels this relationship into increasing prominence. Contrary to the persuasive and widespread mythology that sees 'modern' communication goods and resources as having universalised information availability – the narrative that equates digitisation with a communications cornucopia, or even overload – the rapid rise of communication goods as commercial and expensive technologies enhances and replicates existing inequalities. These goods constitute a sociologically familiar core to patterns of social and economic division in whatever form of capitalist society we are now believed to live in (Golding, 2000).

This all matters because of what has become one of the central and characteristic features of contemporary life, the 'digital divide'. The phrase, whose provenance and meanings are examined in Chapter 2, signals the enduring obstacles that prevent a small but substantial minority of the population from entering the dazzling wonderland of possibilities offered by advances in information technology – obstacles erected by the barriers of economic inequality. That 'the digital divide' is a label that over-simplifies the many reasons for differentiated access to or use of communication services and devices is undeniable. But to argue that disinclination, perverse conservatism, incompetence or ignorance are the principle, or increasingly important, difficulties departs from the unmistakable evidence of enduring and even increasing economic differentiation in explaining the persistence of a digital divide.

The regulatory body in the United Kingdom concerned with this field is Ofcom (the Office of Communications), which monitors people's use and experience of communication services. One such exercise is their regular 'Communications Affordability Tracker', which, as recently as February 2024, found that '8 million households continue to have difficulty in affording communications' (Ofcom, 2024). Moving beyond the organisation's regular concern with disconnections, debt and other points of friction in the communications market, the Tracker finds that 8% of households (nearly 2 million people) in the United Kingdom with fixed broadband find it difficult to afford their service (ibid. and Ofcom, 2021). Having hardware or devices is one step, using them regularly is a further one, but both require expenditure.

The United Kingdom is distinctive but not especially so. In the country many would instantly assume had delivered technological innovation universally to its population, the United States, the persistence of substantial exclusion is readily evident. At the start of 2024, 30% of the US population were not social media users, and nearly 10 million made no use of the internet. Smartphones were common across income levels, but those in households earning $100,000 or more annually were far more likely than those earning less than $30,000 per year to have one; indeed one in five of the latter group did not have one (Gelles-Watnick, 2024). As summarised by the Pew Research Center, 'the digital lives of Americans with lower and higher incomes remain markedly different' (Vogels, 2021). More than 30 years after the arrival of the world wide web into American lives 'About four-in-ten adults with lower incomes do not have home broadband services (43%) or a desktop or laptop computer (41%)'…. while at the same time 'a majority of Americans with lower incomes are not tablet owners. By comparison, each of these technologies is nearly ubiquitous among adults in households earning $100,000 or more a year' (ibid). Similarly, there are large gaps between the lowest- and highest-income Americans in whether they have a broadband subscription. Nearly all (95%) adults with an annual household income of at least $100,000 say they have one. This compares with 57% of adults in households that make less than $30,000 per year (Gelles-Watnick, op.cit.).

The importance of these data and the social circumstances they describe is twofold, firstly, academic, and secondly, and more profoundly, societal. The first argument relates to how we understand and analyse the role and implications of communication technologies and what, in simpler times, were summarily labelled the 'mass media'. The growing tendency within academia for the study of the media as social institutions and of communications as a social process to become ever more specialised and self-contained has, at times, led their investigation and analysis to depart from the contextual understanding of social, economic and political processes. This unintended consequence of the frequent autonomy of these fields of study, reflecting quite properly their importance and growing centrality in scholarship as well as social experience, but detaching their analysis from underlying structural features of society, has often been identified and lamented (Golding & Murdock, 1978; Murdock & Golding, 1991). This book, it is hoped, might contribute to illustrating the difficulties inherent in such undue separation.

Secondly, and more generally, the link between inequality and communications is central to our understanding of the democracies we aspire to live in. A fully functioning and defensible democracy requires its citizens to have some degree of equitable access to the information they need to comprehend and assess the institutions and processes to which they are subject, and with which citizenship obliges involvement. Unequal opportunity or resources to access such information, or to influence it, diminishes democracy. Put simply, democracy needs citizens, citizens need information, and that need is compromised by inequalities. As information and communications goods and services have proliferated and become qualitatively more advanced technologically, inequalities have been replicated and intensified, rather than diminished. The result is an obstruction to what Joseph Trappel describes as 'Access to and participation in the public discourse' (Trappel, 2019: 14).

These arguments are developed in the rest of the book as follows. Chapter 2 sets out the main features of twenty-first-century inequality both within and between societies. The chapter explains the relevance of this to both seeking and disseminating information, in the latter case investigating the rise and importance of public relations and lobbying, and the differential power determined by resource levels. The term 'voice' is introduced and explained to explore the importance of this dimension of communications inequality. The chapter also discusses the concept of the 'digital divide', widely used as a shorthand recognition that new information technologies are unevenly distributed through populations. It challenges the suggestion, however, that this problem is ephemeral or easily eliminated, and shows, using data from the United Kingdom, how ownership and use of new information technologies is significantly and substantially related to basic patterns of material inequality.

Chapter 3 reviews just why this matters in the light of evidence about the insufficiency and even distortions of readily available information, mainly in the news media, about the major processes and circumstances that people expect to learn about from communications media. The lessons of several decades of research into the content and direction of major news media accounts of social process are drawn, underlining the importance of a capacity to seek and use information and ideas beyond those easily and only too readily available.

Chapter 4 addresses the 'myth of the digital solution'. In other words, it examines critically the idea that the rapid growth and extensive availability of new information and communication goods and services have dismantled, or will very soon diminish, the enduring 'digital divide'. On the contrary, the inequitable distribution of such goods and services is replicating and even enhancing existing patterns of inequality. The excessive assumptions of 'cyber-optimism' are examined, and the mixed 'benefits' of digital capitalism are discussed against this background. Chapter 5 explores why it is necessary to have information and communications available, given the limited possibilities of imagining and developing ideas outside those presented and reinforced by existing communications flows. Departing from or challenging existing and dominant orthodoxies is difficult in the face of such constraints, and the chapter shows how potential dissent is managed and marginalised.

The final chapter draws these discussions together, especially around the notion of citizenship. It argues that key concepts like 'the public sphere' and 'hegemony' are enriched by linking them to the matter of communications inequality. The ideal of universal citizenship, the capacity to be engaged, informed and active in thesociety determining one's life chances, is truncated and compromised by communications inequality, and it is clear that well-intended and even effective initiatives to reduce any digital divide will always be limited ultimately by the substantial and insistent boundaries of material mal-distribution. The problem of communications inequality is, at root, the problem of inequality.

2
Inequality and communications

This book is primarily focused on the ways in which people's capacity to be active and participant citizens is increasingly hampered, indeed determined, by patterns of inequality. The information and communications required to perform this role are available in ways that are driven by people's financial resources, and by the contours of power and inequity that shape the society in which they live. In this chapter, the major features of this social topography are outlined to display the extent and nature of the inequalities which govern communications. The concern is primarily with the inequalities within societies. However, we live in a world in which, as Piketty's comprehensive overview of economic trends globally finds, global income inequality is on a scale making richer regions 20 times better off than the poorest (Piketty, 2014: 64). Investment bankers Credit Suisse, who know about such things, report, 'the bottom 50% of adults in the global wealth distribution together accounted for less than 1% of total global wealth at the end of 2020. In contrast, the richest decile (top 10% of adults) owns 82% of global wealth and the top percentile alone has nearly half (45%) of all household asset' (Credit Suisse, 2021: 25). As they point out, the coronavirus disease 2019 (COVID-19) pandemic has had dire effects everywhere, but while the number of millionaires mushroomed, and their extravagant advantages soar away from the pack, the inequalities between nations remain stark and deep. In 2020, total wealth rose by $12.4 trillion(tn) in North America and by $9.2 tn in Europe, while total wealth scarcely changed in Africa, and in India and Latin America, it actually declined (ibid: 8; Capgemini, 2021). It is with the inequalities between nations that we start.

(Some) Nations shall speak unto (some) nations

The BBC's motto, 'Nation shall speak peace unto nation' has a splendid, declamatory ring, and its imagery of a global stream of valued and benign information flows is difficult to resist. The public school headmaster Montague Rendall who, as a BBC governor, suggested it, drew inspiration from the bible and was plainly not thinking of such matters as 'cultural imperialism' in doing so. Throughout the last two centuries, the rapid growth of information traffic around the planet has been a prominent feature of our perception of the development, both socially and technologically, of communications. Yet underneath that comforting narrative has been an insistent reservation that this growth has been grossly unequal, with frequently pernicious consequences. Like so much else, it is a change rooted in and determined by, indeed often a generator of, patterns of global inequality.

The telegraph system of the nineteenth century, the 'Victorian internet', was widely applauded for its capacity to ensure 'All the inhabitants of the earth would be brought into our intellectual neighbourhood' (a dream proclaimed by US educator and soldier Alonzo Jackman, quoted in Standage, 1998: 136). But from the outset, it was both a cause and consequence of the evolution of imperialism. The nineteenth century saw the carve-up of much of the world between the dominant powers of Western Europe and the USA. The fascination with the unprecedented magical potential of the telegraph – its capacity to abolish distance and bring people together – paralleled a growing awareness that the new technology could solve the irritating problems of communication between colonies and imperial control centres. As Tully notes, 'It could take over six months by ship for messages to reach the imperial capital from the colonies. The problem was solved by the invention of the electric telegraph, which could put the least significant British, Belgian, German, or French colonial outpost into almost instantaneous contact with Whitehall, the rue de Brederode, the Reichskolonialamt, or the Quai d'Orsay' (Tully, 2009: 561). For the United Kingdom, the telegraph network and later, wireless, became the 'nervous system of Britain' (Morus, 2001). The tight and unmissable parallels between the geopolitical and administrative lines of imperial control and the spreading telecommunications networks illustrate the centrality of communications to the massive inequities solidified by Victorian imperialism.

Winseck and Pike have examined in great detail how this history evolved, emphasising not so much the links with empire specifically, but with globalisation. 'The growth of a worldwide network of fast cables and telegraph systems, in tandem with developments in railways and steamships, eroded some of the obstacles of geography and made it easier to organise trans-continental business. These networks supported huge flows of capital, technology, people, news and ideas which, in turn, led to a high degree of convergence among markets, merchants and bankers' (Winseck and Pike, 2007: 2). Their research shows the close integration of telegraph expansion with the globalisation of capitalism, rather than solely with the territorial conflicts of imperialist nation-states. But the parallel contours of international communications technology, driven by capitalist expansion as much as nationalist ambition, were deeply and enduringly set.

In the 20th century, the communications inequalities between North and South became steadily more potent, enabling new forms of domination. The new technologies were more likely to increase, not reduce, global inequalities. Gillespie and Robins offer numerous examples, including the EU STAR programme which was intended to help poorer regions but had the opposite effect, with most of the initiatives being driven by the priorities of private investment. As they argue, '[T]he new "electronic highways" of the information society are not, therefore, public thoroughfares but are more akin to a myriad of private roads' (Gillespie and Robins, 1989: 12). In place of the brutal forces of imperial armies or the cruel savageries of slavery, came the 'soft power' of broadcasting, Hollywood, and the international news agencies. Dissatisfaction with this provoked increasing indignation and more from the 'South', voiced most prominently in demands for a 'New World Information and Communication Order' (NWICO). The demands, and the inequalities and forms of domination that lay behind it, were articulated in a report published by

UNESCO in 1980 (MacBride, 1980). The world's superpowers were charged with 'cultural imperialism', imposing their popular culture, political ideologies, language and ways of life on nations previously subject to colonisation and military conquest (Golding and Harris, 1997). Such was the outraged irritation of one or two former colonial masters at these charges that they withdrew from UNESCO, beginning with the United States in 1984, accusing the organisation of corruption and, as then President Ronald Reagan put it, 'endemic hostility towards the institutions of a free society' (Finn, 1986). The USA and the United Kingdom, which withdrew in 1985, were especially vocal about what they regarded as the organisation's dangerous and unwarranted criticisms of the dominant Western-based news agencies, which they castigated as an attack on the free press and as a platform for third world based communists and dictators (see Hamelink, 1997; Roach, 1997).

The disparities behind this dispute remain, and indeed are only too recognisable and familiar, if we leap forward to the digital age. Like transistor radio before it, in its heyday expected to be a 'magic multiplier', the internet and mobile communications have frequently been hailed as the technological facilitators of enhanced equality among the nations of the world. Chapter 4 examines some of the rich mythology that has grown around the role of social media in revolutionary change in some poorer countries, for example. Examining the wealth of a number of countries, indicated by their GDP per capita, compared with the extent in the same countries of ownership of home computers and internet access, reveals a simple but close correlation between the level of wealth and the latter two indicators. To give this claim some precision, calculating the Pearson correlation coefficient between GDP and home computer distribution in a range of countries, using data from various sources, produces a figure of 0.81, and between GDP/capita and internet access it is 0.60 (using 2020 data drawn from IMF *World Economic Outlook* and the ITU Digital Development dashboard).

Having and not having – the basis of communications inequality

The primary focus of this book is on inequality within countries and the importance of this to communications and information. The sheer scale and persistence of material inequalities are well documented, if insufficiently well-known or addressed, and this chapter will not unduly rehearse such readily accessible data. However, three aspects of it are important to note: firstly, the entrenched inequalities of wealth distribution; secondly, the inequitable distribution of incomes, and the consequences of it for spending capacity; and finally, briefly to indicate recent or continuing changes, if any, in such distributions. Most of the illustrative material here is drawn from the United Kingdom, as a representative if sometimes extreme example in recent times among Western industrial nations, of such patterns.

To begin with wealth, wealth has many components, and the wealthy vary greatly in how their privileged affluence is held. Vast estates, sprawling holiday villas in exotic tropical paradises, multi-million pound townhouses, well-stocked savings accounts and a string of expensively fitted out cars in the long drive might be the most obvious signs of prosperity but do not necessarily form its statistical construction. That half of England is owned by fewer than one per cent of the population is the kind of observation that sharply captures the massive and enduring inequalities of contemporary life, though obscuring their more complex and arcane dimensions (Shrubsole, 2019). A careful study for the Institute for Fiscal Studies notes the variety of ways in which wealth is held – business assets, estates, financial portfolios (whose rapid growth has been a major driver of widening wealth inequalities), pension capital and so on (Advani et al., 2021). Existing data, they suggest, probably underestimate the total value of wealth, but demonstrate that, after a period of reducing inequality, recent years have seen a return to growing wealth concentration, both demographically and geographically. The wealthy do not have to do much to ensure their enduring advantages. 'The top three house-hold net wealth deciles held a larger share of wealth in 2016–18 than ten years earlier, and the middle 50% shrank. This has been driven by rising financial wealth relative to property wealth. Importantly, average gains in financial wealth over the past decade are explained more by passive capital gains than by active saving, and wealth gains have accrued mostly to families that already held financial assets' (ibid: 398). Taking a more global view suggested to a group co-ordinating relevant data for the United Nations Development Programme that 'global wealth inequalities are even more pronounced than income inequalities. The poorest half of the global population barely owns any wealth at all, possessing just 2% of the total. In contrast, the richest 10% of the global population own 76% of all wealth' (Chancel et al., 2022: 10). A small part of such inequality of wealth is indicated, as this chapter sets out below, in people's ownership of various communication goods and resources.

Material inequality is also manifest in the wide range of incomes within society, one direct consequence of which is in people's capacity to commit spending to increasingly costly and commercially restricted information. In the United Kingdom, which in recent years has become one of the more unequal societies in the Western world, the income gap between rich and poor has grown substantially in the last decade. The share of total incomes of the richest 1% grew from 7% to 8.3% between 2011 and 2020 (ONS, 2021). As data from the Office for National Statistics illustrate, during the period between 2010 and 2020, income inequality increased by an average of 0.2% points a year to 36.3% as measured by the Gini coefficient (ibid: 3). Measured another way, the ratio of total income received by the richest 20% to that of the rest of the population increased from 5.3 to 6.2 in the same period (ibid: 5). In his review of this stark pattern Dorling begins with the bleak observation that 'Growing income and wealth inequality is recognised as the greatest social threat of our time' (Dorling, 2014: 1). He notes that in 2013, the average salary in the UK was £24,596, but for the top 1% it was 15 times higher (ibid: 6). In the USA, however, he notes that at the same time, the top 1% received almost 20% of all income, a figure last attained the year before the great crash of 1929 (ibid: 10). Taking a wider global perspective, a report from the International Monetary Fund observes that 'widening income inequality is the defining challenge of our time. In advanced economies, the gap between the rich and poor is at its highest level in decades', and that measures of inequality based on Gini coefficients of gross and net incomes have increased substantially since 1990 in most of the developed world (Dabla-Norris et al., 2015: 4, 10). The most recent report from the IMF, mentioned above, shows how these trends have accelerated in the wake of the neo-liberal ideological triumph of the 1980s to the extent that there is, as they put it, a 'dizzying rise in inequality within countries that continues to this day' (Chancel et al., 2022: 3). Put starkly, as a recent summary report from the World Inequality Database puts it, 'the richest 10% of the global population currently takes 52% of global income, whereas the poorest half of the population earns 8.5% of it. On average, an individual from the top 10% of the global income distribution earns €87,200 ($122,100) per year, whereas an individual from the poorest half of the global income distribution makes €2,800 ($3,920) per year' (ibid: 10). Table 2.1 shows the share of incomes received by the top 10% of the population in various countries and regions.

Two social upheavals have accelerated these processes in recent years, the financial crises and subsequent recession of 2008–2009 (and the austerity in public services that followed), and the global pandemic a decade later. By 2015, billionaires in the United Kingdom had seen their net worth more than double after the recession, while average incomes stagnated. The year 2015 'saw the biggest bounce for the UK super-rich in six years, and London [in 2015] has 80 billionaires, up from 72 last year – more than any other world city' (Garside, 2015). By that date, at the other end of the scale, nearly 40% of the UK population was living below the level believed by the wider population to be the minimum necessary for social participation (MacIness et al. 2015). Towards the end of the decade, the richest 1% of the UK population received more income than the bottom 55% combined (Delestre et al., 2022). While some stabilisation occurred in the years after the financial crisis, as data from the USA shows, the crisis entailed a dramatic widening of the market income distribution; market income inequality experienced an increase in the aftermath of the 2007–2008 crisis of approximately 6% between 2007 and 2012 (Almeida, 2015). As the same author comments, 'in 2012 market income inequality was still considerably higher than in 2007' (ibid.).

The second cataclysm was, of course, the coronavirus disease 2019 (COVID-19) pandemic. Despite the colossal volume of deaths and long-term illness the pandemic produced, some were able not merely to escape the most pernicious medical effects, but to come out of it smiling. The Swiss bank UBS's somewhat celebratory account of this perverse outcome is tellingly entitled 'Riding The Storm', and details how billionaires were 'able to decisively pull ahead of the pack as they increased their wealth while others' fell' (UBS, 2020). Rebounds in the stock markets and shrewd investments in desperately needed technological and medical commodities meant that world billionaires saw a rapid increase in their fortunes arising from the pandemic; their aggregate fortunes rising to a record high of $10.2 tn by late 2020 (Neate, 2020).

Table 2.1 Percentage share of income going to richest 10% in various countries and regions (2020)

USA	45
UK	36
China	42
Russia	46
EU	36
Japan	45
L. America	55
Africa	54
S. Africa	66
Middle East	59
World	52

Source: Adapted from World Inequality Database. https://wid.world/data/

It soon became apparent that the pandemic was deepening existing inequalities, not just in health, but in income and wealth. Accelerating existing trends, support from central banks went very disproportionately to the very richest, so that, in 2020, the total wealth of billionaires worldwide estimated by another commentator rose by $5 tn to $13 tn in 12 months, as stock market gains flowed mainly to high-tech companies, and especially to their extremely rich founders and owners (Sharma, 2021). This intensified in the United Kingdom as the 'normal' giant bonuses and extremely high remuneration paid to the hyper-rich in financial sectors returned to pre-pandemic levels. As the Institute for Fiscal Studies reported, in 2019–2022 'earnings growth in finance has dramatically pulled ahead of the rest of the economy. By February 2022, average pay in finance was 31% higher than in December 2019 in cash terms' (Xu, 2022). In the United States, the sheer scale of widening inequalities led a group calling themselves the 'Patriotic Millionaires' to propose wealth taxes, recognising that, despite the implications for their own affluence, the $1.1 tn windfall US billionaires received during the pandemic warranted dramatic intervention (Rushe, 2022). On the other hand, those with worse pre-existing health conditions were more likely to be forced to reduce their working hours or lose their jobs, while their capacity to adapt to online shopping, working from home, accessing leisure facilities or even open space, and so on, were all truncated or non-existent.

The extremes of inequality are startling but represent an indicator of a more extensive inequality of income and wealth right across the population in many countries. These inequalities have consequences, including, as is the focus of this book, for the capacity of citizens to seek and acquire information. Wilkinson and Pickett have painstakingly collated data to demonstrate how 'Inequality seems to make countries socially dysfunctional across a wide range of outcomes' (Wilkinson and Pickett, 2010: 174). Across a whole array of social activities and institutions, the wider the disparity of wealth and incomes in a country the worse their experiences. The link between income inequality and health, or life expectancy, for example, is universal. In the United Kingdom, where the gaps have become larger than in many other wealthy countries in recent years, by 2020. '[f]emale healthy life expectancy at birth in the most deprived areas was 19.3 years fewer than in the least deprived areas in 2018–2020; for males it was 18.6 years fewer' (ONS, 2022). Obesity levels are worse in countries with greater inequality, as are rates of mental ill health, crime rates, educational attainment, violence and even imprisonment (Wilkinson and Pickett, op.cit.: 105, 143, 155, 176). Stiglitz has demonstrated at a macro-economic level how wide ranges of inequality lead to reduced economic efficiency and productivity, wasteful resource use, lower growth, greater instability, and ultimately, in his view, dangerous threats to democratic structures (Stiglitz, 2013: ch. 4). To spell out in detail these links is not the purpose of this book, but the material inequities in which such experiences are rooted are profoundly important for the capacity of people to act as informed citizens, and for their ability to access and respond to information on which that role depends.

One apparent direct consequence of inequality may be in political attitudes and in voting patterns. In work on social and political cleavages, Piketty and colleagues have suggested a simple divide between two sorts of elites in society, the 'Brahmin left', with high education levels but lower incomes, and a 'Merchant right', with high incomes but lower educational levels (Piketty, 2021). The notion has been much criticised, but points up the likely profound consequences for political action and potency determined by income inequality, though much modulated by how such inequalities are understood and explained by those subject to them (see, for example, Therborn, 2021). In other words, material inequality has direct and substantial implications for people's political and social values and attitudes, but these are much influenced by how their circumstances are construed and articulated – a matter of values, ideas and concepts – taking us immediately into questions of ideology and stratified culture. Whether or not the notion of 'false consciousness', that is to say, a construction of the world around you which departs from objective reality, and which might explain the oft-debated apparent enthusiasm among the under-privileged to accept, or even acclaim, the structures, people, political actions or economic initiatives that perpetuate their disadvantage, sufficiently clarifies such apparently perverse docility, the link with communications capacity, and thus to active citizenship, is paramount. To what extent has this changed with the advent of digital technologies into the everyday lives of people in so many societies?

Inequality goes digital

The rapid and accelerating innovations in communications technologies which swept the social landscape of many richer countries in the late twentieth century produced inevitable, and very evident, disparities in social experience across many social divides – age, gender, locality and most especially economic. This was first forcefully acknowledged and described in a series of reports from the US National Telecommunications and Information Administration (NTIA) which used the evocative title of *'Falling Through The Net'*. The first of these was published in 1995, and others followed in quick succession (National Telecommunications and Information Administration, 1995, 1998, 1999, 2000). They cumulatively documented how, in the rapidly and dramatically changing world being sculpted by computers and the internet, the stubborn realities of inequality meant that 'information have-nots living in the economically advanced world are deprived of many of the benefits that cyberspace could offer them' (Warf, 2010: 112–13). The startling transformation in people's daily encounters with the demands of the capitalist order in which they lived was plainly excluding large numbers from the seductive pleasures, increasingly unavoidable routines and innovative potentials of the digital world (Mossberger et al., 2003). The incorporation of the internet into private oversight, hugely advanced in the USA by the 1996 Telecommunications Act, exacerbated this process. An early survey of these trends in the USA documented the great disparities in telephone and computer ownership between different groups socio-economically; generation, urban-rural divides, and ethnicity also all correlated with ownership and use, with the rural poor broadly at the bottom of the digital heap (Brown et al., 1995).

Many governments quickly began to recognise that the wonders of cyberspace were far from universally experienced or accessible among their populations. The 'digital divide' became a focus of policy initiatives in many countries, whether through education, training or even desperate attempts to foster, or engineer through subsidy, the expansion of online activity (Smith, 2002). It rarely worked. Indeed, the desperate urge to get more and more people on board the digital express, meant that dragging the left behind from their exclusion by inter-preting their need as one for training or charitable equipment was questioned sharply by one writer, writing that 'We must wait to see whether "let them have Pentiums" proves more practical than "let them eat cake"' (Attewell, 2001: 257). In these early, cautionary actions the roots of digital inequality in pre-existing economic disparities were very much front and centre of concern. In 1995, just 8% of US households with incomes under $30,000 per annum were online compared with 32% of households with incomes above $75,000. Yet, a decade later, while the poorest income group had increased their presence online by 37%, the increase among the wealthier group was twice as much, 61% (Warf, op.cit.: 118). Paradoxically, the experience of many lower-income groups made them sceptical, or even fearful, of the sup-posedly limitless opportunities being presented on the digital plate. A study of broadband adoption programmes at community-based and public institutions in the United States found that many encountered 'privacy-poor, surveillance-rich' broadband, which provoked myriad anxieties while having few meaningful options to meet their concerns (Gangadharan, 2015).

As time moved on, the digital divide came to be regarded as too crude a description of the very differing use, experiences and benefits of online life for distinct sections of the popula-tion. The demarcations of ethnicity, notably in the USA, and more especially of economic inequality, came to be seen as simply a part and indeed a diminishing feature, of the digital divide. The phrase itself was deemed too simplistic to capture very evident discrepant expe-rience, so that it became commonplace to write of digital divides, in the plural. With increasingly widespread ownership and use, it became a deeply held presumption that the use of computers and online activities were all but universally available so that any apparent gaps in use and enthusiasm could only be explained by wilful abstention (a mythology discussed further in Chapter 4), or by simple incompetence or misplaced wariness.

From this emerged the notion of a second-order digital divide, rooted in the skills (or lack of them) and unduly cautious attitudes of those below the divide (Hargittai, 2002; van Dijk, 2005). Plainly, any residual inequality could only be explained by the characteristics and deficient qualities of the non-users, and policy initiatives could switch to a focus on these difficulties rather than any underlying material inequalities. The problem with this approach lay in three aspects of it. First, the depth of economic divides that was so central to the 'original' digital divide continued significantly to determine patterns of use and ability. This was a simple example in digital form of the 'Matthew effect'. The term had been creatively borrowed from its biblical origins by sociologist Robert Merton, in showing how eminent scientists were given disproportionate credit in cases of collaboration or of independent multiple discoveries (Merton, 1968). As Zillien and Hargittai pointed out, applying this notion when using data from a 2004 survey in the USA, low-income users reaped few benefits compared to more affluent users when encountering the internet, and the benefits of the 'primary' digital divide were reproduced, indeed enhanced, in comparing those either side of the digital divide in its second level (Zillien and Hargittai, 2009). Secondly, the implicit sep-aration of two kinds of divide was unsustainable on closer inspection. In research with low-income US residents, Gonzales suggested that they were faced with a problem of 'tech-nology maintenance' (Gonzales, 2015). Despite near-universal access, her low-income respondents were experiencing unstable access, characterised by frequent periods of disconnection. Being online is in practice a very variable experience, depending on resources to activate and exploit that connectivity. Put simply, lack of material resources 'keep playing their role after a physical connection is acquired' (van Dijk, 2005: 117). Thirdly, newer technologies amplify, rather than eliminate, pre-existing inequalities. In discussing the impact of such arcane delights as the Internet of Things and artificial intelligence, Lutz argues that digital divide analysis should recognise the impact of and integration with existing divides of such innovations and developments (Lutz, 2019).

As Ragnedda has clearly explained, in a valuable overview of the evolution of the 'digital divide', the appearance of a third level was bound to follow (Ragnedda, 2017: 23). This would arise from the advantages accruing from access to and use of the internet. These benefits thus effectively become a form of 'digital capital', reinforcing, enhancing and perpetuating the already existing advantages of those able to be digital citizens, and to all intents and purposes fostering and enabling their assumption of augmented citizenship. Having the skills and opportunities to procure online desired goods and services, not to mention the more mundane but necessary interactions with statutory and regulatory authorities, whether that be in voting, seeking a driving licence or passport, quizzing a political representative, applying for a job, or even surrendering to the inevitable, and buying everyday necessities online (only to discover the most mundane of interactions both requires a password and unleashes a thousand 'personalised' unwanted advertisements), all conflict with the critical and enduring inequities of the 'first level' digital divide. The consequences of the exclusion thus experienced are social psychological as well as material. As Büchi et al. point out, using research data gathered in Switzerland, the experience of falling below the digital divide in this way impacts what they describe as people's sense of well-being, and, in some diffuse way, on their sense of belonging, through the growing role of the internet 'in virtually all domains of everyday life' (Büchi et al., 2018: 3688). In all these various ways, the elemental and enduring roots of the 'first digital divide' determine, and indeed amplify, the accruing advantages enjoyed by those above the line in the 'second' digital divide, and what thereby becomes the 'third' level of digital divide.

The enduring impact of economic inequality on entry to the digital world is illustrated by the data from the United Kingdom in Tables 2.2 and 2.3. The first shows how, even well into the twenty-first century, ownership of the main devices and gadgets endowing access to the magical online world remains unavailable to a significant minority; one in seven households

Table 2.2 Percentage of households with durable goods by income group, UK 2022

	Income group		All
	Top 10%	Poorest 10%	Households
Home computer	99	65	91
Internet connection*	99	83	96
Phone	80	67	79
Mobile	97	86	93

Source: Adapted from Table A46 (ONS, 2022).
*NB figure refers to internet access, not internet use.

Table 2.3 Household expenditure on communications goods and services (UK 2021/22)

| | (£/week) | | As % of all expenditure | | |
	Poorest 10th.	Richest 10th.	Poorest 10th.	Richest 10th.	£/week all
Telephone etc.	4.10	13.70	1.68	1.37	9.70
Internet	0.80	1.10	0.32	0.11	0.80
TV (cable, licences etc.)	3.50	8.50	1.39	0.85	5.80
Newspapers, magazines etc.	1.30	1.50	0.52	0.15	1.40
Totals	£9.70	£24.40	3.85	2.48	17.70
Total Household exp./week	£252.00	£1002.70	n/a	n/a	£528.80

Source: Adapted from Table A6 *Family Spending in the UK: April 2021 to March 2022* (ONS, 2022).

in the poorest decile, for example, having no home internet connection. Interestingly, ownership of a telephone (meaning landline) has declined in recent years among more affluent groups, especially younger households, as they reduce costs without diminishing connectivity through increased use of mobile and smartphones. Once again, the poorest groups are excluded from this enticing option. The importance of these figures is magnified by the widening gaps generally between rich and poor, perhaps especially in the United Kingdom, one of the more unequal of the richer societies, but it is broadly true of most. Such data also disguise the myriad variations in quality of experience behind the simple labels. Ownership of a home computer is very different for someone whose desktop or laptop is fast, gargantuan of memory, jam-packed with the latest software and festooned with dazzling add-ons, compared with a struggling user despairingly making the most of an ageing product, a hapless victim of built-in obsolescence, reduced to cursing unproductively at endless error messages and incomprehensible on-screen obstructions. The frustration of the latter user in finding just how many new items of software and essential appendages, such as printers, are incompatible with their cheaper and swiftly ageing device is unlimited. Equally, having a smartphone is gratifying, but not much use if you can only afford a pay-as-you-go contract and the phone is out of credit.

The second table reveals a pattern familiar to analysts of consumer behaviour in relation to 'essentials' such as clothing, food or fuel, namely that, while the poorest groups spend much less on such goods and services than the better off, that expenditure forms a larger proportion of their 'disposable income'. Table 2.3 shows that the poorest 10th in the distribution of household incomes spend less than a third of the amount spent by the richest decile on the communications services listed in the table, yet it comprises more than half as much again as a percentage of their total expenditure compared to the richer group. If an item of expenditure looms large in a relatively low income, it is inevitably at risk when being considered alongside competing priorities. Thus, what might once have been regarded as essential may well slip into the category of 'nice to have' rather than 'need to have'. Communications goods and services can often sit on the boundary between these categories. As their status as novelties or luxuries increasingly transforms into that of necessities, paradoxically their cost makes them move the other way for those on the lowest incomes.

Two questions arise from the emerging prominence of the digital divide. Firstly, does it create a new form of inequality, comprising a novel calibration of the boundaries and barriers in the social order? Secondly, has it changed, at least in wealthier societies, as access to ownership of new information and communication technologies has become more widespread, even approaching ubiquity? In considering the first question we can see that the inequity apparent in people's use and ownership of these technologies remains driven by the familiar hierarchies of economic inequality. Digital technology changes the character and consequences of social inequality but not its fundamental roots. The technologies and their infrastructures themselves add to the list of needs, indeed increasingly essentials, of modern life, but expand rather than reduce material inequality. In regard to the second question, we must consider the implication of the durability from the earliest times of the cultural capital accruing from access to ICT's (information and communication technologies), including the necessary skills and competences (often arising from ready access and familiarity) to exploit to the full their potential value (see Korupp and Szydlik, 2005; for interesting data from Germany on this). They have, in other words, expanded the many ways in which economic inequality becomes expressed and has an impact in the digital era, but the digital divide does not, in itself, mark a movement from one form of social structural division to another (see also Golding, 2000). Put simply, the lower the income the less the capacity to act fully as a digital citizen, since the means to seek and make use of the information and cultural capital essential for that role are of diminishing availability. This equation of economic capacity with communications consumption at the lower end of the scale is mirrored by its centrality to the production of communications and their dissemination.

Communications inequality and the power of voice

Lack of resources means the capacity to become informed, and to sustain and extend active citizenship as a result, is severely constrained. The more that the information required, indeed necessary, is available through the media, traditional or digital, the more unequal access to these resources has direct implications for active citizenship. The opposite side of this coin is the capacity to be heard, or in a word, 'voice'. Classically in political science, the term 'voice' denotes one of three options open to actors, specifically citizens, in relation to government. In the seminal model developed by Hirschman, if voice is ignored the other options are exit or loyalty (Hirschman, 1970). The term is used here, more simply, to denote the volume and intensity of a given source. Loud voices carry weight, and the ability to be heard bestows enormous power to their owners, while itself resting on wealth and power to nourish such voice power in the first place.

This idea, of course, derives from its roots in Aristotelian political theory and rhetoric (Aristotle, 2016). For a creative and thoughtful development of this notion, see Couldry (2010). I am not concerned here with the distinction made by Aristotle between intelligible 'logos' and the more passive and elemental 'phoné', but the wider sense of these terms, looking at what Rancière describes as a 'distribution of gifts [not aptitudes] of unequal value' (Rancière, 2004: 13). In rhetorical terminology, communication systems allow the amplification of voice, through epimone (persistent repetition) or palilogia (repetition, simply of one term, but here suggesting the use of terms that stick through sheer endless reiteration in public discourse). Political campaigning or simple ideological bluster furnish many examples, from 'scrounger' to 'immigrant' to 'hard working families'. More simply, and cogently, as political theorist Colin Crouch puts it, 'among the many things that the rich can do with their wealth is to control knowledge in order to create climates of opinion favourable to their own interests' (Crouch, 2016: 25). The capture of culture by domination of civic and public voice is at the core of communications inequality, since the amplification and dissemination of information and interpretation, that is of both information and of knowledge, are subject to the resource distribution of communications infrastructure. This section briefly exemplifies these processes at work.

The first aspect of the power of voice to note is the extraordinary growth in recent years of the public relations industry, whose very existence is predicated on the desire to shape public debate and understanding, and whose skills deploy the sophisticated capacity and sheer clout, financial and ideological, to do so. The industry is vast in scale. In the United Kingdom, while the COVID-19 pandemic introduced a blip into the tale of inexorable growth, by 2021 the Director General of the industry's trade association was writing cheerfully that 'salaries are rising again. The industry is confident again' (Ingham, 2021). The report he was celebrating showed that 'despite the disruption of the pandemic, the industry has continued to grow at a steady pace of 6.1% since 2020 and is now worth £16.7 billion (bn). The industry employs 99,900 employees' (PRCA, 2021). Miller and Dinan have charted the growth of this industry from its beginnings, and note that the 'sector seems to have expanded by a factor of 31 between 1979 and 1998' (Miller and Dinan, 2000: 10; see also Miller and Dinan, 2008). They suggest the partnership of this growth in scale with advancing deregulation, neo-liberal ideologies, and, in Britain, the Thatcherite revolution in promoting privatisation and easier movement of capital. The expansion of the industry in the United States has been equally monumental, resulting in eye-watering figures for total spend. Guttman estimates that 'worldwide public relations revenue is projected to grow from $88 bn generated in 2020 to approximately $129 bn by 2025. In the United States, PR agencies generated a revenue of $14.5 bn in 2020, experiencing growth compared to previous years, despite the effects of the coronavirus on the advertising and marketing industry as a whole' (Guttman, 2022), while another estimate suggests that, by 2022, the US industry employed 106,972 people (Ibis World, 2022).

One reason for the growing impact and success of public relations is the shifting balance of power between the sophisticated and energetic 'voicing' undertaken by public relations professionals, and what many regard as the increasing passivity of journalism, reduced over recent years in resources to seek news or investigate received material. In the United Kingdom, there were major reductions in news staffing levels in the years after the millennium, not least in local journalism (Ponsford, 2016). While the total number of people identifying as journalists in various surveys has started to increase again in the last decade, the proportion who are outside London or who are primarily working in desk-based and online journalism has increased (Sharman, 2018). The Cairncross review into the future of journalism, published in 2019, noted that 'the number of full-time frontline journalists in the UK industry has dropped from an estimated 23,000 in 2007 to 17,000 today, and the numbers are still swiftly declining' (Cairncross, 2019: 6). Increasingly, what were previously permanent posts are being replaced by freelancers without access to the full resources of news organisations (Reuters, 2021: 14). The increased volume of PR material has been accompanied by a transformation in its presentation. As one media consultancy noted in advice to their clients, although declining journalists' numbers was not good news for the 'press industry as a whole ...businesses that take the time to create something which can be cut and pasted and immediately work will be rewarded with great coverage' (Full Story Media, 2018).

Summarily expressed, Lloyd and Toogood see these changes as representing a complete reversal in relationships, 'the diminution of public relations' dependence on journalism, and the growth of journalism's dependence on PR' (Lloyd and Toogood, 2015: vii). Crucial to this shift is the strong sense among sources (large corporations especially) of the importance of communications with and via journalism, so that 'many press releases....are now written as news items...such press releases are packaged so that they can be run word for word' (ibid: 31). So endemic has this process become that it has acquired a stark neologism – 'churnalism'. Though sometimes credited to a BBC journalist, the term and the implications of the process were popularised in a book by the British investigative journalist Nick Davies, drawing on research from Cardiff University (Davies, 2008). He defines it as the reduction of journalists to 'passive processors of whatever material comes their way, churning out stories, whether the real event or PR artifice, important or trivial, true or false' (ibid: 59). The process is, he feels, exacerbated by time pressures and by the ready availability of such material online. What is at stake here is more than the effective transmission of advertising and promotional material, however. The shift from active journalism to passive 'churnalism' has been central to the growth in a particular 'voice', or a set of values, ideas and presumptions that mould, or at least frame, a public consensus. The oldest cliché in media research is that the media do not so much shape what people think, as what it is they think about. Thus, a climate of opinion is created in which the most formative and widely accepted ideas are those disseminated by organisations with the loudest 'voice', inevitably correlated with the distribution of deep pockets.

At its most general, this may be seen as the explanation for the widely unquestioned consensus in many Western countries around the economic necessities prescribed by neo-liberal theory. The Australian writer Alex Carey, basing his views on analysis of the USA in the 20th century, suggests emphatically that 'that the people of the US have been subjected to an unparalleled, expensive, 3/4 century long propaganda effort designed to expand corporate rights by undermining democracy and destroying the unions' (Carey, 1996). For Logan, looking more broadly at this history, the rise of public relations in the USA has facilitated a corporate ideology which secures the public sense of the private corporation as a necessary, benevolent and indeed natural institution (Logan, 2014). In examining this notion in the context of British reporting of the financial crises of 2008–2009, Berry argues that focusing on specific and immediate 'effects' misses the larger picture, in which it is through 'the daily repetition of themes and arguments over many years that climates of opinion and ways of seeing are shaped...' (Berry, 2019: 280), in this case to the advantage of the larger organisations in the financial services industries.

Perhaps the most infamous examples of this are in the fields of tobacco and in climate change. In both cases, the media and public opinion have been subjected to intense, colossal and hugely well-funded efforts over many years, to promote a benign view of the effects of tobacco smoking or the impact of fossil fuel extraction and use, on health and indeed human survival, entirely to the benefit of the industries primarily concerned, and against the overwhelming weight of scientific evidence. The tobacco industry and the huge corporations within it have invested vast sums of money, and indeed communications effort, into questioning and opposing the increasing scientific evidence for the association of smoking with ill health, the shortening of life expectancy and fatal disease. The research demonstrating this link had, after all, been established quite firmly in the 1920s, 1930s and 1940s in Germany, in research often unpleasantly linked to the 'degenerative' effects of smoking, and other disturbing aspects of research under the auspices of the Nazis' 'interest' in the scientifically demonstrable links between environment and race (Goldacre, 2009: 235). So, it was no great shock when research establishing the links became more prominent in the 1950s. Nonetheless, it was sufficiently troubling to the industry that their leading figures met and decided to launch a major public relations offensive. In 1999, the United States sued major US tobacco companies for violating the Racketeer Influenced Corrupt Organisation Act (RICO). The suit claimed tobacco companies had violated RICO for decades, by fraudulently misleading American consumers about the risks and dangers of smoking and second-hand smoke. This was reinforced in 2006 when the District Court for the District of Columbia agreed (United States v. Philip Morris USA Inc., et al., Civil Action No. 99-CV-2496 (2017)).

Pressure (powered by enormous levels of funding) grew on the media to present 'both sides of the debate', on scientists to undertake research (generously funded by industry) fuelling scepticism, and on public opinion to keep alive doubts about the soundness and consistency of the evidence for the harmful effects of tobacco consumption. Between 1979 and 1985, one major tobacco company contributed $45million (mn) to scientists to conduct research whose results could be used to defend their product. The relative weight (and consequent 'voice') of such expenditure is illustrated by one example from 1981. In that year the American Cancer Society committed just under $300,000 to research; in the same year, the American tobacco industry granted $6.3 mn (Oreskes and Conway, 2012: 25). As the link between smoking and cancer became increasingly indisputable (though not undisputed), a subsequent 'campaign' arose over the dangers of 'passive' or 'secondary' smoking. Again, vast and expensive efforts were mounted by the industry to promote public scepticism about the pernicious effects of their product. Berridge charts the construction of the concept of 'safe smoking', a fall-back defence given much currency in the United Kingdom, though described by ASH (Action on Smoking and Health, an anti-tobacco campaign group), as comparable in safety to 'jumping from the 36th floor rather than the 39th. floor' (Berridge and Starns, 2005).

One powerful megaphone constructed for the amplification of 'voice' in such areas is the formation of apparently independent and objective organisations to fund research or publish persuasive, if selective, accounts of evidence. These often take the form of research funders or think tanks. Oreskes and Conway, in their tellingly titled book '*Merchants of Doubt*', mention, for example, the Center for Tobacco Research, among others, designed to undertake such work in the United States (op.cit.:139–40). An investigation undertaken by the *Guardian* newspaper in the United Kingdom, published in 2019, suggested that 'at least 106 think tanks in two dozen countries have accepted donations from tobacco companies, argued against tobacco control policies called for by the World Health Organization (WHO), or both...' (Glenza, 2019). The ideological association of dangerous consumption products with freedom of personal choice, or from 'nanny-state' regulation, is a recurrent refrain within such voicing, as in the work of the UK-based FOREST (Freedom Organisation for the Right to Enjoy Smoking Tobacco), founded in 1979, and substantially funded by the tobacco industry (House of Commons, 2000).

This device has been a major feature of the voicing of climate change denial from within the fossil fuel industries over several decades. The dire and potentially existential implications of climate change arising from fossil fuel extraction and use have been known in the scientific community and, significantly, to the oil industry, for many years. In response to the anxieties this fostered the Intergovernmental Panel on Climate Change (IPCC) was established in 1988. The industry was itself a major locus of well-funded and innovative research at a time, in the 1980s, when the overwhelming majority of energy was generated from fossil fuels. As climate change moved up the agenda of public debate, the 'greenhouse effect' was the subject of extensive, authoritative, confirmatory, though confidential research by major oil companies. Their response, through the American Petroleum Institute (API), was the formation in 1989 of a giant consortium of oil companies, the Global Climate Coalition, whose foremost efforts (and colossal resources) were put into insistent and widespread sowing of seeds of doubt, questioning the accuracy and integrity of IPCC reports and of the science behind the growing scientific consensus about climate change, through such methods as planting op-eds, advertisements, press releases, distributing briefing packs, pamphlets and reports, or writing articles in journals and magazines. Much of this was deployed through large public relations companies, notable among them E. Bruce Harrison. As early as 1970 Mobil had been buying space on the op-ed page of the *New York Times*. Between 1975 and 1977 alone, 'Mobil representatives appeared on 365 TV shows, 211 radio shows and gave 80 newspaper interviews' (Brulle et al., 2020: 92). The role of think tanks set up to defend the industry or promote its interests was studied carefully by an American academic group, who focused especially on the production and dissemination of books. This activity was rooted in 'the creation of a sustained anti-environmental counter-movement, institutionalised in a network of influential CTTs [conservative think tanks] funded by wealthy conservative foundations and corporations' (Jacques et al., 2008: 352). These think tanks invested considerable time and money into the production of policy briefs, newspaper columns and so on, but also, and notably, of book-length studies sceptical of environmentalism and the science underpinning it. Of the 141 books the researchers identified as promoting environmental scepticism 130 (92.2%) had a clear link to one or more CTTs, either via author affiliation (62 books) or because the book was published by them, or both (ibid.: 360).

The financial scale and impact of public relations efforts in this powerful example of the relationship between loud voices and deep pockets are daunting. The Chicago-based PR company Edelman, one of the largest PR companies in the world, if not the largest, is reported to have received $359 mn to support climate change denial, including efforts funded by the API to support the creation of a fake grassroots campaign to oppose climate change legislation. 'From 2008 through at least 2011, the firm was paid an average of $68.9 mn a year by the

American Petroleum Institute for advertising that displayed ordinary people...beside a pitch for developing our plentiful domestic energy resources' (Mufson, 2022). Between 2008 and 2017 fossil fuel trade associations spent almost $1.4 bn on PR and related activities, the lion's share of that from the API (Climate Investigation Center, 2018). One study found that in 2015-16 CNN, the major US TV network, 'aired almost five times as much oil industry advertising as climate change-related coverage in the one-week periods following the announcements that 2015 was the hottest year on record and February 2016 was the most abnormally hot month on record' (Media Matters, 2017). Detailed analysis of PR spend suggests that 'beginning in 1997 and continuing through 2004, average annual spending increased markedly to an average of $102 million per year...expenditure averages jumped again between 2008 and 2016, to an average of $217 million per year' (Brulle et al. op.cit.: 93). Brulle's research calculates that the five major oil companies 'spent nearly $3.6 billion in advertising purchases for corporate promotion' from 1986 to the point of publication (ibid: 99). The spend was designed to create, and in many respects effective in fostering, profound doubts about the veracity of climate change science and the real threats of the greenhouse effect. The detail and extent of the research undertaken within the industry, and the extraordinary accuracy of its early forecasts of the dangerous impact of fossil fuel use were subsequently demonstrated through examination of industry internal documentation (Supran et al., 2023).

The construction of widespread doubt about the seriousness of climate change, or its roots in fossil fuel extraction and use, has, in this way, been heavily and effectively fomented by the public relations activities of the large oil corporations. In Egypt in 2022, at the COP27 conference, the annual UN gathering of large numbers of international delegates to address the very obviously growing menace of climate change, no fewer than 636 lobbyists from the oil and gas industries were registered to attend, outnumbering all but one national delegation, that of the United Arab Emirates, hosts of COP28 in 2023. The outcome of the meeting disappointed many climate change activists, who could readily detect the impact of powerful public relations activities by the fossil fuel companies on COP27 decisions. After decades of climate activism, the 2022 conference was opened by the UN Secretary General suggesting starkly that humanity was 'on a highway to climate hell with our foot on the accelerator'. At the same time, the major oil companies were posting unprecedentedly rising profit and dividend levels. By the second quarter of the 21st-century devastating floods in Pakistan, forest fires and hurricanes in the United States, massive melting of polar ice, record temperature highs throughout Europe, droughts, Antarctic heat waves, crop failures and unseasonal freak weather conditions globally, were making it increasingly apparent that the world was reaching, if it had not already passed, irreversible climate catastrophe. Yet in the first quarter of the year of COP27 alone, oil and gas companies made $100 bn in profits. A report published earlier in 2022 suggested that 'the oil and gas industry has delivered $2.8 bn (£2.3 bn) a day in pure profit for the last 50 years...The vast total captured by petrostates and fossil fuel companies since 1970 is $52 tn', leading one commentator to observe that 'these profits have enabled the fossil fuel industry to combat all efforts to switch our energy systems' (Carrington, 2022). The campaigning group Open Secrets, which specialises in monitoring corporate lobbying, produced detailed data in early 2024 showing that oil and gas companies had spent over $35 mn lobbying in the 2024 election cycle year, on target to exceed the $133 mn the previous year, and cumulatively over the period 1998–2024 the energy sector had spent $7,859,088,024 on lobbying. Even this startling figure was dwarfed by the amounts spent by the health industry in the same period – $12,190,924,037 (Open Secret, 2024).

As a New Yorker article succinctly put it, 'if money is the oxygen on which the fire of global warming burns, then PR campaigns and snappy catchphrases are the kindling' (McKibben, 2020). By the time of COP28 the lobbying intensity had grown even further. At least 2,456 fossil fuel lobbyists were granted access to the COP28 climate negotiations (chaired by the president of the UAE national oil company) according to one analysis. Lobbyists for the major oil companies at the meeting outnumbered almost every country delegation and were about seven times larger than the total number of official Indigenous representatives (Lakhani, 2023).

As with tobacco and oil, this also applies to other products. Just one example will suffice, that of children's foods. The marketing and promotion of foods and beverages designed to attract children, regardless of the nutritional effects, is, of course, a big business, and the undoubtedly related consequences of childhood obesity and ill health have become profound (Obesity Health Alliance, 2021). A major multi-national study of this problem concluded that children were exposed to a 'media environment that is saturated by unhealthy choices' (Kelly et al., 2019: 124). Overall, advertising in the hours children would watch TV in the 22 countries studied was four times more likely for foods that should not have been permitted to be advertised to children than those that would. One-third of the food and beverage advertising was from just 10 global companies, with between them a combined market value in 2017 of $994 bn. As the study's authors point out, this rather illustrates what they describe as 'the colossal power of these food and beverage manufacturing and retail industries and their potential to influence country-level government policies' (ibid.: 124).

Public relations is a major vehicle for the use of voice to disseminate images, messages and ideas consonant with the needs of the rich and powerful. It is designed to affect perceptions and public attitudes, sometimes subtly and over time, and therefore to influence both public opinion and political action, not least through the initiatives of policymakers responding to the public mood. The other side of that coin is lobbying, 'the quiet word in the ear'. Not a diverse and highly visible set of actions like advertising or public relations, lobbying nonetheless seeks to affect policy and the climate of authoritative opinion, and to do so needs effective access to decision makers. In this, it is palpably the translation of resources into voice, though in this case the voice is aimed upward as much as down. A loud voice is needed for the quiet word. Large resources are needed for a loud voice, and thus lobbying is another direct consequence and feature of communications inequality. The lunches, texts and phone calls, entertainment, hospitality, persuasive rhetoric over handsome and expensively wined dinners, time-saving and 'helpful' drafting of convenient legislation, all pay dividends – Cave and Rowell cite one US study of a lobbying group that received $1 mn in fees in 2004, while providing assistance worth $1.2 bn to its clients (Cave and Rowell, 2015: 282, fn. 25). The impact of lobbying is, of course, wider than the immediate goals sought by the sectoral interests it seeks to promote. As Parvin argues, lobbying is a means by which substantial power is invested in the hands of those groups able to sustain powerful lobbies, in his view enabling 'norm capture', undermining democracy, promoting the values and needs of the wealthy and powerful, underlining the more pernicious values of free market ideology, and evading the usual constraints of accountability (Parvin, 2022). A report by the WHO in 2024 showed how the commercial power of major companies in areas such as tobacco, alcohol, food, pharmaceuticals and the healthcare industry enables them to influence research and its reception, as well as to dominate consumer attitudes and purchasing choices, in ways that glamourise harmful products, hugely enhance their distribution and consumption, and negatively impact health, particularly non-communicable diseases. Numerous case studies underpin their analysis of lobbying and promotional activities by large companies in these sectors, as well as what they identify as the 'pervasive nature of industry interference in policymaking, which often prioritises commercial interests over public health' (World Health Organization, 2024: xv).

The scale and vast sums of money involved in the lobbying industry are difficult to determine with any certainty. It is, in its nature, and despite attempts to regulate it, a pursuit with ill-defined boundaries and dimensions, a creature of the shadows. In the USA, one estimate suggests that the industry accounted for $3.73 bn in 2021, an increase of nearly 6% over the previous year, and of over 100% since the start of the century (Statista, 2022a, 2022b). These figures are roughly confirmed by Quist and Auble who suggest that 'in the 2019 and 2020 congressional session, interest groups spent $7 billion lobbying the federal government' (Quist and Auble, 2022). Not surprisingly a significant proportion of this spend emanates from a small number of major industrial sectors. The Statista report notes that 'in 2020, the pharmaceutical and health products industry in the United States spent the most on lobbying efforts...' (op.cit). Doering (2021) draws attention to the food and drink lobby among these major actors, while Popiel notes the huge efforts of tech companies devoted to lobbying, which, in their case, he labels a 'proxy for media elite power' (Popiel, 2018: 570). An OECD overview of the lobbying industry concludes that 'well over one-quarter (28%) of total corporate lobbying spending at the federal level in the United States in 2020 was shared among corporate interests in the pharmaceutical, electronics, insurance, real estate, and oil and gas industries, as well as business associations. Among these industries, the top ten spenders account for up to 90% of the total expenditure on lobbying' (OECD, 2021: Fig. 1.1). For a critic like Drutman, the sums required have restricted effective lobbying to only the wealthiest of corporate America, giving it an unparalleled entry to opportunities for influence and persuasion, or in other words, voice (Drutman, 2015).

In the United States, analysis pays much attention to the lobbying that occurs at both federal and state levels, though it is the latter that accounts for the bulk of spending. The efforts required demand significant numbers of people – probably about 12,000 in Washington, or 22 for every member of the House of Representatives and Senate, for example. A particular focus for effort is provided by electoral politics. In the 2015–2016 electoral cycle in the United States, it has been estimated that the finance sector spent $2 bn on lobbying, a substantial rise on the $1.6 bn the sector spent on the 2012 election cycle, which itself had been a record for Wall Street (Bukhari, 2017). In the United Kingdom, the amount of money spent is less daunting, though nonetheless substantial. In 2017 a report in *The Times* suggested that the country's largest companies had committed at least £25 mn in the previous two years to lobbying, though much of that (pre-Brexit) was spent in Brussels. The authors of the study note that hardly any of this money was disclosed in the companies' annual reports (Ralph and Wilson, 2017). What Cave and Rowell label the £200 mn 'commercial influence industry' goes largely undebated; indeed it seeks to be so, making its calibration inevitably uncertain. Despite its relatively small scale by the side of US lobbying spend, the United Kingdom has 'the third-biggest lobbying industry in the world, after Washington and Brussels' and they cite evidence that 'the industry has doubled in size in the last thirty years' (op.cit.: 8). It was, of course, the 'lobby', the entrance hallway of the UK House of Commons, where ministers and politicians could be lapel-grabbed, that gave lobbying its name.

In many countries, the demonstrable link between lobbying and policy development has triggered regulation of the industry. In the UK, the Transparency of Lobbying, Non-Party Campaigning and Trade Union Administration Act was enacted in 2014, which also established an Office of the Registrar of Consultant Lobbyists. A register, owned by the Chartered Institute of Public Relations, was set up the following year, but, as the Institute's own website acknowledges, 'those required to register constituted a small proportion of the UK's lobbying industry. This results in the public unable to access meaningful and accurate information about lobbying [sic]. The CIPR has long taken the view that existing lobbying' legislation regarding the register is not fit for purpose and needs changing. Relevant legislation is widely regarded as loose and ineffectual. One organisation observing the field concluded that 'the UK public is largely left in the dark about who is trying to influence public-policy decisions that affect their everyday lives' (Transparency International, 2015). An OECD cross-national investigation of lobbying concluded that, although, 'in 2020, 23 of the 41 countries analysed provided some level of transparency over lobbying activities…Only a minority of countries globally have addressed lobbying risks in their governance arrangements through transparency and integrity frameworks' (OECD, op.cit: section 2).

In the USA, the 1995 Lobbying Disclosure Act, amended in subsequent years, requires Washington lobbyists to register with the House of Representatives. Here, too, many loopholes enable lobbying vastly to exceed its publicly regulated visibility. For example, an exemption to registration is afforded to lobbyists able to demonstrate they act for no single client more than twenty per cent of the time, a not unduly demanding condition for a competently creative lobbyist. In the United Kingdom, while lobbyists working for private sector consultancy firms are required to register, the very much larger number working in-house for large corporations are exempt. The surfacing of notorious instances, such as when former Prime Minister David Cameron was found to have been texting government ministers on behalf of a financial firm, Greensill, that employed him, almost certainly masks a much larger and endemic flow of communications from lobbyists to policymakers.

One key vehicle enabling this flow to succeed is the so-called 'revolving door'. This is, in the context of the argument provided here, the word made flesh. Communications are made effective by the voice carrying them operating at both ends of the communication process, or in more traditional language, as both source and receiver. In the United Kingdom, investigative journalist Peter Geoghegan calculated that 'A fifth of the new Conservative candidates elected in 2019 had previously worked as lobbyists…In 2018 alone, more than 200 former ministers and senior civil servants took up roles advising and lobbying for different businesses' (Geoghegan, 2020: 179–80). In the USA, the practice is so extensive it has provoked the formation of a research project, the Revolving Door Project, operating under the auspices of the Center for Economic and Policy Research, a left-leaning Washington-based think tank, devoted to this specific activity. Their sectoral analysis details the personnel bases of the practice, concluding, in the case of the major technology companies for example, that 'Big Tech's significant hiring spree of Obama-era officials – both to company jobs and a constellation of influence-peddling semi-independent organisations – leaves Big Tech with well-connected allies ready to coerce old friends and colleagues as necessary' (Moran and Litwak, 2021).

Indirect lobbying, using the media – traditional or 'social' – can be powerful and effective. Sometimes termed 'journo-lobbying', this approach has drawn particular attention because of the use of social media in this way, and as the OECD report on lobbying makes clear, it also highlights the link between lobbying and the ownership and control of the media, and the 'importance of increasing transparency of media ownership as an essential precondition for media pluralism, but also to enable the public to evaluate the information and opinions that are disseminated by the media' (OECD, op.cit.: ch. 2). Indeed, the ownership of the media is a central and salient element of the link between material resources and 'voice' central to this chapter. In crude, but essentially accurate, terms, 'who pays the piper calls the tune'. This hugely over-simplified characterisation of the media, or indeed any social institution, nonetheless captures the essence of one of the central debates in media sociology of the past century (see, *inter alia,* Murdock and Golding, 1974; 1978; Golding and Murdock, 2023).

In the United Kingdom, the first Royal Commission on the press after the Second World War displayed surprising equanimity about the evidence of increased concentration of newspaper ownership. It concluded that 'the present degree of concentration of ownership in the newspaper Press as a whole...is not so great as to prejudice the free expression of opinion or the accurate presentation of news...' (Royal Commission on the Press, 1949: para 672). That sanguine summary has not, however, been the prevailing conclusion since that time, which leans to the view, captured in Kipling's famous phrase (later borrowed by Stanley Baldwin) that the UK media exemplify 'power without responsibility', a phrase borrowed for the title of what has become a much re-published and authoritative account (Curran and Seaton, 1981: now in its 8th edition, 2018). That power is exercised by remarkably few. Newspaper circulations have plummeted in recent years as people have turned to alternative sources, or indeed none at all. The circulation of the major daily newspaper titles in the United Kingdom is shown in Table 2.4. Of the total figure of roughly 3.5 million, roughly 85% is controlled by just three corporations – The Daily Mail and General Trust (*Daily Mail*), News UK (*Times* and *Sun*) and Reach (*Mirror, Express, Star*). In 2020, these three corporations accounted for 71% of the market share by revenue (Media Reform Coalition, 2021: Table 3). The same corporations control about 90% of the national Sunday newspaper circulations.

Local newspapers display a similar picture of corporate and concentrated ownership. In 2021, three corporations owned about 62% of titles. Reach plc., which was known as Trinity Mirror between 1999 and 2018, reflecting its lineage, owns 115 regional or local newspapers in the United Kingdom, in a field that has an increasing number of what is termed 'news deserts' – areas not served by any local paper or where the disappearance of titles under the pressure of competition has reduced local rivalry to local monopoly.

Table 2.4 UK national newspaper circulations in year when last reported publicly

Title	Average circulation per issue (Dec 2019)	As % of total
The Sun	1,215,852	27.8
The Times	370,005	8.5
Daily Telegraph	317,817	7.3
The Guardian	133,412	3.1
Daily Express	295,079	6.8
Daily Mail	1,141,178	26.1
Daily Mirror	451,386	10.3
Daily Star	282,723	6.4
Financial Times	162,429	3.7

Source: www.abc.org.uk

Broadcasting in the United Kingdom poses a more complicated picture, as the very notion of broadcasting, and its consumption, change rapidly with the emergence of a variety of means of accessing and listening to, or viewing, what once would have been described as broadcasts. The BBC remains the dominant source of material viewed, and the ITV network with the BBC has over 50% of audience share for terrestrial television. Major new content providers increasingly feature in this landscape, usually from major international corporations such as Netflix, Disney and Sky.

The massive move towards the use of 'social media' is often regarded as having dissolved any concern about the oligopolistic power exercised by dominant communication organisations. The now somewhat passé terminology of 'mass communication' described a system of few producers and many consumers, and the somewhat derogatory label of 'legacy media', originally intended for largely obsolete forms like floppy disks or VHS cassettes (a term derived from 'video home system'), is commonly applied to things like national newspapers and broadcast radio and television as these are increasingly marginalised by newer forms. The label 'social media', though somewhat dubious, as all media are in some sense social, nonetheless implies a model of the many communicating freely with the many, overturning, it is sometimes suggested, the inherent power of corporate media owners. The use of Facebook, Twitter, Instagram, TikTok and so on as primary news sources has undoubtedly soared in recent years. In 2022, the annual survey by the UK regulator, Ofcom, found that, especially among younger age groups, 'Instagram, TikTok and YouTube are now their top three most used sources for news' (Jigsaw Research, 2022: 6). However, this is substantially compromised culturally by looking more closely at the nature of these 'news' sources. For example, on Twitter two-thirds of its news comes from news organisations; on Facebook, while the BBC remains a primary source, nearly a third of people who use Facebook as a news source do so by accessing the *Daily Mail* or *The Sun* (ibid.: 48).

Many of the dominant media corporations remain under the guidance, or tight control, of extremely wealthy proprietors. In the United Kingdom, the major newspapers are still commonly the property of expatriate billionaires, in a country in which, between 1990 and 2022 'overall wealth controlled by billionaires has risen from £53.9 bn to over £653.1 bn' (Equality Trust, 2022), while, in the same period, the number of billionaires increased from

15 to 177. Viscount Rothermere, a direct descendant of the founder, CEO and chair of the Daily Mail and General Trust, is one of several such men who use their 'non-dom' tax status (he lives in France) to shore up their wealth. Rupert Murdoch, Australian-born but a US citizen, is the archetype of the billionaire media proprietor, with the *Times* and *Sun* in the UK, the *Wall Street Journal* and *New York Post* in the US, and, until recently, through his News Corp and Twenty-First Century Fox, innumerable other media, among vast numbers of titles within his corporate empire. Murdoch has never been coy about his political preferences and ideals, and few would regard them as particularly progressive or egalitarian (see Murdock et al. 2025).

In the United States, national news broadcasting is dominated by 'the big three' – ABC (the American Broadcasting Company), NBC (National Broadcasting Company) and CBS (Columbia Broadcasting System). In recent years, the total dominance of these three has declined, but they remain major players, and their absorption into multi-media conglomerates has enhanced the common assessment that the US media system is largely in the control of five, perhaps six, corporations. ABC is part of the Walt Disney group, which also owns ESPN and is now merged with Warner Brothers under the Discovery umbrella. NBC is part of the Comcast corporate empire, which embraces the DreamWorks film studios and owns the Sky Group, while CBS sits alongside other parts of the Viacom corporation, which owns Paramount Pictures, now Paramount Global, in turn, all part of the corporate structure that is National Amusements.

Newspapers in the USA are mainly city or state-based, though several 'national' newspapers are familiar internationally, including three published in New York (*Wall Street Journal* and *New York Post*, both owned by Rupert Murdoch's News Corp (which also owns the book publisher Harper Collins and Dow Jones) and the *New York Times,* and the DC-based *Washington Post* (owned by Nash Holdings, the company controlled by Amazon boss Jeff Bezos). A handful of major publishers control large numbers of the local newspapers. The Gannett Company runs several dozen such titles, though it has suffered significant financial problems in recent times, resulting in closures and journalist lay-offs. The McClatchy Company has about 30 titles, and a similar number is controlled by Hearst Communications, which also has interests in many other sectors, including magazines, books, and broadcasting (it is part owner of the Disney-controlled ESPN network and has about 30 local television stations).

As in the United Kingdom, atop this map of corporate power are a number of extremely wealthy individuals or families. The communications, media, and increasingly the IT sectors, in the USA as elsewhere, are typically dominated by some of the wealthiest individuals on the planet. Jeff Bezos, owner of the online sales and media group Amazon (and, since 2013, the *Washington Post*), has largely topped the rich list in recent years, while Google's Larry Page and Sergey Brin are fixtures in the top ten (Dolan and Peterson-Withorn, 2022). Rupert Murdoch inevitably features prominently as the owner of newspaper and other media interests on three continents, and with personal wealth placing him comfortably among the richest men in the world. Michael Bloomberg, a former mayor of New York, is probably even wealthier and is CEO of the media and communications giant bearing his name. Shari Redstone is chair of Paramount Global (formerly ViacomCBS) and president of National Amusements; she and her family are majority owners of CBS, Paramount Pictures, and much else. Donald Newhouse heads a corporation owning dozens of US magazines and newspapers as well as a cable company with a controlling stake in Discovery Communications. The list goes on, but most of the major newspapers and communications organisations in the USA are, indeed, owned by billionaires (Lamare, 2017).

The European Union has been frequently and outspokenly concerned about the concentration of media ownership, not unrelated to its unease about the growing presence and ambition of US-based corporations in European cultural space. In 2018, a major report from the EU addressed this, and, linking these concerns to questions of freedom of expression, democracy, journalistic autonomy and citizen rights, suggested that 'the concentration of power of media conglomerates, platform operators and internet intermediaries, and media control by economic corporations and political actors risk causing negative consequences for the pluralism of public debate and access to information and having an impact on the freedom, integrity, quality and editorial independence of journalism and broadcast media' (European Parliament, 2018: para S). A subsequent report by a research group concluded that there was a continuing failure in many European countries to make ownership of media transparent, and a 'failure to protect newsrooms against the influence of owners/managers/advertisers' (Euromedia Research Group, 2022).

The prominence of vast corporate monoliths in the communications universe, not uncommonly, as we have seen, led by high-profile and extravagantly rich entrepreneurs, should not, of course, lead to a simplistic picture of a handful of 'great men' with the communications channels at their beck and call. The problem with the 'great man' theory of history is that there is an awful lot of history and not enough great men (and they usually are men) to explain it. The political economy approach to communications and media has spent much time and effort explaining the far from simple links between ownership and control, recognising that setting a framework is more common than direct intervention (Murdock and Golding, 1991). Media that are themselves significant players in the economic marketplace are unlikely to more than occasionally voice hesitancy or even hostility to the rules and procedures that protect the interests of those best served by that market. James Curran helpfully sets out the many ways in which, what he terms the 'liberal tradition' casts doubt on the more worrying implications of demonstrable concentration of media ownership (Curran, 2002: 130–2). Nonetheless, as he points out, the trend toward increasing concentration, and indeed in some sectors monopoly, 'weakens the assumption of public control through market competition' (op.cit.: 130).

Patterns of ownership and control then, that is the broader political economy of the communications media, are an intrinsic, indeed powerfully determinant, factor in the inequitable distribution of 'voice'. The needs, views, and perspectives of the rich and powerful inevitably frame the driving ideologies of the organisations they own and lead. This is not simplistically to equate ownership with control but to recognise the prevailing limits of fully diverse expression likely to emerge from the media systems predominantly encountered in daily life. The emergence of 'social media' has, it is clear, not fundamentally changed the contours and dynamics of communications inequality.

In this chapter, the international and intra-national scale of wealth and income inequality has been shown to determine directly people's capacity to become informed and to access the means to communicate and obtain information. The digital divide, far from being overcome by the rapid emergence of new 'social media', has in fact extended inequities in this field, and data from the United Kingdom illustrates the extent to which lower-income groups spend a higher proportion of their disposable income, but a lower absolute amount, on communications goods and resources. The other side of the coin, the capacity to produce and disseminate communications, dubbed here 'voice', has become increasingly shaped by the vast growth of the public relations industry, and by the lobbying and policy-shaping that powerful voices, not least in contentious areas of conflict between public need and private interest, are able to affect. Such powerful voices, in the major areas of communications and media, increasingly originate in huge and concentrated corporations, not infrequently run by billionaire individuals. They are the very essence of communications inequality.

3
A partial view of the world

It is the central contention of this book that inequality constrains the capacity of people to seek and obtain the information they need to be active citizens. This need is itself enlarged by the deficiencies in the routine diet of news and information that people receive in their everyday lives, whether they swiftly scan the headlines in a freesheet picked up on a train, diligently read with rapt attention the news available in their daily newspaper, or watch the news bulletins while waiting eagerly for the reality TV show or US crime import to follow.

Characteristically, media studies scholarship succumbs to periodic episodes of self-flagellation, conceding a great deal of the obloquy to which it is regularly subjected, and agonising over its 'failures' to accrue large amounts of certainty and knowledge. Journals offer special issues on 'whither' the field is going (it was in 1983 that the major American *Journal of Communication* published a widely discussed special 'Ferment in the Field' issue), and a guilty sense of uneven and insufficient cumulative analysis pervades the field. Nonetheless, we now have, after many decades of research and discussion, a substantial body of work that attests to the imperfections, to put it mildly, of the news about major social issues and institutions, readily available to citizens through leading news outlets. This is not just a problem of partisanship, but of systematic trends in emphasis, selectivity, framing and focus, that render the availability of common knowledge through the media about the world around them problematic for citizen-users.

The purpose of this chapter is to review what we know about such flows, using mainly UK research, leavened with occasional allusions to research from elsewhere. In doing so, it will review the nature of the information about and characterisation of major institutional areas which are routinely made available to people. It cannot review all such areas, and in that sense is not a 'long march' through the institutions. However, it does seek to summarise the available research on most of the areas which would form the basis for people's judgements and consideration in their role as citizens of the world being surveyed.

The political world

Surveillance of the polity in which the citizen lives, enabling considered and informed deliberation from which rational action, demands and reactions can be derived, is a primary task the media claim to fulfil, both news media and more generally. The notion of the media as a 'fourth estate', as watchdogs on behalf of the citizenry, both holding the powerful to account and shedding light into the murkier corners of power, is a central and prevailing myth for producers and audiences alike. Yet research has consistently and repeatedly demonstrated the restricted, partisan or partial flow of information about policy and politics provided by most media in most countries to most people. I cannot here review all of this material, but it is often displayed most evidently in studies of communication during election campaigns, which are prone to attract both intensified political coverage and extensive research.

Five features of such research illustrate the general point. First, the range of issues brought to the attention of voters is usually limited and dominated by the top few (e.g. Deacon et al., 2001). In the 2015, UK General Election issues such as foreign policy, transport, public services, crime, health and the environment each received less than 1% of news coverage in both television and press (Loughborough Centre for Research in Media and Culture, 2015: Table 3.1). In the 2024 election campaign, the Loughborough studies show that none of education, Brexit, defence, law and order, employment, foreign policy, housing or social security received as much as 5% of coverage in five weeks of the campaign (Loughborough Centre for Research in Media and Culture, 2024). Research consistently shows a focus on very few issues while many others are either reduced in scope or completely absent. While elections crystallise such a focus, and it could be said (and often is) that the media can only report what political parties choose to air, coverage between elections, in 'normal times' displays a similar circumscribed range (see Negrine, 2016).

A comparably limited range of issues was found to be reported in the 2016 EU referendum in the United Kingdom, which resulted in a vote for 'Brexit' (Jackson et al., 2016). A common complaint during and after the referendum was that people felt uninformed about the EU in general and about the implications of remaining or leaving in particular. Attempts to seek 'balance' during the referendum campaign led to particular problems for the BBC, which, in seeking to sustain balance between 'remainers' and 'leavers' found itself giving copious air time to these two positions as articulated from within the Conservative Party, by Members of Parliament and campaigners, while the Labour Party and its leaders all but disappeared from view (Gaber, 2016). News about the issues involved inevitably became coloured by the partisanship of the media reporting them. As Barnett summarises it, 'most of our national press engaged in little more than a catalogue of distortions, half-truths and outright lies: a ferocious propaganda campaign in which facts and sober analysis were sacrificed to the ideologically driven objectives of editors and their proprietors' (Barnett, 2016: 47).

Recurrent surveys by the EU and others have discovered a widespread sense of ignorance about the EU, especially in the United Kingdom. Past Eurobarometer surveys have found near-zero knowledge and understanding of the functioning of the EU and that the institutional workings of the Union and how decisions are taken are matters of nearly complete ignorance. In attempting to answer three relatively simple queries about the EU only 28% of respondents in the United Kingdom could offer correct answers in 2015, the lowest figure for any country other than Latvia (European Commission, 2016: 131).

Referendums ought, in theory, to allow a simple and effective provision of information to people who are being required to make a fairly straight yes/no choice about propositions put to them. Similar to the EU referendum was the Scottish referendum of 2014, inviting Scottish voters to say whether their country should or should not become independent of the United Kingdom. Yet, even here, the shaping and limitations of news coverage left those who were able to vote far from fully informed about the possible consequences of their doing so (Blain and Hutchinson, 2016).

Second, research has demonstrated a reduced attention span within, especially, broadcast coverage of electoral issues, in what is sometimes termed a drift towards a 'sound-bite' format for political quotes or material generally (Hallin, 1992). Subsequent studies, both in the United States and elsewhere, have documented the diminishing time or space devoted to interviews, descriptions of policy initiatives, and so on, as election coverage has steadily restricted the length and space of individual items. A third feature is what has been termed the 'horse-race' preoccupation of political communication, especially in elections, when the latest polling results and the performance of political parties and actors as they near the electoral finishing line outweigh what many would consider the more substantive aspects of the messages and issues at the heart of the political debate. This was a matter of considerable comment in the earliest analyses of electoral reporting, for example in the United States (Graber, 1976), and has remained a feature universally. Sometimes interpreted as a fascination within the media for their own role in the political process, a recent example in the United Kingdom was observed in the 2015 general election, in which coverage of the electoral process itself far outweighed any other issue reported (Loughborough Centre for Research in Media and Culture, op.cit).

Fourth, and most obviously, at least in newspaper coverage of politics, is the partisanship displayed by news media. Broadcasting, and especially public service broadcasting, is often regulated by strict requirements ensuring at least superficial, and often carefully calibrated, impartiality as to time and space devoted to participating parties. Newspapers are rarely governed by such restraints, leading to the type of concern expressed by the Second Royal Commission on the Press, which suggested in 1962 that while 'there is still a considerable range of choice in the national daily and Sunday press…it is less than it was in 1949 and it would be better if there were more' (Royal Commission, 1962: 18). In the 2015 UK general election, the Loughborough study cited found more or less 'stop-watch parity' in broadcast coverage, but a very wide dominance in pro-Conservative coverage in the press. Finally, consistently demonstrated by research on media coverage of politics, is what has been termed 'personalisation', that is to say, a palpably greater interest in the personalities and people in the political game than the policies, processes, and institutions behind them (on this process in Italy and France see Campus, 2010). Many would argue that this process reached a zenith in the election of a former reality television presenter to the Presidency of the United States in 2016, and again in 2024.

One consequence of such restricted flows of political information may be citizen disengagement, itself a complex phenomenon beyond the scope of this chapter. The Hansard Society run an annual survey on this, a recent version of which notes that prior to the 2016 UK EU referendum only 38% felt knowledgeable about the EU, and although in 2015, a general election year, as in previous election years, interest in and claimed knowledge of politics peaked, even in such a year it was little above half the population who claimed to be so interested or informed, and in most years it has been rather below half (Hansard Society, 2016: 20, 36). By and large voter turn-out both in national and EU elections has steadily declined in recent years (to a near-record low in the United Kingdom 2024 general election of just 60%, or 52% of the adult population, the lowest since 2001), for which, of course, there are many and varied explanations and causes.

The economy

A major example of the limitations of mainstream media provision arises from accumulated evidence about the presentation of the economy and economic issues. As John Corner has perceptively pointed out, news seeks to be narrative as much as expositional, and in this area particularly, what he terms the 'narrative/expositional tension' may often 'let the "poetic" dimension of news obscure the extent of its "referential" obligations' (Corner, 1998: 54–5). In other words, in seeking to keep interest alive much of the basic explanation of what is going on in 'the economy' may be lost. I cannot here attempt to summarise this extensive and complex field. However, three aspects of economic news are salient; its dependence on a restricted range of authoritative commentators, its much-discussed failure to explain or predict such monumental events as the 2008–2009 financial crash, and its apparent adherence to a consensual, and often neo-liberal set of assumptions about the economy.

Like environmental news, financial and economic news has relatively recent origins as a specialist area in mainstream media, although the business and financial press has much longer roots in many countries, meeting the needs and interests of an ever-rising commercial and mercantile class. Most TV bulletins now would see the need to solemnly announce the latest fate of national stock market indicators, or exchange rates, in much the same way they might ritualistically impart the weather news, though with only the most limited explanation or purchase on audience comprehension. Where economic news is provided more analytically, it commonly deploys the help of 'expert' commentators to assist the reader or viewer. Research has frequently shown the quite limited range of 'accredited witnesses', to use Stuart Hall's phrase, who provide this commentary. Never in any way labelled as *parti-pris*, City financial elites or international bank economists provide the required explanation, and act as arbiters as to whether an event should be construed as 'good' or 'bad'. Indeed their views, or the reaction of some apparently impersonal entity, such as 'the markets', are themselves often the substance of the story (see, for example, Deacon et al., 2005).

Economic and financial journalism is often regarded as having failed to predict, or indeed explain, the financial crash of 2008/2009, though this might perhaps be regarded as a stern demand. It was the Queen of England who famously, if mischievously, asked economists (at a seminar at the London School of Economics) why they had failed to see the credit crunch coming (she had, after all, probably seen about £25 mn disappear from her own personal fortune). If news aspires to provide explanation, full description and thus the means of understanding the economic environment, then analysis of its coverage of the most dramatic events of recent Western economic history has been harsh in its judgement. In studies of both BBC and press, Berry demonstrates that coverage was dominated by elites, unchallenging of their orthodoxies, and unquestioningly accepting austerity as the solution (Berry, 2016a, 2016b). The presumption of austerity as the 'normal' solution framed coverage of government economic policy (Kay and Salter, 2014), and in general journalism failed to provide the public with either a warning or explanation (a judgement of the US media provided extensively, if harshly, by Starkman, for whom the public was 'left in the dark about and powerless against complex problems that overtake important national institutions' (2015: 1).

For Knowles et al., in a comparative study, these failings were but a stark example of a more general deficiency, reflecting reporting of earlier events such as the recession of the late 1990s and the dot com boom in 2000. They claim that their interviews and empirical evidence indicate 'a decline in mainstream financial journalism standards since the 1980s, as the media have faced increasing institutional, ideological and industrial pressures' (Knowles et al., 2015; more generally see Schiffrin, 2015). All these analyses, and others, see economic news as provided by media locked into a neo-liberal consensus as to financial and economic processes and solutions. Not least this leads to almost complete failure to report much of the economic environment, including the failings and misdeeds of the corporate sector (Doyle, 2006). In part, this arises from the demarcation of economic and financial news into separate, and indeed specialist sections – *Money Mail,* the *Financial Times,* Bloomberg Television, Fox Business Network and so on – which has evolved continuously.

In a comprehensive study of how the British media presented the financial crisis of 2008 onward, and more generally the financial world in which this crisis originated, Mike Berry showed how, despite some variation in coverage, there was a uniform acceptance that bank bail-outs were the solution, while any larger picture of the role of the finance sector in the UK economy was very rare (Berry, 2018). His study embraces content analysis, audience research and interviews with journalists, and concludes that the unprecedented scale and significance of the crisis explained a lot of the coverage and the insufficient audience communication that resulted. The inappropriateness of anything other than private sector bank ownership, and the necessity of austerity as a policy solution, were consensual and unquestioned. Newspaper readers, using newspapers driven by ideology and politics, 'were provided with incorrect information on the UK's public finances as well as misleading international and historical comparisons' (Berry, op.cit.: xx).

Poverty and inequality

One area of the economic environment whose media coverage has attracted much attention is that of inequality itself, or more especially news about poverty and the poor. Castigating the poor, and implicitly underwriting a distinction between the 'deserving' and 'undeserving' poor, has long historical roots culturally, and is given rhetorical emphasis in media portrayals (Golding and Middleton, 1982; Bullock et al., 2001). Research has replicated this finding in Ireland (Devereux, 1998), Canada (Redden, 2014) and more widely (Lugo-Ocando, 2014). Bringing research in the UK up-to-date Morrison has shown how the deep roots of this distinction in UK poverty policy have persisted in the most recent rhetoric, where it has surfaced as the distinction between 'shirkers' and 'workers' (Morrison, 2018).

In research undertaken at the height of the 'scroungerphobia' excesses of the late 1970s, we found widespread belief that welfare benefits were too generous and too easy to get, even fraudulently. Roughly four in five of the respondents to the research survey thought too many people were dependent on benefits, and just under a third thought people who claim social security should feel guilty about 'living off tax-payers' charity' (Golding and Middleton, 1982: ch. 6). The popular media portrayals that formed the basis for much of this punitive belief system were palpable. The life of 'welfare claimants' was one of unearned luxury and habitual petty criminality. Of all lead stories in the press examined as part of this study's content analysis no less than 21% dealt with 'abuse', and the figure rose to 31% of all news stories about social security – over a third of which were front page news (ibid. ch. 5). The apparently eternal cultural need to separate 'gods poor and the devil's' continued to shape popular attitudes, but more importantly media portrayals of the fate and circumstances of society's most impoverished. The moral reaction and righteous indignation aroused among the nearly poor by such constructions have been constants in this area of policy news.

While in recent years there have been occasional signs of a less severe popular perception of the poor, the range of the 'undeserving' has increasingly embraced more groups, including those with disabilities (see below). Political rhetoric has amply reinforced these views. The then United Kingdom Chancellor, George Osborne, asserted in 2010, in commenting on one of his first budgets, that the 'lifestyle choice' as he put it, of those on unemployment benefit 'is going to come to an end', adding by way of justification the rhetorical question: 'Where is the fairness, we ask, for the shift worker, leaving home in the dark hours of early morning, who looks up at the closed blinds of their next door neighbour sleeping off a life of benefits?'

To the historically rooted and pernicious mix of stereotypes and inaccuracies perpetuated about poverty and welfare in the media, television has in recent years added the potent format of what is sometimes known by the po-faced term of 'factual welfare television' or perhaps more generally as 'poverty porn'. Neither term does justice to the inherent bear-baiting ridicule inherent in the programmes' presentation of poverty, linking cheap production costs, voyeurism, and poverty stereotypes in an unholy but highly successful mix. A five-part series called *Benefits Street*, hosted shows such as *Tricia* or *Jeremy Kyle*, Channel 5's *In Benefits and Proud*, the BBC's *We All Pay Your Benefits*, and their like have all been hugely successful. *Benefits Street* gave Channel 4 the highest viewing figures it had had for years, and its progenitors, Love Productions, attracted the attention of Rupert Murdoch's News International who took a 70% stake in the company. The format had international appeal: Keo Films who made a series called *Skint*, franchised the format to Australia as *Struggle Street* (on these series generally see Paterson et al., 2016; De Benedictis et al., 2017). As an eviction officer was shown telling a tenant in a Channel 5 episode of *Can't Pay, We'll Take It Away*, 'say whatever you like, just give it some wellie, it makes good television'.

As noted earlier, misleading and malignant stereotypes are of course far from unique to the UK media. A study of news photos in five US news magazines between 1993 and 1998 was found to show black women with numerous children and the non-working poor over-represented (Clawson and Trice, 2000). A study of the *New York Times* and *Washington Post*, from 1994 to 1996, looked at 319 articles and found that welfare recipients were overwhelmingly shown negatively – as lazy or feckless. Over 55% of people in the stories had three or more children. As the author concludes: 'The poor are often a lightning rod in our society, shrouded in myths and the symbolism of the "other", often blamed for their poverty in language that implicates their very morality' (Lens, 2002: 13). Many similar studies, from many countries tell a similar story. One comparative study of United Kingdom and Scandinavian newspapers finds the UK press more severe than others but also notes the considerably more 'liberal' tone of Danish and Swedish papers is not immune to 'moral panics' (Larsen and Dejgaard, 2013).

Alongside the miseries, ineptitude and calculating delinquency of the poor, the daily lives and doings of the rich and super-rich receive little exposure. Research into people's perceptions of inequality tends to suggest their perceptions are shaped by a relatively restricted purview of social structure, limited to those around them, and that this leaves most people believing they themselves are rather 'middling'. Penetrating this by qualitative research, Irwin has suggested it probably understates people's capacity to adopt moral positions in relation to inequality, as well as their sophisticated understanding of the role of agency in changing social position. Nonetheless, her research makes no mention of the indirect (mediated) source of images about inequality and suggests by default the continuing importance of these in relation to direct experience (see Irwin, 2018). Other than in the fantasy world of greed and grope familiar from past TV successes like *Dallas* and *Dynasty,* or their more recent successors, the daily lives of those in oak-panelled boardrooms or in the luxurious hideaways of tax havens or gated cities are seldom exposed to widespread gaze. The result is that the sheer scale of economic inequality is both hidden and unexplained if the major source for its understanding is the mainstream media. While wealth appears glamorous, exceptional and related to innate allure and style, poverty is inextricably linked to feckless inadequacy, casual criminality, and the blinkered generosity of a lax and bloated welfare system.

Social policy: health and education

Vaccination against measles, mumps, and rubella (MMR vaccine), all highly infectious diseases, was introduced for very young children in the United Kingdom in 1988. In the ensuing years these conditions, despite very occasional outbreaks, became rare. A research paper published in 1988, in the highly respected *Lancet* journal of medical research, suggested that the vaccination could lead to autism and to colitis. The paper was subsequently found to be fraudulent. It had been written by a doctor who, many years later, was found guilty by the General Medical Council of dishonesty and irresponsibility (he was, among other things, receiving funding from legal firms seeking to pursue vaccine damage cases), and struck off their list. The disgraced doctor concerned seemed to have eventually converted his notoriety into some form of celebrity success when he surfaced years later in the United States as a popular supporter of campaigns against the big drug companies and as a consort of a famous Australian supermodel. His 1988 paper received very widespread news coverage at the time, and vaccination rates plummeted. Headlines such as in the *Daily Express* (February 5, 2008), 'Parent' Anger Over New 'Evidence' That The MMR Jab Is Safe', fuelled parental unease about the vaccine (see, inter alia, Boyce, 2007). Worryingly this media-fuelled myth returned with a vengeance over a quarter of a century later. As rates of infant vaccination slumped again, a number of surveys found widespread distrust of their efficacy, notably in Europe. The director of one of the surveys identified 'social media' as an 'amplifier of doubt', and suggested that medical staff could not counteract the diffusion of disinformation, in commenting on findings that, as childhood rates of measles surged, a global survey showed that only 59% of people in Western Europe believed vaccines to be effective (Wellcome Foundation, 2019).

Incomplete or misleading coverage of medical initiatives is not uncommon, even if the MMR case was an exceptionally dramatic example. News is somewhat inevitably enthralled by 'breakthroughs' to the point where oscillation between the euphoria of a discovered cure for some major disease one week and its rejection the next is common-place. Some commentators have characterised this as the 'medicalisation' of health in the media. Reviewing the US media coverage of health, Signorelli highlights the focus on the glamour of miracle drugs or high-tech machinery, with very little attention to the social and economic contexts of ill health and disease (Signorelli, 1993). The curious invulner-ability of so many of the fictional characters portrayed in the media to ill health, or indeed any minor blemishes, is complemented by an insistent picture that stresses the culpability of individuals rather than their economic circumstances, environment or industry for any ill health they endure. Examining US media coverage of obesity (tending towards epidemic proportions in some richer countries), Kim and Willis, writing in 2007, concluded that 'over the last 10 years, mentions of personal causes and solutions significantly have out-numbered societal attributions of responsibility...Findings also indicate that television news is more likely than newspapers to mention personal solutions, but less likely to attribute the responsibility to society' (Kim and Willis, 2007).

A study by the King's Fund in the United Kingdom examined media coverage of health and illness in 2001. It found that coverage emphasised health services rather than health as such. Using a slightly ghoulish 'deaths per story' measure, it found that '8,571 people died from smoking for each smoking story in the news. It took only 0.33 deaths from vCJD (a brain disease associated with eating beef from cattle with BSE) to merit a story. Both the BBC's news programmes and the newspapers' news pages showed strong contrasts between the frequency of news stories on a particular topic and the mortality risk associated with that condition. The number of reports on relatively small or unproven risks such as BSE and MMR vastly out-weighed reports on such major killers as obesity and mental health problems' (Harrabin et al., 2003: 14). More generally Seale, in a review of all media portrayals of health, both fictional and non-fiction, concluded that acute illness is overrepresented in relation to chronic illness and that the health issues present in media coverage were, as he puts it in a slightly under-stated summary, 'different' from those experienced' by the populations of the countries he examined (Seale, 2002: 48). Occupational health is almost invisible, as is the widening 'health gap' between the better off and the rest, while the role of industry is barely reported (Berridge and Starns, 2005).

It is important to include here two aspects of health whose coverage in the media has large implications for public knowledge and for policy, namely mental health and disability. On the first, as Philo summarised it in reviewing a number of studies collated for a 1996 publication, 'the key issue here is the gap between this experience [of serious mental distress] and the manner in which mental illness is so often portrayed in media accounts' (Philo, 1996: 212). Writing some years later, and covering a wider canvas, Michael Birch arrived at similar conclusions, stressing the worrying implications for both those who suffer mental distress and those seeking to offer them help and support (Birch, 2012).

Mental illness is most likely to make news when associated with crime of some sort. Looking at a 20-year period (1995–2014) of US news about mental health, McGinty and colleagues found that compared to news stories in the first decade of the study period, those in the second decade were more likely to mention mass shootings by people with mental illnesses. The most frequently mentioned topic across the study period was violence (55% overall). Fewer news stories, only 14%, described successful treatment for or recovery from mental illness (McGinty et al., 2016). Simon Cross has brought this into sharp focus in the United Kingdom, noting the frequent association, particularly by the UK tabloid press, of mental illness with criminality. His study notes the prominence of the mentally distressed among reports of criminal offence, and the simplistic combination of 'mad and bad' in tabloid reporting (Cross, 2014).

News coverage of people with disabilities is equally deficient. A study of the UK media found that there had been a growing anti-disability rhetoric between 2004 and 2011, especially in aligning the disabled with 'scroungerphobia'. The topic was far from hidden; there had been a 43% increase in articles where disability was mentioned. But much of this was due to the repeated association, again notably in the tabloid press, of receipt of sickness and invalidity welfare benefits with what the papers characterised as 'soft touch Britain' (Briant et al., 2013). In the view of the *Sun* newspaper: '...countless thousands are having a laugh at the expense of *Sun* readers and others who do get out of bed, turn up for work and pay taxes to fund the £12.5 bn. bill for their feckless lifestyles' (op.cit: 883). Between 2010 and 2014, the authors found that fraud steadily increased as a central theme in tabloid coverage. In summary, they suggest that 'this framing has seen the emergence of disabled people, or at least those claiming benefits, as a new "folk devil"'(op.cit. 881). A study by the charity Disability Rights UK found that disabled people increasingly feel the press is discriminating and contributing to disability hate crimes and abuse. In a survey among people with disabilities, they found that over three quarters (77%) of respondents cited negative press articles about disabled people; only a third (35%) named a positive story (Disability Rights UK, 2012).

The association of mental distress with crime, and of disability with fecklessness, suggests that in neither case is the health dimension of principle concern in coverage. Yet, as we have seen, in the wider field of health and medicine it would be hard to suggest that readers and viewers are provided with an adequate diet of information and analysis to fuel an informed judgement about this major area of public policy.

Beyond health and medicine lies a whole array of activities and institutions which we might regard as the province of 'science and technology'. It is an unhelpful cliché to point to the increasing prominence of technology in all our lives, but it is nonetheless of major importance that its underlying institutional imperatives and activities are open to public scrutiny. To assess how far this is resourced sufficiently by the media would be an extensive task, and is not attempted here. One of the most scathing critics of such material, Ben Goldacre, has summed up his own review of such work in the title of his book, *Bad Science* (2008). In his view, supported largely by his own focus on coverage of health and medicine, 'The greatest problem of all is dumbing down. Everything in the media is robbed of scientific meat, in a desperate bid to seduce an imaginary mass who aren't interested' (Goldacre, 2008: 338). He concludes that the media have failed science, and indeed the public, massively. The media imagery of the scientist as either unworldly boffin or white-coated genius is difficult to escape, from Disneyfied stereotype to summary news item.

A striking example, rather away from Goldacre's primary fields of concern, is that of genetically modified crops. The use of plants whose DNA had been 'engineered' to increase yield or improve their nutritional value, increased enormously in the second half of the twentieth century. The debate about their huge contribution to yield increases, herbicide tolerance, and so on, and the relative benefits of such matters when considered against their safety, environmental impact, or actual potential for farming and consumption, especially in poorer countries, became widely apparent in much public (though not mass mediated) material. Whatever the rights and wrongs of this debate (and they are complex and not judged here), analysis of mass media coverage shows a substantial leaning in one direction, fuelled by considerable melodramatic excess.

In a study of UK media, it was found that presentation was organised around a constructed debate contrasting the good sense of the public to resist GM crops with the determined insistence of an intransigent government to introduce them (Agoustinos et al., 2010). This study notes the widespread use of the evocative term 'Frankenstein crops/foods' in popular newspaper coverage of the topic, typified by a *Daily Mail* headline (10 March 2004) 'Frankenstein Food: You'll Be Made to Like It'. As Hammond has shown, the Frankenstein myth is commonly deployed in popular discussions of the risks and threats of scientific and technological development, hinting at the inevitable dangers stirred by 'playing God' (Hammond, 2004). Morse studied global newspaper coverage of the issue between 2006 and 2013. He finds a slight increase in positive coverage in this period (Morse, 2016). Petersen, however, studying media coverage of biotechnology issues more generally, including GM crops, but also cloning, stem cell research and other matters, found them almost entirely constructed for public consumption through metaphor (Petersen, 2005).

Most of us go to school, an increasing proportion of us go through further or higher education, and many of us have children who go to school. Finding out how these institutions are run and the policies that drive their development might seem like a primary need for the informed citizen. Educational expenditure is a far from minor feature of most industrial societies' budgets. The National Center for Education Statistics suggests that in 2014 spending among OECD countries on education was typically about 5% of the total, though the UK, Denmark, New Zealand, Korea and the USA all spent above this figure (National Center for Education Statistics, 2018). Yet education is a very minor topic of news or press concern. Studies of the most recent UK election campaigns, for example, found that in 2015 education in all its aspects provided the substance for just 1.3% of coverage, and while it rose in subsequent elections it was still only 2% of the total in 2024 (Loughborough Centre for Research in Media and Culture, 2024). For Malcolm Dean, for many years, a leader writer for the *Guardian* newspaper, and a doyen of UK journalists writing about social policy matters, the sheer lack of education correspondents and the consequent lack of knowledge among journalists about what went on in the world of education, came as a shock when he came back to the United Kingdom after two years in the USA (Dean, 2012: 98).

Even when it does attract attention coverage can be less than exhaustive. One of the most controversial and contested developments in UK education in recent decades was the establishment of 'grant maintained' or 'opted out' schools – terms applied to schools that were able and encouraged to detach from local authority (local government) control after 1988. While the issue was aired considerably in a few 'quality' newspapers, the research concluded that coverage was characterised by a 'discourse of omission' as much as, if not more than by a 'discourse of derision'. In other words, while a lot of the relevant educational research was dismissed or derided, more was simply ignored (Pettigrew and MacLure, 1997). The education establishment has often felt obliged to seek to hit back at the dismissal of its concerns by media and political leaders alike.

Alongside this neglect is research that suggests teachers, though rarely, or only occasionally, represented, are much maligned or misrepresented. In a study of teachers' press images in the United Kingdom in the second half of the twentieth century, Cunningham notes the insistent presence of 'attacks from the political right and their development in the media' (Cunningham, 1992: 55). Yet he notes, as do others, the continuing regard for teachers in popular opinion despite such disparagement of them, and perhaps especially of their union representatives. The latter is highlighted in much US research. For example, a study by Goldstein of media coverage of teachers' unions suggests that the notion of teachers' unions as 'bullies' 'reflects much of the discourse revealed in data analysis' (Goldstein, 2011: 556). A British study by Warburton and Saunders of press cartoons in the UK suggests they play on a number of images that they serve to cement, including that there are two types of teacher, 'traditional' and 'progressive', and that teachers' own standards are poor, or that parents are 'worried sick', and so on (Warburton and Saunders, 1996: 320). It is not surprising that Dean quotes David Bell, a former head of the national schools' inspection service Ofsted, who. in commenting on a welcome increase in specialist correspondents, suggests they could counter the 'fact-free and prejudice-rich who witness the casual slandering of state education that permeates our newspapers' (Dean, op.cit.: 373–4).

The environment

Climate change and the environment, are of a different order to some of the other areas of public life considered here. While the occasional subject of 'event' stories, notable in exceptional natural events (volcano eruptions, violent storms, tornadoes and forest fires), the palpable and increasingly (though not universally) accepted importance of climate change is a challenge for the media in many ways. It is not surprising that the issue was barely evident in media output in earlier decades, although the 'anthropogenic' character of climate change, that is its causation by human activity, has been known, or at least discussed, for some considerable time. Occasional news about reports by international bodies, or the latest meteorological data showing yet another improbably hot year, or even dramatic films of forest fires across the globe or unlikely and disastrous flooding, are all important bases for news stories, but amount to a good deal less than the informed citizen might wish or need to know about such an important and increasingly apocalyptic subject.

In past times, few media would have had 'environment' correspondents or have thought about it as a news category. Despite spikes of concern in the 1960s, not least prompted by the publication of Rachel Carson's *Silent Spring* in 1962 (see Kroll, 2001), most such posts were created in the 1980s, though often lapsed again a decade later as the subject declined in political prominence (Hansen, 2010: 76–9). The cyclical rise and fall of coverage of the environment, or more particularly climate change, has often been charted (for a useful summary see Boykoff, 2011: 20–28). The issue rose significantly in press and TV reporting in the late 1980s, not least through the prism of prominent personalities or political announcements. The emergence of climate change denial, and promotional lobbying designed to question the scientific evidence, followed swiftly in the 1990s, prompting what was to become one of the primal dilemmas of news reporting in this area. In seeking 'balance' between two apparently contradictory views – that climate change was indeed 'anthropogenic', or that it was not, or even that its very existence was dubious, invited many media to see these two positions as requiring balanced presentation by offering equal prominence to each. Such slavish adherence to one of the apparently basic requirements of journalism, in practice, gave the overwhelmingly consensual scientific view of the seriousness and human origins of climate change no greater prominence than the very much smaller and sectional, if vociferous, denial of such concerns. For the citizen seeking clarification, active pursuit of information and evidence became essential if not to be becalmed by this apparently reassuring balance (Boykoff, ibid.: 124 et. seq.).

The whole debate about climate change and its impact or causes is, of course, problematic for news media to convey. Journalists working in this field are often unusually committed and engaged with their topic, but, perhaps for that very reason, wrestle with the means to inject it into mainstream coverage. As Gibson et al. have noted, this may explain why public engagement with the issue, at least in the United States, has lagged somewhat, as specialist correspondents have sought to develop strategies to convert events, concerns, and warnings into the stuff of news stories (Gibson et al., 2016). Research into coverage in *The New York Times* and *The Washington Post* from 1980 to 1995 suggested that an early, almost apocalyptic concern with global warming, needs to be considered within a narrative growing over time and that the outcome of the 'master story' of global climate change may have discouraged later attention to global warming (McComas and Shanahan, 1999).

It was not until 2011 that the British Social Attitudes Survey, run annually since 1983, included a question about belief in climate change. This was not least because numerous earlier surveys had suggested that public concern about the environmental impact of climate change had fallen to historically low levels. By the time of the 2011 survey, however, 76% of respondents agreed that climate change was indeed happening and that human activity is, at least in part, responsible.

The complexity of the arguments also makes this an area of media output unusually dependent on material from sources. These could include scientific 'experts' in an age when expertise and its spokespersons are increasingly suspect, or the less overt but certainly powerful sources in the nuclear, fossil fuel, or oil industries.

It is not surprising then that 'The environment, more than many issues, brings to the surface some of the most persistent anxieties surrounding news media practices…' (Lester, 2010: 59).

News is about events, not process, yet climate change is very much the latter. One US study published in 2010 found that the US media were continuing to suggest climate change problems were exaggerated. Their findings suggested that in providing, where they did, 'both sides' of the climate change debate, one potential such 'side' – suggesting in line with increasing evidence that climate change was becoming even more hazardous and widespread than hitherto feared – was largely ignored in the US media (Freudenburg and Muselli, 2010).

The requirement of 'balance' seems otiose when the scientific consensus is overwhelmingly behind one position, so that 'balancing' it with the contrary view gives the reader/viewer an inevitably misleading sense of the relative weight of explanations on offer. The concerned citizen, anxious to explore what has become one of the most profound, some would argue the fundamental, issues of our age, would certainly need to be an active seeker for information and analysis to get to grips with the topic in any sustained manner.

Crime

Being made aware of transgressions of social norms and laws is plainly a civic need as well as a long-established staple of both news and fiction. The 'penny dreadfuls' of Victoriana and the gothic high drama of the contemporary police television series have formed a major part of media provision and audience diet. But if imagery, narrative and reporting of crime are plentiful, the sum picture of the world of crime, the penal system and policing is far from a complete or sufficient provision in this central area of public policy. Crime is probably the best example of one of the two paradoxes of news, in that its most dramatic or extreme instances receive prominent coverage, inevitably creating an exaggerated impression of their frequency. In general, news reports the unusual, but in so doing recurrently contributes to a culture that is likely to overstate the prevalence of such events (see Golding and Elliott, 1979). The example considered above, the environment and culture change, exemplifies the other paradox, that news reports events rather than processes.

Research into crime news is voluminous, and I do not here propose to review or summarise all this literature. But three characteristics illustrate its departures from any full account of criminality or criminal justice: the rate of crime events, the nature of crimes committed and the perpetrators of crime. One of the more creative theoretical advances in analysing crime coverage was the development of the notion of the 'moral panic', initially in Cohen's study of riots in England in the 1960s and 1970s, described in his analysis of their news coverage and the emergence into common usage of 'mods' and rockers' to describe the antagonists (Cohen, 1972). Schematically, a moral panic is created when the reporting of a series of acts by a minority increases the apparent frequency and significance of the action so as to give it a threatening prominence that changes perceptions and public concern. This is achieved by a 'deviancy amplification spiral' (Wilkins, 1964) which increasingly labels and characterises the 'crime' and its perpetrators, and in so doing foments a culture of both fear and recognition of the newly labelled problem. In different periods young people generally, women, social security claimants, single mothers, black youth, immigrants and others have all been so labelled and the central figures in such 'moral panics'. Drawing, not least, on the common penchant in journalism, perhaps especially in the popular press, for the implicit or explicit expression of moral outrage, such cycles serve to reinforce and to mobilise the moral boundaries of cultural conventions.

Crime news has repeatedly been shown to overstate the volume and frequency of crime. Of course, this immediately prompts the question 'compared to what', quite properly to recognise that 'official' statistics are themselves a social construct, attracting as much quizzical comment as news coverage. Yet, as Carter Wood notes, in a compendious review of relevant accounts, 'crime news has consistently offered a distorted view of crime, with the greatest attention being given to those crimes that least frequently appear in official statistics' (2016: 301). Combining human interest with dramatic appeal, crimes fulfil many of the most important requirements of a medium straddling information and entertainment. Taking the long view of this, Rowbotham and her colleagues, having analysed news content in the UK local and national press over more than a century, conclude that the urge to entertain and thrill with such news has left the United Kingdom the 'most ill-informed society (in terms of its comprehension of laws) in modern history' (Rowbotham et al., 2013: 6). It would be difficult, however, to be sanguine about this problem elsewhere, research generally having discovered very similar trends in many other countries.

A second feature of crime reporting is its emphasis on violent crime, which is repeatedly shown to be significantly over-reported compared to property crime or other forms of non-violent criminality, such as fraud (Dailey and Wenger, 2016). More emphatically, Lin and Phillips (2014), restricting themselves to coverage in the US of capital crimes, sum up the coverage as presenting 'a distorted reality in which brutal crimes tend to be committed by minority offenders against vulnerable, worthy victims'. In the cliché long associated with newsroom decision making, 'if it bleeds it leads'. While far from adequate as a summary of the sociology of journalistic practice the phrase simply, if crudely, identifies a primary news value. This is not only a feature of news media of course. In analysis of crime films over time Allen and colleagues have shown that films released between 1945 and 1991 demonstrate a steady increase in the violence of the crimes portrayed (Allen et al., 1998). One consequence, much investigated, of such portrayals and reporting is the emergence of 'fear of crime', often disproportionate, indeed even contrary to, the likelihood of victimhood among the groups most prone to such fears (see Jewkes, 2015, chapter 6 for a useful overview). The relationship between media presentation of crime and fear of crime is obviously a complex one. But as Dowler concludes, in a review of this complexity in the context of the USA, 'there is an overemphasis on crimes of violence...murder and robbery dominate while property crimes are rarely presented' (2003: 121), and while the direct effect of this on fear of crime is uncertain and unproven, it is an undoubted factor.

Thirdly, it is important, as the summary by Lin and Phillips (op.cit.) suggests, to note the demography of the perpetrators of crime portrayed in the media. It is a not uncommon conclusion, notable in the USA, to write of the 'racialisation' of crime, and Mancini and colleagues (2015) suggest 'media accounts and policy discourse have presented Blacks and criminality as virtually synonymous...'. They note that the direct impact of such 'stereotyping' is substantially mitigated by direct experience and contact between Blacks and whites, a finding fairly generalisable about much media coverage.

The media portrayal of crime is, of course, about much more than crime news, and includes the portrayal of the various stages of the criminal justice system. Police (along with private detectives) have been staple and central figures of drama for centuries, and remain among the most popular fulcrums around which fiction is formulated in most media. Their efficiency at solving crime is inevitably higher in such fiction than in 'real life' – unresolved conundrums are an unlikely basis for satisfying drama – one among many features separating the fictional from the 'real' (Rhineberger-Dunn et al., 2016, see also Leishman and Mason, 2003). At the end of the judicial process is sentencing, and much research has suggested uneven coverage has a detectable effect on public views and attitudes about sentencing. Hough and Roberts argue that 'the news media rarely makes any attempt to explain the judicial reasoning underlying the decision, or to place the sentence imposed in some statistical context' (1999: 23), and from their survey conclude that, as a result of press reporting, people believe sentencing is softer than it really is and if asked to suggest a sentence actually propose one similar to or even softer than that actually given.

There now exist enormous quantities of research and debate about the nature and consequences of crime portrayals in the media. The point here is to underline its departure from any comprehensive or even account which would enable the citizen to deduce well-founded and informed conclusions about the infringement of society's legal and moral boundaries and the consequences and causes of it.

As these examples suggest, in all such areas of reportage the trend towards the fusion of entertainment and information, much analysed in research into 'tabloidisation' is not new. The first Royal Commission on the Press in the UK recognised that the commercial success of a popular title necessarily depends 'on something other than the authoritative discussion of public affairs; they depend on the power to interest and entertain a wide variety of readers whose concern with politics is limited and intermittent' (Royal Commission, 1949: 41). Not surprisingly the Commission concluded, perhaps coyly, that 'we have found some evidence of willingness to be satisfied with what at best corresponds only roughly to the truth...' (ibid.: 150). The broad conclusion from such research is well summarised by McQuail, who suggests that 'the net effect on the news of the factors outlined risks transforming "reality" into a new form (often called "infotainment") that is not primarily designed to meet the informational needs of audience or society' (McQuail, 2013: 115).

More than this, however, it is difficult not to conclude from any such survey of the nature of information available to citizens about any of the areas of public life on which they might wish or need to deliberate, that their life is seriously under-resourced by the provision of the mainstream media on which people by and large depend. To act as an informed citizen necessitates the capacity and means actively to seek information well beyond that routinely provided by the news media on which most people directly or indirectly depend. How far this is equitably possible is the subject of this book.

4

The myth of the digital solution

In a prolonged diatribe against the evils of the Communist menace behind the iron curtain, former US President Reagan assured a London audience in 1989 that 'the Goliath of totalitarianism will be brought down by the David of the microchip' (Rule, 1989). Reagan's characteristically home-spun saw provided, as ever, the kind of cowboy aphorism that was at the heart of much of his thinking about the rise of digital technology. Amidst the dizzying advances changing all our lives in the late twentieth century, the rapid expansion of digital communications loomed largest. For many other seers, too, it seemed that a whole new way of life, even a different kind of society, was incipient, prompting everything from lofty analyses of the rise of the 'digital age', to everyday preening by 'early adopters' annoying friends with tales of incomprehensible new online adventures and equally mysterious neologisms and acronyms that were soon to become all too familiar.

It was the age of cyber-optimism; the belief that the onset and rapidly increasing prominence of digital communication, and especially the internet, would so profoundly change our lives as to render obsolete lingering and increasingly irrelevant concerns with such problems of a previous age as inequality, political division and social decomposition. In this chapter, the claims of such cyber-optimism are examined, not simplistically to arrive at an equally callow conclusion of determinist pessimism, but to assess whether the unquestionable and huge impact of digital communication on our lives has solved, or rather, in some respects, simply refashioned, or even deepened, the enduring contours of social structure and inequality.

Reagan was lecturing to the English Speaking Union, during a private visit to the United Kingdom that nonetheless saw the red carpet rolled out for him, dinner with the British Prime Minister Margaret Thatcher, and lunch with the Queen. His speech was focused on the revolution in communications technology, and the ways in which it would enable 'electronic beams to blow through the iron curtain as if it were lace'. In deriding these comments some twenty years later the Russian-born American internet scholar and columnist Evgeny Morozov scornfully suggested that they must have had China's microchip manufacturers '...laughing all the way to the bank' (Morozov, 2011: 49).

A new world beckons – the promise of the digital utopia and political reality

The apparently rich promise at the dawn of the internet age drove many a starry eyed visionary to their newly potent keyboard. Bill Gates, the progenitor of Microsoft, and swiftly becoming the world's richest man for many years around the turn of the century, set out his own vision for 'The Road Ahead' in 1995 (Gates, 1995). He was convinced that 'just about everything will be done differently' (7), not least because of 'The availability of virtually free communications...' (251). The deep divides and disturbing inequities of the past would soon be overcome – 'The information highway will be available to everyone, and if they don't have a home PC then there's the library, post office etc' (256). The fully developed information highway will be affordable – almost by definition. Once people are on the highway, they will enjoy full egalitarian access to vital online resources (257). Technologist entrepreneurs like Gates were often the most vociferous (and undoubtedly, very often genuinely committed) believers in the utopia they were so energetically, and profitably, creating. Nicholas Negroponte, founder of the influential Massachusetts Institute of Technology Media Lab, was convinced that 'the information superhighway is more than a short-cut to every book in the Library of Congress. It is creating a global social fabric' (Negroponte, 1995: 183). In his view, 'The access, the mobility and the ability to effect change are what will make the future so different from the present. The information superhighway may be mostly hype today, but it is an understatement about tomorrow' (op.cit.: 231).

The elimination of inequality was but part of this vision. Digital communications, notably on the internet, would mean what the distinguished British academic and journalist Frances Cairncross called 'the death of distance' (Cairncross, 1997). As Negroponte envisaged, 'We will socialise in digital neighbourhoods in which physical space will be irrelevant and time will play a different role' (7). So, too, for Cairncross, 'the death of distance will bring to many more people around the world the privileges and pleasures that up to now have been available only to the rich' (op.cit.: x). For all these seers, and many like them, the digital world would mean an enormous expansion of opportunities, to learn, to obtain knowledge, and, not least, to erode the basic structures of inequality to which such prophets were, to be fair, often anything but insensitive. The optimism was real if occasionally a little hyperbolic and even self-interested. It certainly had uncomfortable myopia, reflecting too often the attractive vistas of middle-class west coast America rather than the real and painful lives of many in industrial societies, not to mention the large parts of the globe for whom such magical visions were of rather less interest that a reliable supply of safe drinking water or a day's food.

Not surprisingly, therefore, the hype generated much doubt and scepticism. In an entertaining diatribe, a Californian astronomer wrote a much-cited book on 'silicon snake oil' (Stoll, 1995), in which he argued, perhaps somewhat emphatically, that 'while the internet burns brightly, seductively flashing an icon of knowledge-as-power, this non-place lures us to surrender our time on earth' (op.cit.: 4). His doubts were large: 'As I contemplate this silicon navel I see a wide gulf between the real networks that I use daily and the promised land of the information infrastructure' (10). 'The vast majority of people don't own computers, so they're excluded from the online democracy' (32). 'And as governments provide their information online, those who are wired to the net will continue to become more powerful, those without modems will become even more disenfranchised' (34). While politicians like Al Gore, US Vice-President from 1993 to 2001, and a major promoter of IT development and legislation, were lauding the potential of the 'information superhighway' at every turn, sceptics were a significant undercurrent in public debate. For Andrew Keen, writing a little later, Silicon Valley, the southern Californian hub of high-tech companies, whose name became metonymic for the locale of digital inventiveness, was a place 'where doing good and becoming rich are seen as indistinguishable' (Keen, 2015: 6). Morozov sardonically identified what he termed 'the Google doctrine', 'the enthusiastic [and in his view deeply mistaken] belief in the liberating power of technology accompanied by the irresistible urge to enlist Silicon Valley start-ups in the global fight for freedom' (Morozov, op.cit: xii). Growing doubts about the enormous power of the new high-tech companies, of the persistence and even deepening of 'digital divides', the dilution and incremental elimination of privacy, and the surveillance and marketing potential exploited by the political and economic titans of online life, all began to generate unease about, or outright hostility to, the potential of digital aspirations, as we shall see later in this chapter.

Blaming the victim

The allegedly inevitable benefits of the onset of digitisation, and the enveloping of the globe by the World Wide Web, led many to the confident conclusion that any blemishes on the otherwise flawless panorama arising in this new world could only be explained by the failings of its inhabitants. Such was the mind-set among many senior European officials in the early part of the twenty-first century, frustrated that exciting plans for 'e-everything' would fast-forward European society on all fronts – education, welfare, politics, culture, health and economy (Golding, 2007). The notion of an 'e-Europe' arose from the June 2000 European Council declaration 'to make the European Union the most competitive and dynamic knowledge based economy with improved employment and social cohesion by 2010' (European Commission, 2002). Regretful and weary disappointment marked the recurrent observations among the progenitors of a variety of ambitious plans that their systems designed for online life were being obstructed, or simply left unused, by the obstinate conservatism or stubborn inabilities of those who seemed unable to recognise the benefits being provided for them. In part this became a wider reflection on the 'democratic deficit', describing the growing disenchantment with the EU becoming ever more evident in many countries, and finding later assertive expression in the 'Brexit' vote in the United Kingdom in 2016. It led to a recurrent weary yearning among enthusiasts for reluctant consumers and workers to avail themselves of the technologies and training required for them to make the best use of the undeniable advantages and opportunities being created for them.

Further initiatives from the EU emerged frequently in subsequent years. The failings of citizens to avail themselves of either the technology required or the training necessary to use it, became a persistent refrain in the laments issued periodically by the European Commission that plans were somehow not being realised (Golding, 2007: *passim*). While surveys recognised the continuing gaps in broadband provision and internet access, especially between countries and regions, the familiar inequities of income and wealth, enduringly stark in much of Europe, explained much of the inability of European citizens to grasp the many delights of 'e-Europe' eagerly formulated by its more ambitious visionaries and architects. In 2005, only 10% of the EU-15 population had a broadband subscription when broadband was available to about 88% of them. This figure fell to 8.6% if the enlarged EU was included (Golding, op.cit.: 730).

The concept of 'e-democracy' has had a special allure for techno-optimists. As Matthew Hindman has discussed, the expectation that the internet would revolutionise politics, give voice to the voiceless, and inevitably enhance democracy, became an axiom of early twenty-first-century debate, finding simple expression in the Delaware Supreme Court conclusion that 'the internet is a unique democratising medium' that allows 'more and diverse people to engage in public debate' (Hindman, 2009: 3). There are several difficulties that complicate this otherwise attractive aspiration. First, the widespread use of internet possibilities, notably in online 'social media', has often generated huge problems of abuse, anonymous 'hate speech', and mindless denunciation, at least as frequently as hopeful conclusions that it has enabled otherwise unlikely political mobilisation and radical action ('digital activism', as reviewed for example in Diamond, 2010; Fenton, 2016; Castells, 2015; Barassi, 2017). Secondly, existing platforms – the 'legacy media' of broadcasting especially, continue to dominate the consumption of even technologically equipped and capable consumers, as well as being the primary source, and indeed often owners, of newer platforms.

There are two further difficulties that dull the otherwise sparkling allure of digital democracy, however. One of the visions of the early enthusiasts for such advances was its direct nature. People could vote from the security and comfort of their own homes and regularly register their needs or demands online ('push-button democracy' as some have termed it, cf. Wilhelm, 2000: 103). Missing from such a scenario, however, was the deliberative and more complex nature of political demand-making and opinion-forming. As political scientist Stephen Coleman has argued, political action requires consideration and examination of unfamiliar arguments and evidence in order to enrich democratic decision-making. Instant pressing of a button or clicking on a website are weak and callow substitutes, facilitating the façade of participation but with little substance. As a keen enthusiast for the potential of the internet for enriching democracy, Coleman nonetheless notes that deliberation and the capacity to seek and review relevant information are the crucial tools of enhanced democracy, which could be, but are as yet not delivered by the arrangements of digital provision now in place (Coleman, 2017). This weakness was, of course, familiar to early enthusiasts of digital democracy. Reviewing experimental attempts to foster a more deliberative use of this exciting new opportunity, Dahlberg notes how far from realising the ideals of a democratic public sphere it was because of the commercial and political realities of existing arrangements (Dahlberg, 2001). Some early commentators were forthrightly sceptical. Lockard sourly notes that 'true believers who tout the internet as democracy actualised, as an electronic town hall meeting, live with class blinders in a muddle of self-delusion…Access to cyberspace is effectively divided between self-financed, institutionally financed, and unprotected non-access'. The net result, he concludes, is that cyberspace is a 'democratic myth' (Lockard, 1997: 220).

The dystopian view of the oft-claimed contribution of the internet can be quite radical, as in the subtitle ('how the internet is killing democracy...') of a book by Bartlett, in which he warns, grimly, that 'unless we change course, democracy will be washed away by the tech revolution, and join feudalism, supreme monarchies, and communism as just another experiment that worked for a while but was unable to adapt when technology evolved...' (Bartlett, 2018: 206).

Right at the outset, while many were fascinated by the seemingly epochal advances in democracy the new technologies could enable, others voiced much caution, as in Arterton's conclusion, after reviewing thirteen early experiments in 'teledemocracy' that 'the real problems are political in nature' (Arterton, 1987: 197). Such reservations are often enhanced by worries that 'direct democracy' would bypass the existence of parties, trade unions and other collective mechanisms for political action, emphasising a very individualistic and fragmented form of politics. This can, of course, be regarded as a benefit, allowing the individual citizen to break free of the smothering embrace of top-down programmes and political party domination. This might be true if such individual action were based on equity of opportunity, or if politics were little more than opinion polling. However, increasingly the 'disintermediation' of politics is regarded by many as diluting rather than enriching democracy (among many discussions see Sussman, 1997). Most salient, in the context of this book, is the problem of inequitable availability of the resources to act politically via digital means.

Internet use and non-use: choice or digital divide?

One way of blaming the user for the failure of the internet to liberate and empower is the charge that non-use is voluntary, even wilful. There have been many studies of non-users who might otherwise seem perfectly able to acquire online services and use them, but among these groups appear a hard-core of assertively disconnected citizens whose non-use is as much a lifestyle statement as a form of social detachment. Beyond a grumpy antipathy to all technological novelties, some people assert their independence from the internet as a positive declaration of intent. The Norwegian media scholar Trine Syvertsen has examined such behaviour in detail, noting how it can manifest a desire to show 'authenticity' in political expression and action, in a way that online activity fails to do. Such people have moved beyond dislike, to active abstention, and, indeed, if reacting to previous use, they appear to display what Syvertsen describes as 'digital detox' (Syvertsen, 2017, 2020), often periods in which users impose on themselves a calculated, though sometimes delimited, period of non-use of digital media. In many cases, this can become little more than another, somewhat up-market, American style of fashionable behaviour pattern akin to 'mindfulness' and self-realisation of various kinds. Resistant to the perceived addictiveness and dependency-creating character of smartphones and email, disengagement becomes a positive display of individual detachment from the capture of the consumer by online manacles, or what the American psychologist Sherry Turkle has memorably described as being 'tethered' to the internet (Turkle, 2012: 171). This is possibly a more mundane though likely explanation than the possibility that 'disconnection promises a potential liberation or redemption from the contradictions of contemporary digital capitalism' (Treré et al., 2020: 606).

Such absenteeism from the online world is the exception, not the rule. Attitudes to and use of the internet have changed over time and reasons for non-use vary greatly (see, for examples and an overview, Helsper and Reisdorf, 2017). But it remains the case that by and large, internet use is significantly determined by access to, and ability to afford, both the hardware and the continuing costs of being so connected. This was examined in detail in Chapter 2. Even by 2021, when internet use was regarded in many richer countries as having become almost universal, studies by the regulatory agency in the United Kingdom, Ofcom, showed that about 2 million UK households struggled to afford internet access. The same research showed that, despite some low tariffs, 2% of broadband customers and 3% of mobile customers were in arrears, while between January 2020 and January 2021, total debt among broadband and mobile customers increased from £475 mn to £550 mn (Ofcom, 2021). The research confirms a repeated concern of this book, the higher proportion of their household expenditure required by low-income consumers to enter the communications market-place, compared to more affluent consumers. It concluded that 'The 3.3 million households with the lowest incomes in the United Kingdom spend on average over 4% of their disposable income on fixed broadband, nearly four times more than the proportion of an average household' (ibid.: 4).

The consequences of limited or non-access were graphically, and even tragically, made abundantly clear in the fate of millions of children during the lockdown periods of the coronavirus (COVID-19) pandemic in the Spring of 2020 in the United Kingdom. With all schools closed in March, home-schooling became a necessity, and for many parents a cause of huge anxiety, uncertainty and effort. Local provision, of course, varied according to the ingenuity and determination of particular schools, and the often heroic efforts of local authorities and individual teachers. Inevitably, inequities of home resources – parental time, private space and support equipment (even basics like paper and playstuff) determined the differential experiences of the nation's children.

Prime among these inequities were the availability and quality of online facilities, as school teaching staff worked tirelessly to provide digital materials for parents to access and for teachers to assess and support. Some schools, mindful of this, even factored into their diligent attempts to help and support their pupils an awareness that a significant minority would be unable to access anything they distributed online. One summary of early surveys suggested that one-fifth of pupils – over two million children – did no schoolwork at home, or less than an hour a day, and the proportion of children in receipt of free school meals who were able to spend more than four hours a day on schoolwork was 11% (Green, 2020). Not surprisingly 31% of private schools provided four or more online live lessons daily compared with just 6% in state schools. Of course, the stresses and burdens arising from school closure meant little schoolwork of any kind was being done at home by large numbers of children, but the differences in experience fostered by digital inequality massively exacerbated this.

This problem was interrogated by the UK Parliamentary Education Committee in generally assessing the impact of the pandemic. As the committee chair pointed out, 'one particularly stark figure I saw was that 900 head teachers said that 700,000 pupils were not doing any school work at home'. Posing this observation to the Children's Commissioner prompted her reply that 'Certainly…, 700,000 children do not have access to broadband or a laptop…You can imagine that if a home has five people in it and one tablet, no one can dominate that all the time' (Education Committee, 2020: qn. 387). In evidence to the same Committee the Sutton Trust also expressed concern about inequitable access to online learning. Citing their own research, they suggested that 'In the most deprived schools, 15% of teachers report that more than a third of their students learning from home would not have adequate access to an electronic device for learning, compared to only 2% in the most affluent state schools' (Sutton Trust, 2020: 2.1). They also underlined the gap in experience between different groups in citing their finding that, just before the schools shut down, 'three-fifths of teachers in independent schools …already had access to a platform to receive work, compared to under a quarter of those in the most deprived schools' (ibid.: 2.3). Research by the National Foundation for Educational Research (NFER) found that over a quarter of pupils had little or no IT access and that levels of engagement with education were starkly diminished for those with limited access to IT at home (NFER, 2020: 6–7; see also CPAG, 2021).

Acknowledging the problem, the government committed £85 mn to a scheme to provide schools with 200,000 laptops or tablets, but as the summer of 2020 approached it became increasingly clear that this (like many other such declarations it must be said) was an aspiration that failed to get translated into action. By August 2020 nearly two-thirds of disadvantaged children had not benefitted from the government scheme (Simpson, 2020), and in October schools received emails from the government informing them that allocations had been slashed. The consequences were predictable. The Sutton Trust research found that only 15% of the most deprived schools had been able to provide devices to pupils in need. The already vast gulf in educational experience and opportunity between children at different socio-economic levels was being intensified even further by the digital solutions being sought, and it became a matter of recurrent comment that the pandemic had both revealed and exacerbated the fact and impact of the digital divide (Office for National Statistics, 2021). The educational charity Teach First concluded that there was a continuing and increasing digital divide provoked by the pandemic, and the long-term consequences of nearly a year of disrupted learning in that context mean that there was, by late 2020, a difference of seven months' learning for both reading and maths between disadvantaged primary school pupils and their richer peers (Teach First, 2021).

The manifest failure of the scheme, and the inequities it revealed, provoked considerable comment and reaction. Many schools realised that education online, while an understandable and, indeed, hugely demanding, attempt to meet the exceptional needs created by school closure, would exclude many of their most disadvantaged pupils, and attempted to complement online provision with other forms of remote contact. A Yorkshire firm repaired hundreds of laptops to provide to poorer children in Leeds, citing the poignant case of a student apprentice sitting on a bus for two hours to use its free Wi-Fi as he had none at home (Blackall, 2021). But for many the pandemic and school closure had highlighted, not created, the depth, enduring impact and economic foundations of the digital divide.

The severity and visibility of the educational digital divide brought back into some prominence the continuing disadvantages of exclusion from regular and ready access to the internet; access which was fast becoming a necessity for everyday life, and which was, after the arrival of COVID-19, magnified and intensified by the domestic isolation imposed by the pandemic lockdown. Those without the means to make the most of online schooling were almost certainly the same households struggling to obtain the weekly shop – their lack of cash was an economic inevitability, not a technological choice. An immediate example of this was the fate of the 'unbanked', who could no more manage their finances online than fly, in the absence of the means to do so, and yet who were increasingly faced with the baffling and demanding requirements of a 'cashless' society (a fate already becoming obvious much earlier, see Toporowski, 1996). Approximately 1.2 million people in the United Kingdom (in 2020) had no bank account, and with over 3,000 bank and ATM closures in rural areas of the United Kingdom in the five-year period to 2020, many, especially those on lower incomes, found themselves increasingly excluded from the most mundane and necessary daily financial activities, even buying essentials (Kale, 2020).

For very similar reasons online shopping, an attractive luxury for the asset-rich and time-poor, became an increasingly familiar part of everyday routine for millions during lockdown. It remains predicted to be an enduring 'benefit' of the many changes in life and work habits occasioned by the pandemic, extending and intensifying the already diminishing role and prominence of the traditional 'high street'. For those with the means (a credit card, and the resources to facilitate online browsing and purchasing), the advantages of online shopping became recurrent and cumulative. For those without such resources, the opposite was true. These various rapid accelerations of online activity (education, consumerism and financial management) all impacted onthe same groups in the same way. Similarly, and not surprisingly, health inequalities loomed large during the pandemic. Not only have poorer groups been most stricken by the COVID-19 virus, but waiting lists for medical attention and access to family doctors (increasingly a matter of online consultation for many) have enlarged already existing health inequalities, and healthcare generally has become increasingly inaccessible to the digitally disadvantaged (Stone, 2021). In all these ways the digital divide is pervasive and cumulative.

Cyberspace and the internet: deep, dark and dangerous?

It would of course be a mistake to swing from the naïve, yet in so many ways entirely understandable and admirable, cyber-optimism of 40 years ago, of the kind illustrated at the outset of this chapter, to a technophobic hostility to all advances offered by the rapid growth and widespread availability of the internet and World Wide Web. The temptations to a quasi-luddite distaste for the often dehumanising or debasing consequences of online life can, if over-indulged, be simply nihilistic, and ultimately regressive. Yet, equally, it would be incomplete not to notice at least four adverse aspects of the internet's importance in the lives of twenty-first century citizens.

First, attention must be given to the 'dark net'. The very phrase conjures a hinterland of nefarious, dubious and often contemptable practices which have been fostered and enabled by the new possibilities for transaction and communication afforded by the internet. The sheer murkiness and unsavoury doings to be found behind the more familiar online activities can fuel anxiety that it is the technology itself that has unleashed a wholly new potential for the baser greediness and exploitations of human sordidness. Bartlett's extensive account of this largely hidden dimension of online life notes how the labels 'dark net' and 'deep web', often used interchangeably, have 'become a catch-all term for the myriad shocking, disturbing and controversial corners of the net – the realm of imagined criminals and predators of all shapes and sizes' (Bartlett, 2015: 3). The image, and indeed the reality, is of an electronic playground inhabited by pornographers, paedophiles, drug dealers, money counterfeiters, illegal gun markets, hackers, scammers and political extremists.

At its simplest, the deep web (which in reality is probably well over 90% of the internet) is that part of the internet beyond the indexing power of search engines. Guccione (2021) helpfully distinguishes the two terms 'deep web' and 'dark web'. It is the latter that is intentionally hidden, often using a readily available browser, TOR, whose very purpose, since its development by computer scientists at the US naval laboratories in the 1990s, is to render untraceable a net user's location. It is the dark web that Guccione describes as providing a 'memorable glimpse at the seamy underbelly of the human experience' (ibid.). In turn, this should not be confused with what used to be described as 'darknets', semi-private systems designed to enable sharing, often illicitly, of music or other copyright material (Zittrain, 2008: 197).

Second, and perhaps closer to the light of day, and to familiar experience for many, is the internet's capacity for disseminating, and indeed for facilitating easy dissemination, of 'hate speech', whether directed at individuals or groups. In research published by the UK regulatory agency Ofcom, it was found that, of people who used online video-sharing services, roughly one in three had encountered hate content directed at racial groups, or at people in certain religious groups, transgender people and those of a particular sexual orientation. A quarter had been exposed to bullying or abuse (Ofcom, 2021b). The internet's capacity for fostering or amplifying the dissemination of hate speech in its various forms has been a major cause of scepticism about its benefits. The ability to threaten, abuse or offend either individuals or groups has unquestionably been eased and widened by the availability of communication via the internet. Groups and organisations, from the Ku Klux Klan to lesser-known abominations were, indeed, early adopters and enthusiastic users of the net, as described by Jessie Daniels (2009) in looking at the activities of white supremacist groups. Banks notes that the anonymity, immediacy and global nature of the internet have made it an ideal tool for extremists and hatemongers to promote hate (Banks, 2010). As he puts it, 'The internet has become the "new frontier" for spreading hate, as millions can be reached through an inexpensive and unencumbered social network that has enabled previously diverse and fragmented groups to connect, engendering a collective identity and sense of community' (Banks, 2010). Reviewing this area generally, Costello and Hawdon (2020) note that there were at least 11,500 such groups online by 2011. Interestingly, they reflect on some curious national variations in this. Finnish websites attacked immigrant status or sexual orientation, in the UK and USA race and ethnicity were most commonly targeted, while in Spain it was mainly sexuality and gender. But overall, online hate speech, they find, is predominantly right-wing in temper and ideology.

Of course, the difficulty in regarding the internet negatively as a locus of hate speech is how readily it becomes a temptation to control and restrain. The distressing parallels between internet curtailment and library policing or book burning are palpable.

Banning book publishing because some books may contain anti-social or even horrendous content is plainly to attack the wrong target. Similarly, the hostility attracted by the internet for its role as a facilitator for hate speech can easily reflect a lazy technophobia, or enable evasion of the legal and moral complexities of public regulation inhibiting 'free speech'. The problem has become massively intensified by the rapid diffusion and very widespread use of 'social media'. One complication, readily and often ingeniously exploited by large internet-based corporations, is the fostering of what is sometimes termed 'cyberlibertarian' ideology – the association of digital communications with free speech, and the latter in turn with free markets and property rights. One further complication is that regulation by nation-states of inherently international activities deposits a legal minefield in the path of the best of intentions. It is possible to find material accessible but illegal in one country but which is entirely legal in the country from which it originates. In 2016, the European Union agreed on a Code of Conduct with four of the largest information technology corporations. As one commentator notes, a dilemma was immediately prominent in this and similar attempts to regulate such material. The Council of Europe Committee of Ministers' Declaration on freedom of communication on the internet underlined the necessity to ensure freedom of speech, but it also stressed that "freedom of communication on the internet should not prejudice the human dignity, human rights and fundamental freedoms of others, especially minors" (Alkiviadou, 2019: 19).

In 2021, it became known that Instagram (a photo and video-sharing 'app' owned since 2012 by Facebook) had been studying the possible deleterious impact of its use by teenage girls. The research demonstrated the largely unhealthy consequences for this group in such areas as body image but had been kept under wraps by the company (Gayle, 2021). The claims were vehemently denied by the company. This echoed a number of other studies questioning the possibly unhappy outcomes of use, or at least excessive use, of social networking, especially among younger users, which had been repeatedly emerging in the first decades of the twenty-first century (Turkle, 2012; Fox and Moreland, 2015; Aral, 2020). The uncovered Instagram research led to US Senate sub-committee hearings and was one in a series of similar public worries about the consequences of widespread use of 'social media', and exploitation of users by the companies providing them. The hearings were the latest occasion on which Facebook had been forced to send executives to testify about accusations against it, including misinformation and antitrust concerns. Hundreds of companies withdrew advertising from Facebook in a campaign, 'Stop Hate for Profit', initiated in 2020 by civil rights organisations (https://www.stophateforprofit.org). Legislation to regulate and minimise 'online harms' was also produced in the United Kingdom, following widespread debate and legislative concern (Woodhouse, 2021). Following revelations in the *Wall Street Journal* in 2021, in a series headlined 'The Facebook Files', the company found itself facing authoritative accusations that its appetite, indeed greed, for monumental profits, was entirely overwhelming any sense of discretion, need for regulation, or active intervention, that might be expected to curtail harmful information flows (*Wall Street Journal*, 2021). President Joe Biden was even quoted as saying companies like Facebook were 'killing people', when invited to comment on the growing impact and availability of anti-vaccination material on social media.

The most dramatic and substantial evidence of the extraordinary power and questionable influence of Facebook came in 2018 with the Cambridge Analytica scandal. Cambridge Analytica was a UK-based political research and consulting organisation that worked for, among others, the 2016 Donald Trump campaign in the USA and the Brexit campaign in the United Kingdom. In 2018, it became known through a Canadian data analyst whistle-blower that, over several years, the company had collected, without their consent or knowledge, up to 87 million people's Facebook data, which was used to construct psychological profiling to assist targeted political campaigning and advertising. In 2019, Facebook was fined $5 bn by the US Federal Trade Commission due to its privacy violations, and in the same year paid a £500,000 fine to the UK Information Commissioner's Office for exposing its users to a 'serious risk of harm'. Nonetheless, faith in the company and enthusiasm for using its services seemed not to be dented (Hinds, et al., 2020; Lupton et al., 2017).

Paradoxically, the growth of social networking, of 'social media', has frequently been celebrated as a major and entirely new vehicle for political mobilisation and organisation, not least among groups previously silenced or oppressed. Far from being condemned as an unfortunate or even pernicious aspect of internet growth, social networking has therefore often been acclaimed as a progressive, even revolutionary, unleashing of the potential for popular political expression. This was never more so than during the period of the 'Arab Spring', a sequence of anti-government uprisings in much of the Arab world in 2010–2011, resulting in fundamental regime change in some countries. The role of social media in several of these events was highlighted at the time and has been much commented on since.

For Castells, reviewing these events a few years later, 'There is no question that the original spaces of resistance were formed in the internet' (Castells, 2015: 57). The severe and often cruel and punitive measures of the security forces and police in these countries forced organisational communication underground, making a premium of what was, in effect, a digital form of *samizdat*. He was writing specifically about Egypt, where 'the internet provided the safe space where networks of outrage and hope connected' (ibid.: 82). Certainly the Egyptian government acted very much in line with this view, blocking texting and demanding internet service providers to effect disconnection. In Tunisia, the fact the country had one of the highest penetration rates of mobile phones and the internet in the Arab world, and a high rate of internet use, including both domestic connections and community use in places like schools and cybercafés, meant that 'the connection between free communication on Facebook, You-Tube and Twitter and the occupation of urban space created a hybrid public space of freedom that became a major feature of the Tunisian rebellion' (ibid.: 23). The sense that the internet had facilitated, even been a prime, and in a sense, real locus of revolutionary expression and mobilisation, rapidly became a widely held view.

Yet doubts were never far from the surface, even at the time. Twitter had been regarded by many as housing the essence of dissent over the elections in Iran in 2009, to the extent that the notion of events in Iran having been a 'Twitter revolution' became commonplace. At the same time, as one reflection suggested very soon afterwards, 'opinions remain divided about the extent to which these and other protests were in a narrower sense led by activists using social media to express their views and orchestrate resistance' (Bruns et al., 2013). That is, they were a valuable extension of existing forms of organisation and dissent. Similarly, in Egypt and

Tunisia, the undoubted importance of social networking, and the energy and ingenuity put into using them to bypass official attempts at suppression and intimidation, nonetheless leave 'questions about whether Twitter was a stable means of coordinating demonstrations on the ground or primarily a channel for international observers to discuss the uprisings' (ibid.; Barrons, 2012). Generalising the subsequent research and considerable hindsight applied to these events, Wolfsfeld and colleagues concluded that the use of social networking media followed rather than enabled intense political organisation and dissent. In their simple phrase, 'politics comes first' (Wolfsfeld et al., 2013). Coming at the same topic from a slightly different angle Gerbaudo suggests that, rather than being naturally a force for progressive and even revolutionary politics, 'social media' may indeed be a vehicle for 'the peoples' voice, but lend themselves naturally to an individualistic populism, a product of the ideologies of Silicon Valley corporations, in a manner that he describes sourly as providing 'a means for disaffected individuals to express themselves and…a space in which disgruntled internet users could gather and form partisan online crowds' (Gerbaudo, 2018: 751).

It would plainly be unwise to be overly sceptical about the role of the internet and social networking in enabling and enhancing radical dissent and popular political movements. Equally, however, it may be premature to unduly celebrate the liberatory and even revolutionary capacity of such forms of communication in and of themselves. To voice doubts is not to leap to the equally uncertain conclusion that the internet is a technological threat – neither a means nor a determinant of popular political action. But the internet's uncertain and perhaps as yet not fully tested, potential in either direction, requires its limitations to be noted in any assessment of its social benefits.

A further question raised by the rapid growth of the internet and its networking of information across vast populations has been its assumed role in the rise of 'fake news'. The notion of 'fake news' became especially associated with the rise of Donald Trump to the leadership of the Republican Party in the USA and in turn to the country's presidency (to which he was elected in 2016). Of course, news distorted or even entirely manufactured to influence public opinion is far from novel to the internet. Famously the UK *Daily Mail* published a letter shortly before the 1924 general election, purporting to come from the head of the Comintern in Moscow, instructing the British Communist Party to disrupt public life. Its 'advice' on radicalising the British working classes was inevitably found offensive by many. The 'letter' is now agreed to have been forged, but to have played a major role in the ensuing election result, a Conservative landslide victory (Bennett, 2018). Despite this, and many other perhaps less dramatic instances, the volume and speed of dissemination of fake news has massively accelerated in the internet age.

Trump's recurrent condemnation of 'fake news' was predominantly targeted at what he saw as one or two of the TV news networks and elite newspapers in the USA. His infamous torrent of tweets denouncing their negative coverage of him as 'fake news' became a familiar undercurrent to his presidency and popularised the term (Lind, 2018). The existence of 'fake news', of course, certainly pre-dates both Trump and Twitter, as the Zinoviev letter illustrates. Research into the practice of journalism and the content of news, as examined in chapter three, has demonstrated how both are the product not just of 'bias' or prejudice, but inevitably of occupational ideologies and routines. They are social constructs.

Nevertheless, the internet and social networking using the net, have enormously multiplied the dissemination and impact of fake news of one kind or another. The relative ease with which unfounded or speciously substantiated material can be lodged into public debate and even, in the jargon, made to 'go viral', has made the internet fertile terrain for unfounded 'information' and dubious comments. This became a major concern during the COVID-19 lockdown periods, with millions poring over screens providing an array of conspiracy theories and alarming assertions. Vast numbers of social media users found themselves reading daunting but compelling accounts of how vaccination could enlarge their gonads, distort or destroy their fertility, or be used covertly to insert microchips inspired by Bill Gates into their bloodstream. An Ofcom survey series found that, early in the lockdown period in the United Kingdom, a quarter of respondents had come across misinformation 2–4 times a day, and nearly half (46%) had come across information in the previous week they thought false or misleading (Ofcom, 2020b).

The myriad mythologies dispersed on the internet about COVID-19 – that it had been deliberately cultivated and released, or alternatively was entirely a hoax designed to render compliant populations docile and inert, proved problematic for social media corporations. YouTube (owned by Google) removed 130,000 items related to coronavirus vaccination in 2020/21 and stepped up its attempts to remove similar video items in 2021 (Milmo, 2021). In an attempt to forestall criticism, Facebook had distributed funds in 2017 to 'fact-checking' journalist groups and organisations, whose work quickly mushroomed. More broadly this particular large-scale internet pollutant paralleled a wider and enormous flow of claims, many associated with the far-right Q'Anon conspiracy theory organisation, initially mainly in the USA, especially circulating theories about paedophile rings and 'deep state' undermining of Donald Trump. Climate change deniers were also, predictably, keen users of this communication route. One report found that climate change denial advertising had been viewed by over 8 million people in the USA in the first half of 2020, although only one of the 51 advertisements looked at had been taken down by Facebook (InfluenceMap, 2020).

Finally, it is impossible to acknowledge the many dubious consequences of the spread of the internet without looking at the rise of what is sometimes termed 'unreason', or, more generally, popular wisdom of an often pernicious, and, either deliberately or inadvertently, anti-social character and questionable derivation. The concern prompted by this trend is about the threats to and undermining of the 'enlightenment project', a presumed advance in human thinking in which reason and progress in knowledge rooted in science prevailed over prejudice, superstition, and irrationality. The precise construction of this notion and its links with philosophical movements of the late eighteenth century and beyond, matter less here than the sense that publicly disseminated assertions and arguments have become tainted by the pervasive availability and influence of irrationality occasioned and enabled by the internet.

The strange hinterland of popular beliefs now often designated as 'unreason' or even (and increasingly in the days during and since Donald Trump's rise to the presidency) 'post-truth', is certainly not, in itself, a product of the internet. But the accelerated distribution of some very odd certainties among, at least, western populations in recent times is difficult to ignore. Astrology has been growing in popularity for many years, with proliferating dedicated 'apps' building huge and loyal user bases, convinced that horoscopes will reveal truths and guidance to which they should commit. The sense that reason is in retreat is much documented, and frequently lamented with a desperate loyalty to what is regarded as the superior thought process of science (see, e.g. Taverne, 2005, who argues that we are increasingly vulnerable to rejection of the evidence-based approach, leading to a culture of suspicion, distrust, cynicism, dogmatism and intolerance). The consequences are sometimes dismissed as evidence of the harmless gullibility of the masses, but also sometimes as something much more sinister. As Wheen puts it, 'The sleep of reason brings forth monsters...the proliferation of obscurantist bunkum and the assault on reason are a menace to civilisation...' (Wheen, 2004: 7). Flat-earthers, climate change deniers, neurotic worriers that we are all about to be enslaved by alien lizards, or that we are controlled by shady conspirators, people convinced that AIDS was designed in an American laboratory, or that the moon landings were staged video acts, that the holocaust never happened, mobile phone masts cause the spread of coronavirus; all these, and many more, can be found to decorate the rich tapestry of human beliefs and opinions.

The role of the internet, however, is identified by some as having contributed to a new and much more intense diversion along these odd byways of conviction. At one level this is 'simply' a worry that excessive use of computers will substitute a narrow data-processing model for the broader, and more satisfactory, imaginative creativity of the human mind, especially in education (Roszak, 1988). The real culprit is even more explicit for others. Thompson suggests that 'In the long term the real menace of the internet is its ability to carry the virus of counterknowledge to societies that are not protected by evidence-based methodology' (Thompson, 2008: 129). In other words, while in the West, with our sophisticated and expensive education systems, we are protected from much of the injurious flow of post-truth internet myths, the same cannot confidently be said for much of the world. The reason is clear; 'the new medium has speeded up the privatisation of knowledge, and increased our ability to incorporate elements of fantasy into our "work in progress". Thanks to the internet millions of people have absorbed postmodern relativism' (ibid.: 27). That is, the existence of what Wheen describes as 'mumbo-jumbo' is not new, but 'in the internet age, conspiracy theorists prosper... never before has the dissemination of information been so simple or so cheap'.... [Deeply suspect claims] 'acquire a spurious truth through repetition and exposure that they would have struggled to acquire in the age of the salon and the printed pamphlet. We live in the era of the instant, self-proclaimed expert' (Hanlon, 2013: S4). The paradox is very clear to some commentators. Grimes, for example, points to the plethora of new voices the internet carries, but, despite what he terms the heady optimism of its early diffusion, 'the reality is somewhat murkier. We live in an age of algorithmic filtering and directed advertisement' fostering the dissemination of irrationality, conspiracy theory, disinformation and propaganda (Grimes, 2019: 253). While the internet might not be the cause or originator of the strange and possibly dangerous cacophony of unreason, its very ubiquity, and the speed of distribution of information it facilitates, are seen by writers such as these as seminal contributors to the entry of 'counterknowledge', 'mumbo-jumbo' or 'unreason' onto centre stage in the human drama.

As ever, in the context of the concerns of this book, the question posed is how far this places a premium on the capacity of information seekers and users to obtain the diversity of material required for intelligent and coherent consideration. That the internet is home to, indeed the enabler of, widespread dissemination of hate speech, unreason or dangerous mythology, does not necessarily lead to the conclusion that it is their cause. While the internet and digital communication networking are not 'the solution', neither are they necessarily 'the problem'. The further exploration of this conundrum takes us to a more material, and perhaps more familiar, characteristic of the internet age.

Digital capitalism and the new oligopolies

While the internet has brought unprecedented benefits to large numbers of people, radically accelerating the speed of distribution of information and entertainment, as well as massively enlarging their availability, as the last few pages suggest the picture is not one of untrammelled progress. The notion of the 'digital age', or more generally of the internet and the World Wide Web having not just enhanced and embellished industrial societies, but taken them into a new epoch, is probably premature. As I have argued elsewhere, much has changed, but not the more entrenched and underlying character of the society in which we live; a late capitalist order in which there are established and enduring fissures of inequality and of power (Golding, 2000).

The internet's maturation into a vehicle of unparalleled commercial energy is an oft-told story (see, inter alia, Abbate, 1999; Greenstein, 2015). It is a story of a development driven initially by the 'cold war', and harboured within, primarily, military centres of innovation and investigation, moving on to become, in Schiller's trenchant phrase, a 'new neoliberal paramountcy' in which large corporations 'sought to harness the web for advanced capitalism's most sacred social purpose: selling' (Schiller, 1999: 203–4). Using his succinct label, we have entered comprehensive 'digital capitalism' (ibid.).

The origins of the internet are firmly rooted in the frosty soil of the 'cold war', involving large-scale US government investment in institutions like the National Defence Research Committee and the Defence Advanced Research Projects Agency (among many accounts see Keen, 2015: 37–9). Full-scale commercialisation began in the 1980s, and the ensuing years, in Baran's summary, witnessed a 'transition from federal funding to full private commercial operation of the internet' (Baran, 1998: 126). The military and Cold War drivers of technological innovation are crucial, but it was the liberalisation of the US telecommunications industry that facilitated 'an increasing premium on market-led development' (Schiller, op.cit.: 12), a process in which, as Schiller describes it, the internet 'is only a leading element in the hurricane of destructive creativity that has cascaded through telecommunications' (ibid.: 37). With the arrival of what Mosco describes as 'the next internet', based on cloud computing, big data, and the 'internet of things', the process is all but complete – 'under this model the market is the leading force shaping decisions about the production, distribution, and exchange of information, and corporations with market power hold the most influence' (Mosco, 2017: 64).

The scale and dominance of those corporations – 'digital behemoths' in Mosco's phrase – (ibid.: 64), are certainly startling, as is the swiftness with which both have multiplied. But central to the core mythologies of the tech giants that now dominate internet use is a story of humble and folksy origins. The image of a couple of nerdy Californian I.T. students launching a hopeful start-up from their bedrooms is evocative, and possibly even partly true.

Bill Gates recalls how it all started 'on a day when, as a college sophomore, I stood in Harvard Square with my friend Paul Allen and pored over the description of a kit computer in *Popular Electronics* magazine' (Gates, 1995: xi). Amazon started life in Jeff Bezos' garage as an online bookshop (Robinson and Martin, 2010), though he was by then (1994) a well-paid hedge fund executive. Facebook was named after the photo booklets of fanciable students kept by Harvard undergraduates around the turn of the century, and even then condemned by the student newspaper as 'catering to the worst side of Harvard students' (Kirkpatrick, 2011: 24). It was developed, initially possibly illicitly, by a geeky undergraduate called Mark Zuckerberg, before becoming the digital colossus of less than two decades later. Google began as an experiment by two doctoral students at Stanford in 1996, the name arising from either an inadvertent or, more generously, a deliberately inventive corruption of googol, the mathematical term for the number ten to the power of one hundred.

The mythology survives in the oft-hyped cultural aura of casual, 'cool', laid-back but creative work settings of the tech giants, drawing deeply from the wells of Californian hippydom and cosy Silicon Valley luxury. Many small start-ups have evolved, in Darwinian fashion, very quickly to a small number of technological – more especially internet-based – giants. Barwise and Watkins explain the economics of this process, in which digital market concentration evolves in a winner-takes-all procedure. The major factors, as they outline them, are economies of scale, important user and employee brands, direct and indirect network effects, big data and machine learning, and, of course, a corporate culture of ambition, innovation and strength, buttressed by ingenuity in tax avoidance (Barwise and Watkins, 2018: 30, 41). The market share of the winners is truly vast. Bilic et al. note that, in 2020, Google had over 90% of the market in web searches, Facebook had a global market share of social media of over 60%, Amazon had half of the US e-commerce market in 2018, and led the global cloud infrastructure market, and so on.

As a consequence, the tech giants whose names keep appearing here operate on a scale unprecedented in human history. In part, this is through a process of acquisition, as the largest companies swallow up competitors. GAFAM (that is Google, Apple, Facebook, Amazon and Microsoft) made 723 acquisitions between 1987 and 2019 (Bilic et al. ibid.: 169). The companies concerned have become not just monumental organisations within their sector but economic giants dominant in the capitalist economy as a whole. Table 4.1 shows that these

Table 4.1 World's largest companies by market capitalisation (as at July 2024)

Rank	Company	$trillion
1	Microsoft	3.31
2	Nvidia	3.22
3	Apple	3.22
4	Alphabet (Google)	2.19
5	Amazon	1.94
6	Saudi Arabian Oil	1.78
7	Meta (Facebook)	1.27

Source: Hayes (2024). Market capitalisation is the company's stock price multiplied by the total number of shares outstanding.

high-tech companies (Google was restructured in 2015 to create Alphabet as a holding company for it) are the world's largest companies measured by market capitalisation.

There is no crime in bigness, but the scale on which these few, totally dominant, companies operate is daunting and historically unparalleled. Wallach suggests that 'Apple's market capitalisation is larger than 96% of country GDPs, a list that includes Italy, Brazil, Canada, and Russia...Microsoft ...would be the 10th richest country in the world if market cap was equivalent to GDP [and] ...Amazon's market capitalisation has grown to $1.7 tn, larger than 92% of country GDPs' (Wallach, 2021; see a similar analysis in Lishchuk, 2021).

The immense economic scale of these corporations is reflected in the size of their user base, or market share. Perhaps the most startling is the profile of Facebook. With a revenue in 2020 of $86 bn, Facebook had nearly 2.9 billion monthly active users by the second quarter of 2021. By early 2021 3.51 billion people (in a world population of about 7.95 billion) were using at least one of the company's products (Facebook, but also WhatsApp, Instagram, and Messenger, all owned by Facebook) each month (Statista, 2021). Amazon, 'the everything store' (Stone, 2013), had over 140 million Amazon Prime members (about two-thirds of the total number of Amazon consumers) in the USA by 2020, and, illustrating the company's move well beyond its origins in book-selling, by 2021, in the USA, its share of customers ordering groceries online amounted to nearly 36%, while it commanded 49.1% of all e-commerce in the USA, compared to 6.6% for eBay in second place (Finances Online, 2021). The coronavirus pandemic significantly intensified these trends. The five companies discussed here saw their stock value rise sharply during the pandemic period and by mid-2021 constituted between them about a fifth of the US stock market's total value (Wall Street Journal Staff, 2021).

One surprising feature of the tech giants is their relatively small workforce (Amazon, as a very large-scale retailer being the exception). As van Dijck notes of Facebook at the time of its initial public offering in 2012, 'With 2000 employees and 15 offices worldwide, the company's size was surprisingly modest in relation to its net worth of almost 100 billion dollars' (van Dijck, 2013: 57). Keen, writing just a couple of years later, notes that 'Google is around seven times larger than General Motors, but employs less than a quarter the number of workers' (Keen, 2015: 62). Even more dramatically, as Srnicek has recorded, 'WhatsApp had 55 employees when it was sold to Facebook for $19 billion and Instagram had 13 when it was purchased for $1 billion' (Srnicek, 2017: 4). The point, as we shall see below, is that so much of the labour from which the wealth of the companies is generated, is delivered by their users, in a business model in which consumers receive services for free, but only if they have the capacity to be online, in return for which they are providing detailed data enabling sophisticated marketing and advertising from which the companies derive their vast profits.

As with the myth of origin, the imagery surrounding employment at these corporations can be remarkably rosy, a confection of relaxed luxury, rapid promotion, and the potential for very high salaries. At the same time, however, they have increasingly attracted negative comments on, and frequently angry denunciation of their labour practices. Microsoft has been characterised as a 'velvet sweatshop', and a book by two investigative reporters about its founding CEO, Bill Gates, is tellingly, and with deliberate ambiguity, entitled 'Hard Drive' (Wallace and Erickson, 1993). Apple, the world's largest technology company by revenues, has been mired in accusations of sweatshop labour conditions for many years, the most serious relating to its connection with Foxconn, a huge Taiwan-based company where many of Apple's devices are assembled. Suicides at the Foxconn plant in 2009–2010, and regular accounts of dire working conditions, have been a continuous backdrop to the analysis of Apple's operations (Chan et al., 2020). Google often presents itself as a model and highly desirable employer but has also been the target of many accusations of union-busting and anti-union activities. The company's famous motto, 'Do No Evil', has been much lampooned. In 2013 residents in San Francisco attacked a bus taking employees to the company's local plant, 'the campus', in protest at their displacement by Google employees resulting in 'gentrification' of local neighbourhoods to the detriment of 'real' locals (Rushkoff, 2016). Though the company is not named in a hugely entertaining novel by American writer Dave Eggers, his dystopian satire is about an online company, based at 'the campus', that increasingly takes over the world and whose employment routines include the gradual removal of all privacy, and continuous monitoring of its employees (Eggers, 2014).

Perhaps the most severe revelations of harsh employment conditions have come in relation to Amazon. Vehemently anti-union, the company has regularly been accused of intimidation and exploitation of its workers, both in its warehouses ('fulfilment centres') and delivery staff. Automation of its warehouses, increasing pressure on the rate and scale of deliveries, and punitive sanctions and work condition policies have produced regular revelatory accounts, including broadcast documentaries with images of, for example, workers camped in freezing conditions outside a plant in Scotland to reduce the need and time for commuting, while regular reports of drivers forced to use plastic bottles to urinate into in their vans due to lack of time to seek a public toilet, have become iconic. A report in 2020 by the UK Trades Union Congress noted 'reports of the unsafe working conditions in their fulfilment centres across the globe. In the US, in Spain, in France, in Italy, in Poland, in Germany and in the United Kingdom, workers raised the alarm and unions demanded they do better, organising strikes to try and bring Amazon to the table when they dragged their feet or refused to introduce essential safety measures to reduce the risk to these key workers. Several workers in the US who raised the alarm did so at great personal cost, resulting in their sacking' (Trades Union Congress, 2020: 4).

To the charge list against these internet-based tech giants must be added their successful exploitation of the many loopholes built into national taxation systems, resulting in massive tax avoidance. The sheer scale and inherently international basis for much of their operations have allowed the major internet-based corporations enormous leeway for creative use of shell companies, tax havens, inter-company licencing arrangements, and similar devices to reduce their tax liabilities. That they are engaged primarily in the movement and management of information and intellectual property rather than goods, factories or large-scale physical products, adds to the ease with which tax avoidance is organised. This has aroused the fury and frequent legal challenge of many national governments and has particularly attracted the hostility of the European Union. A report by the Dutch delegation of left parties to the EU in 2017 concluded that the tax paid by Alphabet Inc. (Google) as a share of their revenues outside the EU was between 6% and 9%, whereas in the EU this ratio was only 0.36%–0.82%. They note that until 2015, Amazon's European revenues were recorded in Luxembourg (Amazon EU Sàrl) and were therefore only taxable in the Duchy, while it has several national websites elsewhere.

In Luxembourg, a special arrangement resulted in the company having nil tax obligations to Luxembourg (Tang et al., 2017). Facebook has profitably managed many of its tax affairs by routing revenues through the Republic of Ireland. A report by the lobby group Fair Tax Mark on the 'silicon six' (the five companies being considered here plus Netflix), concluded that in the period 2010–2019, these companies had managed to avoid paying tax to the tune of one hundred billion dollars, a sum that had not reduced when the group updated their analysis two years later (Fair Tax Mark, 2021). Subject to many and frequent legal disputes, the tech titans nonetheless continued to minimise their tax obligations with great success. The implications of this, given their remarkable achievements financially during the pandemic, have drawn inevitable comment. ActionAid, in a report on the five companies discussed earlier, suggested that 'G20 countries may be losing as much as \$32 bn annually in taxes from just five of the world's largest tech companies' (ActionAid, 2021). The report is understandably exercised by the scale of this loss, and the difference it might have made if spent on health care during the pandemic – as they calculate, it could have paid for a full two-dose COVID-19 vaccination for every human on earth.

The so-called 'tech-lash' against the tech giants has been predictable and increasingly vociferous, and the literature demonising and revealing the less admirable practices of these companies is voluminous (Weiss-Blatt, 2021). A leading body seeking to curb the ever-growing power of the tech titans has been the European Union. In 2017, the EU fined Google \$2.7 bn for monopolistically exploiting its dominant position, and, despite often voiced fears in the USA that European regulatory inhibitions would hobble the growth of the US tech sector, the position of the companies has caused, and will continue to provoke, considerable disquiet and political resistance. With a broad context of revelations about fake news, political manipulation, tax evasion, dubious employment practices, privacy breaches, monopolistic domination, psychological harm and unfair competition, the social and economic role of the 'big five' has become a topic of major concern to the EU, in what van Dijck describes as 'a big struggle over public values and the common good' (van Dijck, 2019: 3). As she notes, the 'dominant platform eco-system' is 'rooted in neoliberal market values' (ibid.: 2).

Among the most significant consequences of development in digital technology and of the internet has been the immensely enhanced potential and power of surveillance, both by the state and commercially. The first of these has been much discussed and is not the primary focus here. If digital communication allows for radical networking and mobilisation of otherwise massively under-resourced dissent, at one and the same time it affords statutory oversight and control of enormous potency. As Fenton notes, 'just as digital media are used for liberatory ends, so they are also used to suppress dissent through state censorship, internet filtering and surveillance...' (Fenton, op. cit.: 18). The use by oppressive or authoritarian regimes of digital networking to monitor or record the activities of dissident groups and individuals has certainly grown alongside its use by such people. Equally, the shutdown of internet access and use has become a tool of state oppression. One rights organisation alert to this reported over 50 internet shutdowns in 21 countries in the first half of 2021 alone (AccessNow, 2021). Surveillance, whether using hacking of smartphones, monitoring or interception of email traffic, cameras with facial recognition capacity, or many other such methods, has become very much part of the armoury of state control of unwanted dissidence in the twenty-first century. The potential of the internet faces both ways. As Diamond puts it, 'Liberation technology enables citizens to report news, expose wrongdoings, express opinions, mobilise protest, monitor elections, scrutinise government, deepen participation, and expand the horizons of freedom. But authoritarian states such as China, Belarus, and Iran have acquired (and shared) impressive technical capacities to filter and control the internet, and to identify and punish dissenters. Democrats and autocrats now compete to master these technologies' (Diamond, 2010: 70).

The context of this trend is frequently documented, with many reports noting ever-rising numbers of internet shutdowns by repressive states, and their increasing use and collection of private data (Shahbaz and Funk, 2021). The extent to which the internet affords new means for oppressive regimes to contain dissidence is spelt out by Gohdes, who notes how the expanded opportunities for citizens to communicate with each other and organise also create massive amounts of information that oppressive states can obtain and use for ensuring their own safety and survival (Gohdes, 2020). Indeed, many would argue that the internet has afforded an almost Orwellian expansion of state surveillance, fundamentally rooted in a wider expansion of state power over the individual of which the new technologies are an enabler, but not the cause (Giroux, 2015). The metaphor frequently reached for is that of the 'panopticon', a term originating in the design for observation of prisoners developed by the English eighteenth century philosopher Jeremy Bentham, but seen by some as inadequate to capture the potential of modern state use of internet technology (Manokha, 2018). All this is a far cry from the 'cyberlibertarian dreams' sometimes conjured by the more optimistic of earlier analysts (Hintz et al., 2019: 31).

The primary focus in the context of this book, however, is *commercial* surveillance – the collection and use of huge amounts of data about consumers by internet-based corporations of the kind described above for economic and marketing use. The technical arguments this prompts arise from the difficulty of defining what 'users' do. Is it labour? For many commentators, the time and effort contributed by users of networked 'social media' create the raw material, information, that corporations can use to extract value from their activities (for debates on this see Fuchs et al., 2012). The focus of inquiry is how users of these services allow their 'leisure activities to become commodified as inputs contributing to the wider business model of surplus value extraction'. Put more simply, every time someone inputs information to a Facebook or Twitter ('X' as it now is), they are contributing to a vast and sophisticated digital archive of what might once have been termed market research data, facilitating unparalleled opportunities for targeted promotion and advertising. The result is the constant surprise many have when their computer seems unnervingly knowledgeable about their leisure habits, shopping records, or online browsing for possible Christmas presents.

The process thus unleashed is simply summarised by Srnicek: 'revenue is generated through the extraction of data from users' activities online, from the analysis of those data, and from the auctioning of ad space to advertisers' (Srnicek, 2017: 56). The consequence of this, setting aside for the moment the more arcane discussion it prompts in debates about political economy or Marxist theory, is the emergence of what has been termed 'the age of surveillance capitalism'. In a much-discussed book with this title, Zuboff expands the idea behind it comprehensively (Zuboff, 2019). In her view, our lives are being 'plundered for behavioural data' in order to feed the appetite of giant corporations for growth and profits (ibid.: 53–4). This can mean, for a company like Google, a '180-degree turn from serving users to surveilling them' (ibid., p. 84). Zuboff stresses that these developments are matters of choice and policy, not technological inevitability. She writes of the period following Facebook's appointment of a former Google executive to be its CEO, that the latter led to 'Facebook's transformation from a social networking site to an advertising behemoth' (op.cit.: 92). For Google itself, predictions about user behaviour are its actual products, with search engines being a means to feed the ever-evolving capabilities of the compilation by artificial intelligence of consumer profiles (op.cit. p. 95), or what van Dijck had earlier described as 'precious information on social trends and consumer preferences' (van Dijck, 2013: 35).

Zuboff's thesis is not without its critics, including analysis from the left as it were, which sees it as misreading the true political economy of the internet giants. Lucas, for example, argues that these corporations derive the bulk of their revenue from advertising. He poses the rhetorical question: 'Who is it that purchases these ads? Largely other companies – meaning that advertising in general is a cost to firms, and thus a deduction from their overall profits in the terms of classical political economy, it is one of the *faux frais of production*...' (Lucas, 2020: 139). Of course, it could equally be argued that those costs are simply a means to boost overall profit extraction – a means to an end. Certainly, a prominent characteristic of giant internet corporations is their collection and use of data about their 'users', so that 'the extraction and commodification of this data ...is a new method for the generation of economic rents' (Blakeley, 2020: 101). An example of just how extensive this data can be is offered by Mosco, who cites a 'partial list' of no fewer than 75 characteristics about its users gathered by Facebook, from such basics as age, location, gender, and education to sports and travel preferences, political leanings, credit history and even grocery preferences (Mosco, 2017: 163–5).

This does not add up, however, to what writers like Zuboff regard as 'a new economic order'. The extraordinary scale and sophistication of data gathering from online users, and its complex and large-scale exploitation for ever more focused and subtle selling and profit maximisation, mark an extravagant advance in the technologies and capabilities of an economic order, but not its transformation into something different. The relevance here, then, is to see the many and much-discussed qualities of the dominant high-tech companies as an enhanced, perhaps even qualitatively inflated, facet of the economic system in which they exist. But the deep and persisting contours of inequality and powerlessness that are a focus of this book remain crucial to understanding their capacity to inequitably shape and control the life chances of those who live in the societies in which they operate. The motif is one of continuity rather than epochal change (cf. Golding, 2000). Jeff Bezos' annual letter to shareholders includes a copy of the first such letter he sent out in 1997, with his proud proclamation that 'This is Day One for the Internet'. The 'day one' motif is often presented as an adventurous call to arms, demanding a constant refreshing and innovative approach to the core businesses. But it also states with utter clarity the importance of the internet to the emergence of the tech titans in the last three decades.

The internet – neither the problem nor the solution

Tim (or to give him his proper title since he was knighted in 2004, *Sir* Timothy) Berners-Lee, is widely regarded as the inventor of the World Wide Web, arising from his ingenious linking of hypertext with the internet when working at the European Organisation for Nuclear Research (CERN) in Geneva in 1990. As he and many others are at pains to explain, the World Wide Web and the internet are not the same thing; the web is an application that runs on the network (the internet) enabling the distribution of vast amounts of information between computers. But the aspirations for both that are loosely conflated as 'cyber-optimism', of the kind illustrated at the start of this chapter, are similar. In 2010, Berners-Lee wrote an article in *Scientific American* lamenting what he now saw as the 'Threats to the internet, such as companies or governments that interfere with or snoop on internet traffic', a problem he felt would 'compromise basic human network rights' (Berners-Lee, 2010). In addition, he foresaw with considerable foreboding the dangers of a drift towards monopolies in the world of social networking, search engines, or browsers.

In much of this book, the concern is with inequities of access to the cornucopia of information and innovative social interaction that the internet provides. The dramatic growth of the internet, and of its many applications, plainly holds the potential and promise of previously unheard of actions and possibilities in most domains of human life. Yet assessment with hindsight often leads to the broad conclusion starkly expressed by one writer, who suggests that 'the tremendous promise of the digital revolution has been compromised by capitalist appropriation and development of the internet' and notes the 'great conflict between openness and a closed system of corporate profitability' (McChesney, 2013: 97). The point here is to recognise the essential continuity of the social order, despite, possibly even because of, technological advances. The ambivalent benefits of digitisation and the internet can be experienced by the poorest, not just as unaffordable desiderata, but even as new forms of punitive intrusion. Eubanks, for example, writes of what she terms 'the digital poorhouse', in describing surveillance and monitoring of welfare recipients in the USA in programmes adopting automated procedures for scrutinising eligibility and compliance (Eubanks, 2017).

The notion that the internet could liberate, galvanise, and open up every aspect of experience, from politics to education, to consumption, is readily shown to be just one potential pathway. The reality seems to be one of unprecedentedly powerful monopolies, ever more exploitative employment practices, and tax evasion and avoidance on a colossal scale. Whether characterised as 'digital capitalism', 'surveillance capitalism' or 'platform capitalism', there is a common theme. While we cannot, and should not, disregard the very real promise, and the frequent progressive and liberatory outcomes, of internet use, its proper analysis can only be complete with recognition of the continuities and impact of inequality in the societies in which it is embedded.

5
Managing dissent

I am arguing in this book that to be an active citizen requires the capacity to seek and then consider substantial amounts of information and understanding that are routinely unavailable through the mainstream media that most of us consume. To be able to do that involves, at least tacitly, comparing what is with what might be, that is to say, at least being aware that other ways of organising our affairs are possible. Imagining otherwise is the minimum capacity of citizenship since it compels us to compare what is with what could be, using our knowledge and awareness of the alternatives to, as well as the deficiencies of, the arrangements, policies and conventions which frame our civic lives.

Obviously it is possible to idealise a utopia in which we all, as a matter of public duty, consider the full range of alternatives available, and engage in some kind of continuous review of our requirements as members of a political community. Society is not a debating society, and life is rather more imperfect than such a romanticised picture of us all constituting some kind of permanent citizen's assembly might imply. However, that we are routinely denied narrative and insight into the potential forms of alternative societal arrangements, or are presented with them in ways that accentuate their undesirability or impossibility, is a serious concern for the viability of civic life, and it is that proposition which this chapter addresses.

Throughout history, radicals and progressives have torn their hair out at the apparent failure of the under-privileged to recognise, let alone condemn and oppose, their disadvantages. For Marx, of course, this was a major feature of his notion of the evolution of class consciousness, as, firstly, awareness by the working class of its common position and collective form emerged, to be followed, he predicted, by the necessary action to forge, or force, organised and irreversible revolutionary change. The very notion of 'false consciousness' was developed to describe and explain the frustrating frequency with which the dispossessed accept and even acclaim their lot. Such responses have remained an abiding worry for both political activists and academic theorists. One consistent line of thought has been the increasing insistence of both rich and poor to compare their position with those nearest to them rather than those more considerably in better or worse circumstances. This may have become exacerbated by the growing geographical and social demarcations between groups in diverse circumstances. The comparisons made, and the consequences of the manner and limits of such comparisons, were expertly examined, for example, in a fine piece of research undertaken by W.G. Runciman in the United Kingdom in the relatively halcyon days of the 1960s (Runciman, 1966).

The political and theoretical debate this simple observation has generated, through such concepts as that of the Italian Marxist Antonio Gramsci's idea of hegemony (considered in the next chapter), to structuralist ideas about ideological state apparatuses, is not the focus here. Rather, the aim of this chapter is to explore the problem at the heart of this debate by assessing the nature of mediated provision about dissent. The central argument is that opposition to the prevailing order is, effectively, managed by major news media. Any kind of dissent offering more than marginal criticism, or that apparently indicates widespread and potentially trans-formative demands, is thus in various ways minimised or undermined in scope and effect, or presented as manifestly unacceptable or excessive. In developing this account the chapter will look at two significant and indicative cases. The first looks beyond the United Kingdom to coverage of the rise of various radical movements in Europe in the last twenty years, notably in southern Europe. The second compares the 'Jarrow Crusade' in 1936 (and the 'hunger marches' of the preceding period) in the United Kingdom with the 'Day of Action' organised by the British Trades Union Congress in 2011.

The 'Protest Paradigm'

So commonplace is the role of the media in emasculating or even masking dissent that researchers have evolved the notion of the 'protest paradigm' to describe the manner in which this commonly occurs. Protests, almost by definition reactions to political events, sometimes quite specific ones, are of course some way short of full-blown movements demanding wholesale or radical change, though they are often motivated by similar political views, and indeed are expressed by similar populations. However, the common character-istics of the 'protest paradigm' appear in media coverage of many such events and actions. These include describing the motives of the participants as suspect or marginal, their actions as unduly violent, illegitimate, or possibly anarchic, carnivalesque or irresponsible, and their support as restricted or narrow. The concept arose from Todd Gitlin's account of the work of the Students for a Democratic Society (SDS) in the USA in the 1960s (Gitlin, 1980). Coverage of their activities, and of the American New Left in general, raised questions and concerns well beyond this particular set of events in, mainly, the American West Coast. Gitlin's essential argument is that 'the media helped *contain* the movement in the course of diffusing images of it' (ibid.: 245). This was exacerbated, in Gitlin's view, by repetitive coverage of a negative kind, so that attentive audiences were even more recipients of discrediting imagery than incidental ones. Growing dissent and opposition were thus demeaned and under-mined, reducing their potential and impact. The concept of the protest paradigm was crystallised in the analysis of events in Hong Kong in the 1970s (Chan and Lee, 1984), focusing on the ways in which the political and ideological presumptions of the news media directly affected their coverage of such protests.

Writing over 30 years after Gitlin, Weaver and Scacco used the concept of the 'protest paradigm' to analyse coverage of the 'Tea Party' in the USA (Weaver and Scacco, 2013). They note that many studies in the intervening period had addressed coverage by mainly right-wing media of mainly left-wing protest, but in looking at coverage of the far right fringe Tea Party they found many of the same characteristics – emphasising spectacle (marches and demon-strations), actions (rather than policies) and the protesters themselves rather than their pur-poses, in coverage of protest and dissenting groups. Di Cicco examined US media reporting of protests of one kind or another between 1967 and 2007, and detected a general tendency to treat such activities as a 'public nuisance' (Di Cicco, 2010). Boykoff's study of US media coverage of the World Trade Organisation protests in Seattle in 1999 and the World Bank/IMF protests in Washington, DC in 2000, found what he describes as five dominant frames in the coverage: the violence frame, the disruption frame, the freak frame, the ignorance frame and the amalgam of grievances frame. None of these could be remotely construed as sympathetic to or supportive of the protests (Boykoff, 2006). A similar study by Rauch and her colleagues found that in the years following the 'battle in Seattle', there was some evolution in US media coverage, though the Seattle events became a primary reference point in coverage of later anti-globalisation actions. While this change represented some degree of growing sophistication, both of coverage and of protester media savvy, generally, what the researchers term the 'delegitimising language' of confrontation, 'circus', and the protest paradigm, endured (Rauch et al. 2007). Despite any such growing sophistication, in research into Wisconsin newspaper reporting of protests over a 40-year period, Boyle and his colleagues suggest the press became progressively less interested in protest of limited vehemence, becoming 'more critical of less deviant activity', with social-issue protests being met with increasingly critical coverage (Boyle et al., 2005: 650).

In looking at media coverage of such protest and dissent three themes emerge. Firstly, the coverage is generally sceptical and selective, in the ways the 'protest paradigm' indicates, though this is much shaped by the political expectations and presumptions of the media reporting the dissent. Of course, it is a fact of communications and political life that most mainstream media in countries like the USA and indeed the UK sit some way from the left of the political spectrum, and also that dissent is often expressed from a left position so that coverage of protest is inevitably largely of the left by the centre or right. Participants are commonly disparaged for their appearance, unappealing demeanour and homogenous demography (i.e., suggesting they are far from typical). However, an extensive study of protest movements in four European countries between 2010 and 2012 found a range of social demographics and political affinities among the protesters surveyed, and much difference between 'old' and 'new' forms of protest (Peterson et al., 2015). News coverage is less discerning and 'sociological'. In an Irish study of protests in Ireland in 2014 against rising water charges, it was found that the protest paradigm remains alive and well, and the authors note the distinction between 'reasonable people' and the 'sinister fringe' to be found in much news about the protesters (Power et al., 2016). This distinction is an important one, to be discussed more extensively later in this chapter.

Secondly, analysis of reporting of such kinds suggests significant variation depending on the form and affiliations of the media describing the protests, as illustrated by looking at the coverage in various countries of dissent of this kind. Much of the research into the emergence of newer social protest movements is primarily interested in the use of new 'social media' to facilitate unprecedented scale, velocity and form in political mobilisation among their participants (see, for example, work mentioned in Castells, 2015). *Podemos* became the identity for left-wing political parties in many countries, notably in Spain in 2014 following the '15-M' or 'Indignados' movement protests, mainly against austerity and the 'Euro crisis'. The Indignados first became evident in Madrid in 2011, and inspired similar activities with similar names and slogans elsewhere, not least in Greece. In a study of coverage in two main Spanish newspapers Labio-Bernal shows how the movement/party was extensively demonised, especially in associating it with Venezuela, Bolivia, Cuba and more broadly with a bogy image labelled 'communism' (Labio-Bernal, 2018). Comparing coverage in the Spanish and Greek media one study notes the continued salience of the 'protest paradigm', emphasising the spectacle and 'theatricality' of the protests (Kyriakidou and Olivas Osuna, 2017). The authors acknowledge the increasingly sympathetic character of coverage over time, but caution against overstating such positive coverage, and note also that sympathetic coverage was heavily weighted towards the centre-left press in both countries.

Thirdly, analysis of this kind of news suggests that greater tolerance is shown of dissenting and protest activities at some remove from the media and their audience. Of course, this is in the context of the relative paucity of news about the wider world in the news media of most countries, the parochialism of which has become exacerbated by the rising costs of international newsgathering. Sanz Sabido and Price conducted a survey of coverage of anti-austerity protests in the UK press between 2011 and 2015. They note how coverage was oriented towards overseas rather than UK events, and was concentrated in newspapers with political sympathies leaning to the left. Coverage of events closer to home was much more likely to accord with the protest paradigm, focusing, for example on the violence of protesters and the negative consequences of protests. The contrast with the restraint and responsibility of UK-based police and authorities in what was sometimes coordinated Europe-wide protests was a theme frequently appearing in news reports (Sanz Sabido and Price, 2017). In a study of protests in the Brazilian, Indian and Chinese media, Shahin and colleagues note just how much the political affiliation of the media, and the history of protest and political action in the countries concerned, need to be understood and addressed in reviewing the role of the 'protest paradigm' in the media of differing societies. They emphasise the extent to which national media covering protests elsewhere do so through the prism of local priorities – the familiar parochialism of 'home news abroad' (Shahin et al. 2016; Golding and Elliott, 1979: 156). In countries where there is a history of political change rooted beyond the usual consensual structures of political management, more media tolerance is likely. In more 'formalised' political cultures, such as in the US, this is less likely. Their conclusion is that 'ideological affiliation with the government of the day, rather than the tenets of a particular ideology, makes news organisations more likely to follow the protest paradigm' (Shahin et al.: 159).

One of the most widespread and rapidly developing such protest movements in recent years was that which gradually acquired the rubric of the 'Occupy Movement'. Rooted in rising awareness of and indignation about the economic crisis after 2008, the 'movement' emerged initially in the USA, most dramatically with a protest in 2011 on Wall Street, the financial centre in New York. Prompted by the dissemination of awareness of the concentration of wealth in the country (the top 1% nearly trebled the proportion of national wealth they held in the period since 2007), the protesters evolved the effective and evocative slogan of 'we are the 99%'. The Occupy Wall Street events were replicated throughout the country, with several hundred similar protests taking place in relatively short order (see, among many accounts, Castell, 2015: pp. 159–210; Gitlin, 2012).

The Occupy Movement very quickly generated international replication, not least because of its swift exploitation of the possibilities of networked and digital political mobilisation and organisation (see, for example, Costanza-Chock, 2012; Kavada, 2015). There have been numerous studies of how the Occupy Movement (if such it was) came to be portrayed in news coverage. Looking specifically at the *New York Times* Gottlieb suggests the paper focused on 'the conflict instead of the protest issues' (Gottlieb, 2015: 18), though he argues that this does not settle the observation that news frames delegitimise protest, and urges protesters to be innovative in their strategy and tactics in order to solicit better coverage and wider public interest. That the language used to describe the Occupy activities was less than helpful to them is widely analysed. Linguists Gregoriou and Paterson, examining a range of English language media, concluded that Occupy and its supporters were predominantly portrayed negatively, in language suggesting aggression, conflict and even violence (Gregoriou and Paterson, 2017). Winslow takes this one step further and discovers a 'pathologising' of the Occupy Wall Street protesters in the use of language redolent of 'an aesthetic of disgust', with recurring attention to the hygiene, moral impurity, and generally unappealing aspects of the Occupy encampments (Winslow, 2017).

The ultimate impact of this coverage, and indeed of the 'movement', remains uncertain. Gaby and Caren concede that the movement 'fizzled out' almost within a year of its first emergence, but their analysis of US newspapers claims that one legacy of the protesters' efforts was increased attention given to matters of inequality in the press, a 'lasting discursive influence', a trend which they detect increasing in newspapers published throughout the period between 2002 and 2013 (Gaby and Caren, 2016). They also note, however, how much more sympathetic coverage is obtained by activities demanding 'reasonable' change, a theme to be examined in the next section.

Of course, the 'protest paradigm' is a simplified description of how active and sometimes widespread dissent is reported in the news media. Increasingly, changes in both political action and communications capacity and processes have made this an insufficient diagnosis of the way media report dissent. It is over a decade since Cottle, for one, described the many ways in which such changes demanded renewed and more nuanced attention to the 'changing media politics of dissent' (Cottle, 2008). The rapid escalation in the use and availability of digital media increasingly has enabled the political organisation and mobilisation of demonstrators in many countries and situations, while the globalisation of news and political rhetoric has enhanced the visibility and effectiveness of their actions. Widespread dissatisfaction with 'conventional' institutions of political resource allocation and action, whether parties, parliaments or traditional authority structures, has become translated not only into various forms of populism but also into a continuous challenge for the kind of conventional response described by analytical constructs like the 'protest paradigm'.

It remains the case, nonetheless, as Cottle observes in his cautionary review of this research, that 'some demonstrations are more politically acceptable to sections of the news media than others' (ibid.: 857), and while, on occasion, this may find unlikely actions receiving unexpectedly supportive reporting, the continuing and general tenor of the media with which most people come into contact remains one that subtly distinguishes the legitimate from the illegitimate in dissent, and in so doing manages its potency.

Cottle is asserting the extent to which changes in the focus and *modus operandi* of more recent protest movements and actions require a change in our analytical approach to them. However, if we compare mass media representation of protests in the 1930s to protests in the present day in the United Kingdom (as I shall do later in this chapter), then we are struck not by the novelty of protests and media representations but by the continuities and parallels. Protesters in the 1930s deployed a great deal of media savvy designed to win support from the public via influencing media representations. They engaged in demonstrative action precisely for this purpose. The targets of dissent remain very familiar. The key mobilising slogan of the Occupy Movement, 'We are the 99%', is clearly about the maldistribution of income and political power, not the politics of identity. Finally, the dominant frame of the news media remains that of law and (dis)order and of maintaining the legitimacy of liberal capitalist democracy.

Responsible and Unacceptable Dissent: Two Case Studies[1]

Central to the argument of this chapter, then, is the notion that the media play a vital role in managing dissent, most effectively by distinguishing its presentation into forms of opposition that are acceptable and within the realms of responsible and suitable expressions of disagreement with public policy, from those that are readily labelled as outside this consensus, and beyond what should be accepted by the public at large. The boundary between those two is rhetorically constructed by the media in an effective and self-sustaining operation of ideological distinction, which has the effect of limiting the potential and credibility of radical dissent. This process of legitimising and delegitimising is, at root, what is described in the 'protest paradigm' outlined above, and in the context of this book it underlines the importance of the capacity actively to seek information about and accounts of public conditions, beyond those easily and cheaply available. This distinction is made very apparent in comparing two major events in the United Kingdom in the twentieth century. The first is what has become remembered as the 'Jarrow Crusade' of 1936; the second is the 'Day of Action' in 2011, largely organised in the United Kingdom by the umbrella body for the country's trade unions, the Trades Union Congress.

Poverty in the United Kingdom had increased and became increasingly a concern in the period before the First World War, and the long-held differentiation between the 'deserving' and 'underserving' poor was readily and recurrently brought into service to justify the many punitive limitations placed on unemployment benefit support (Golding and Middleton, 1982: ch. 2). The very notion of proper citizenship, of the 'better sort of labourer', lay at the heart of this distinction, and the press was frequently prompted to express concern that policy should recognise the division to be made between those so intemperate and indolent as to deserve their impoverished fate, and those for whom sympathy and support might reasonably be expressed. As the *Daily Express* had put it in 1909, 'The genuine unemployed workman has a strong distaste for all these futile demonstrations' (15 February 1909).

---

[1]This section draws on research undertaken with Prof. John Downey and Karen Williamson, whose contribution I gratefully acknowledge.

The 1920s and 1930s were the 'hungry years', and also the period in which the mass circulation of popular press exploded in scale and impact. National daily circulation more than trebled between 1918 and 1939, by which date it was nearly 11 million (Murdock and Golding, 1978). Anxiety that public spending, not just on 'the dole' but on services generally, was 'running out of control' was crystallised in the Geddes Reports of 1921–1922. Sir Eric Geddes (a Conservative politician and businessman) was chair of a Committee on National Expenditure, and the 'Geddes Axe' cut huge swathes of such expenditure. While education was a primary target, the continuing need to exercise discriminatory caution in welfare benefits, not least in imposing a 'genuinely seeking work' test in administering them, buttressed the public sense of propriety expressed in much of the press in the face of severe adversity experienced by millions. Against this backdrop, the 'hunger marches' organised by the National Unemployed Workers Movement (of which there were six major such events between 1921 and 1936) aroused much ire (see Hannington, 1938). Press hostility and government exploitation of press animosity to the NUWM were a prominent background to these events, and indeed overt antipathy to the 1934 march became the prompt for the founding of the National Council for Civil Liberties. But in the years leading up to the Second World War, reviving economic fortunes began to make unemployment, and the anguish of those it hit hardest, increasingly cries in the dark.

Shipbuilding was one of the great success stories of British industrial supremacy in the nineteenth century, not least in the northeast of England. But increasing international competition meant that, while in the late nineteenth century over three-quarters of the world's new ships were built in the north-east of England, by 1934 this had fallen to under 7%, and between 1930 and 1937 28 firms closed, including, in 1933, Palmers Shipyard in Jarrow, a single-industry, one-company town on the River Tyne near Newcastle. The town, that had been prosperous up to the 1920s as a result of Palmers, became increasingly more destitute with its closure. Unemployment levels were among the highest in the country. As Ellen Wilkinson (the radical socialist Labour MP for Jarrow), notes in her book, '*Jarrow: The Town that was Murdered*', 'six thousand are on the dole and 23,000 on relief out of a population of 35,000 . . . Jarrow in that year, 1932–1933, was utterly stagnant. There was no work' (1939: 238). Wilkinson was a central figure in what was to become a national symbol of protest, the Jarrow Crusade (generally see Perry, 2005).

The Jarrow Crusade, a march to London of about 200 people selected from about 1,200 volunteers, was self-consciously different from the 'hunger marches' that preceded it, and became, at least eventually, an establishment-approved, 'apolitical' demonstration. The (decidedly political) decision was taken by its leaders to present the Jarrow March as non-political, as a march not like the others in their wider grievances aimed at capitalist-produced crises, but rather as a march about a specific industrial and local tragedy. This was, to a large degree, in tune with the town's history. As Purdue reflects, Jarrow was in many ways a model of working-class conservatism. As a parliamentary constituency, it had mostly been a stronghold of Liberalism and support for the Conservative Party grew during the 1930s. Left-wing militancy was rare in the town, and the march to London to demonstrate the dire straits of its population was not conceived as militantly anti-government (Purdue, 1982a; 1982b). The organisers of the Jarrow Crusade (a term much preferred and selected by the organisers as less provocative and more indicative of their intentions than 'march') set out explicitly to avoid the negative publicity of the Hunger Marches (the last of which coincided with the march from Jarrow to London) by stressing their non-political, non-violent and traditionally English way of expressing a grievance to the government. Its public image was a primary concern; one of the four committees for the Crusade's organisation was devoted to media handling.

The march became, and has endured as, a symbol of this kind of sympathetically received and politically acceptable concern. The marchers were welcomed in London by locals, lodged in the east end, went to watch the parade leading to the state opening of Parliament (though, having scrubbed up for the occasion they found it cancelled due to rain), and went to a public meeting they organised in Farringdon. On November 4th, the following morning, a petition was presented on their behalf to Parliament, but a Cabinet meeting, by all accounts, ignored the Jarrow issue, and while some of the Crusaders went for tea at the House, a lingering sense that the Crusade had failed accompanied the marchers as they returned by bus and train to the north-east the following day.

National press coverage of the march shows that while the means of protest were approved, success in achieving the marchers' aims was regarded as ultimately always doomed, particularly following a government-issued statement indicating it had no intention to receive their deputation. The descriptive headlines of both the left-leaning *Daily Herald* and *The Times* make this clear. In the former, the headline was 'Precaution following information of attempts by Communists and fascists to "get at" the Jarrow Marchers and win them from their pledge not to indulge in politics' (*The Daily Herald*, 3 November 1936), while the latter noted that the Crusade would be 'Non-political in character' (*The Times*, 2 November 1936). Most newspapers covered the story of the Jarrow Marchers from the day the 200 unemployed men, and their organisers left Jarrow for their 268-mile trek to London. Each had a series of relatively short articles covering a host of largely insignificant, often 'human interest', details including how far the marchers had travelled, where they were to be accommodated overnight, the food, drink and entertainment offered to them by their accommodators, and the health of their black Labrador mascot, Paddy. In the course of the march, The *Daily Mirror* had ten articles; the *Daily Express*, six; *The Times*, five; and the only left-wing newspaper, *The Daily Herald*, had eight articles about the Jarrow Marchers between their departure from Jarrow and arrival in London on the 29 September 1936.

Contrast with the unacceptable nature of the hunger marches was frequent and explicit. The 1932 'National Hunger March Against the Means Test' had been especially characterised as beyond the boundaries of acceptable decency and restraint. Before the event *The Daily Herald* (26 October 1932) reported that 'Police have warned against encouraging or lending assistance to any overt acts that may occasion a breach of the public peace'. The events in Hyde Park the following day received predictable coverage: 'Clash Between Mounted Police and Rowdy Demonstrators' (*Daily Express,* 28 October 1932); 'The Police and the Agitators' (*Daily Mirror* editorial, 28 October 1932), and so on. Large photos of the baton-wielding police confronting dangerously uncontrolled demonstrators were commonplace (and very similar to those taken at the 1968 anti-Vietnam War demonstration in London analysed in Halloran et al., 1970).

Three aspects of such events are highlighted in the coverage – unacceptable rowdiness and violence, the misdirection of innocent dupes by extremist leaders or interlopers, and the futility of such protests. As the *Daily Mirror* reported of the 1932 march, 'we regret very much that several thousand of our unhappy unemployed should have been led (or misled) into the utterly useless demonstration known as a "hunger march"…we in no way blame these deluded unfortunates who have been set marching and shouting. We ask who are those who play upon their distress? We blame their unscrupulous leaders' (27 October 1932).

With this background, coverage of the Jarrow March was able to bring into relief its essential decency (and impotence). At the outset, it was greeted simply as 'intended to provide an opportunity of describing to a London audience the facts about a town which has suffered from industrial depression' (*The Times* 2 November. 1936). The human interest generated during the march was prominent among the limited national coverage it received en route. On October 7th. *The Daily Mirror* reported that 'Two Boys Run Away to join 260-mile March'. The marchers' mascot was regularly featured (*Daily Herald* 15 October 1936, 'Dog Leads Jarrow March'), not least when the papers reported that Paddy was out of sorts because her foot pads were slightly inflamed. Curiously, this vocabulary translated readily into reports that, once in London, there were careful precautions to 'prevent the marchers from becoming the catspaw of any political organisation' (*Daily Mirror* 2 November 1936). *The Daily Express* offered a familiar refrain when reporting of the marchers' arrival in Luton that they were 'warned of attempts to turn their march into a political Crusade' (29 October 1936). Unlike the 1932 'mob', 'these men – clean, decent, orderly, self-disciplined, with their poor but well-darned and carefully patched clothes' (*Daily Herald* 31 October 1932) were in a march that was admirably non-political. In the rainy demonstration in London they remained orderly and cheerful, and were applauded for taking part in a 'pilgrimage [that] is not one of violence' (*The Times* 5 November 1936). As the same paper noted the following day, it was one that showed no suggestion of disorder even though extremists were mingling with the demonstrators, as shown by their being able to 'advertise their presence not only by crude banners but also by the noisy shouting of slogans'.

The success of the Crusaders in obtaining relatively sympathetic coverage was as notable as their failure to obtain any change in government policy. The Jarrow Crusade, however, has become an enduring symbol and rhetorical badge for particular forms of popular protest, notably engendering imagery of cast-down involuntary poverty, respectable if distressing expressions of need, and acceptable and 'proper' forms of popular expression. As Perry notes wryly, the legend has bequeathed 'five plays, two musicals, an opera, three pop songs, two folk songs, ….a cuddly toy, a real ale, a public house…' and much more besides (op.cit.: 2). This has cumulatively provided a blue-print for respectable, legitimate, media approved protest through acts of accommodation with the dominant ideology. Its modest intentions and non-political stance have since been the source of its celebration by the Labour Party, the Trades Union Congress (TUC), and the British establishment, i.e. in education, the BBC and the church. As Perry argues 'selective nostalgia for protest allows such institutions to act as arbiters of what constitutes legitimate protest in the past and present… It is an irony of history that the same institutions celebrate the Crusade and discourage present day protests …' (op.cit.: 182). The myth persists. In 2011, *The Socialist* greeted a Youth Fight for Jobs demonstration under the banner headline 'Join the Jarrow March', anticipating the organisers' plans to replicate the 1936 action (5–11 May 2011). In August 2014 a march from Jarrow was organised in support of public funding for the

National Health Service. On 5 December that year the *Daily Mirror* introduced critical coverage of Conservative Chancellor of the Exchequer George Osborne's autumn budget with a large picture of the Jarrow Crusade. Many such examples, often with no accompanying explanation, testify to the enduring mythology and symbolic resonance of Jarrow.

My second case study is the 'Day of Action', also the 'March for the Alternative', organised by the TUC. This was a large demonstration in London in March 2011, driven by opposition to the Conservative-Liberal Democrat coalition government's austerity plans and public spending cuts. It was widely estimated to be the largest such demonstration in the United Kingdom since the Iraq war nearly a decade earlier. The demonstrators (variously estimated to number between 250,000 and 500,000, many bussed in from all over the country) marched along Whitehall, via the Houses of Parliament, to Hyde Park, where a rally was addressed by speakers including the TUC General Secretary, Brendan Barber, and the leader of the Labour opposition, Ed Miliband. Small splinter groups, however, targeted the west end of London, and over 200 people were arrested in incidents including the occupation by UK Uncut of the up-market store Fortnum and Mason in protest against its alleged avoidance of taxes.

The press made the distinction between the orderly march and the disorderly direct action central to coverage. As the *Daily Mail* approvingly observed of Barber, he was 'A quietly-spoken Merseysider,... a standard-bearer for new style trade unionism, operating through partnership with government and employers, rather than conflict' (17 March 2011). The violence of the minority, however, was both foregrounded and forecast. On the day of the march, even in early editions, the *Sun* headline was 'Riot on March', while on the day after the march, the *Mail on Sunday* provided an article headlined 'Thugs Killing their own Cause', suggesting protests are only helpful if they are 'dignified and well-controlled'. Once again the shadow of Jarrow three-quarters of a century earlier is readily invoked; a *Times* editorial argued, of the 2011 marchers, 'They know, too, they don't have the public support to turn this into the General Strike or the Jarrow March' (25 March 2011). Anticipation of likely violence (and thus framing of the event before it happened as predominantly about its character rather than its aims) was extensive. The London *Evening Standard* (25 March 2011) carried the headline 'Extremists Vow to Hijack March and Bring Chaos to the Streets'; and *the Sun* warned (26 March 2011) that 'violent extremists' were likely to turn the march into a battleground. Not least among the more salubrious events at presumed risk was the royal wedding of Prince William and Catherine Middleton scheduled for 29 April 2011. Several press reports raised the alarming prospect that this event might itself become a belated victim of the likely violence and anarchy afoot. As the *Daily Mail* worriedly suggested (28 March 2011), 'Royal wedding celebrations were last night being singled out for a campaign of violence by extremists intent on repeating the mayhem that swept London at the weekend...'

The malign role of agent provocateurs, presumably exploiting the innocent and naïve for their own political ends, was much highlighted. The *Daily Telegraph* (18 March 2011) demanded that the 'union-sponsored, unrepresentative Popular Front is not allowed to pass itself off as the British public', and the following week reported that police 'have been warned that today's mass demonstration in London against government cuts might be hijacked by extremist groups intent on violence' (26 March 2011). And after all, the participants had little to complain about; 'They are entitled to the full largesse of the welfare state, and many of them drink deeply of it' (*Daily Telegraph* 30 March 2011).

In addition to displacement that deflects attention from the purpose of the march, there is also a rationalisation of government policy. In the same manner as in the 1930s, the march was portrayed as counter-productive because there could be no sensible alternative to government austerity, which was, in any case, quite modest. 'What has been represented ... as a dramatic and dangerous change of course is, in fact, no more than a relatively small but firm and determined touch on the financial tiller', wrote the *Daily* Mail (26 March 2011), elsewhere the same day suggesting that 'Today's March for the Alternative (ill-named, because there is no alternative) will only be the start of it'.

As outlined in Chapter 3, behind much of the reporting is a tacit, and sometimes explicit, presumption that even Keynesian approaches to economic crisis, requiring government expenditure and investment rather than retrenchment, are impracticable, while more radical calls for fundamental change to the structure of the economy are absent or dismissed. Reporting of the Day of Action itself classically highlighted the futility of the action, its marginal violence and disorder, and its exploitation by 'extremist' manipulators. As Williams dejectedly reflects, 'The sad fact is that the impact of media coverage of events in London means it will be remembered for the mayhem in Oxford Street and the police action in Trafalgar Square, rather than the massive mobilisation of half a million trades unionists and supporters' (Williams, 2011: 4).

Conclusion

Both the events whose media presentations have been outlined in this chapter display a number of features that persistently characterise the portrayal of radical and active dissent, not least in a political communication environment with a distinct political leaning as found in the UK national press. Such presentation is testimony to the boundary-maintaining and policing role of the news media, managing dissent by presenting eruptions of it as acceptable, legitimate and effective, or as unacceptable, illegitimate and futile. Where dissent is perceived to be threatening to an existing consensus its manifestation is likely to be reported with the latter of these frames.

Of course, the deep-seated reservations of the largely right-wing UK national press about radical opposition are hardly unfamiliar, and the weaknesses of the press generally as a reliable witness to history have received regular and multi-faceted analysis. The largely laudatory report of the first UK Royal Commission on the Press, in 1949, while rejecting, and indeed often dismissive of, many of the accusations of influence, bias, and inaccuracy it received, nonetheless could not resist coyly concluding that 'we have found some evidence of willingness to be satisfied with what at best corresponds only roughly to the truth' (para 553), and acknowledging that as a matter of realpolitik 'it should be readily understood that newspapers' treatment of public affairs is...frankly partisan' (para 555) (Royal Commission, 1949). That largely right-wing proprietors pursued largely right-wing agendas through their newspapers was a fact of political life, captured most succinctly in the bravura assertion by Lord Beaverbrook, one of the archetypal 'press barons' of early twentieth century Britain, whose political as well as industrial career was founded on the huge success and influence of his *Express* newspapers, that (as he told the Royal Commission on the Press) he ran his paper 'purely for the purpose of making propaganda, and with no other motive' (para 87).

The antipathy of much of the UK press to any perceptible drift to the left, and to the Labour Party in particular, is a familiar part of the political landscape. This is often rooted in a sense of 'moderation', 'common sense' and the centre ground being a space occupied by journalists and readers alike, who are rhetorically yoked into a hegemonic political culture that, in fact, makes specific assumptions about the rectitude and inevitability of such propositions as neo-liberal economics, the impracticability or undesirability of regulation or public intervention, and the superiority of private over public services (Williams, 1970 comments on the historical evolution of this particular kind of popular journalism). Gaber suggests that 'broadcast journalists, and particularly those based at Parliament, have been so suffused with a culture of politics that is oriented around some mythical centre ground that they are unable to treat fairly politicians (and parties) that are seen to lie outside this consensus' (Gaber, 2019: 230).

This position was most vehemently, and at times extremely, deployed in coverage by the press in the 1970s of the urban left. Strident and often simply vitriolic coverage of the 'loony left', especially in London, has been exhaustively documented in research by Curran, Gaber and Petley (2019). Though the effect may often have been limited (Curran suggests that the right-wing press did not secure complete public support for the emasculation of local government, at least not at the time – see ibid.: 135), the 'loony left' image had an undoubted major impact on the electoral fortunes of the Labour Party as a whole. The picture was increasingly elaborated, however, after a period of relative infatuation with the 'moderate' policies of the 'new Labour' Blair years, after the Labour Party elected the more left-wing Ed Miliband as party leader. That his father had been the socialist academic Ralph Miliband led the *Daily Mail* to cover its front page with a pen portrait of 'The Man Who Hated Britain' (27 September 2013), making the links between the newly elected younger Miliband to his marxisant academic father both obvious and threatening.

This approach became even more insistent following the election of Jeremy Corbyn as leader of the Labour Party in 2015. His personal demonisation as a 'sex-pot Trot' (relating to past relationships and invariably portraying him wearing a Lenin-style hat), with odd habits and hobbies (an interest in manhole covers), suspect appearance (routinely described as scruffy), and as a threat to national security (his lack of obvious adherence to proper nationalist loyalty was illustrated by expression of extended doubts about his ability or willingness to sing the national anthem or go through the proper formalities of becoming a Privy Councillor), were all frequent and indeed recurrent aspects of his press presentation after the 2017 election. In the final days of the pre-Brexit period, as the possibility of a general election became seriously considered, the *Mail on Sunday* devoted a whole front page, and many inside pages, to the worry that this 'joyless fanatic' was 'Unfit for Office' (10 February 2019), its deduction from a reading of a book 'every voter must read'. Research by a team at the London School of Economics, examining in detail coverage of Corbyn in 2015, concluded that the news media had severely failed the needs of their audience. The research found a great deal of Corbyn criticism but little case for the defence, and a surprising absence of his own 'voice' in coverage (well over half of the coverage of Corbyn contained no direct quote from its subject). In summary, their analysis shows 'most newspapers systematically vilifying the leader of the biggest opposition party, assassinating his character, ridiculing his personality, and delegitimising his ideas and politics' (Cammaerts et al., 2016: 12).

Such political tendentiousness is the stuff of press politics, and the right-wing 'bias' of the UK national press is far from unfamiliar, though surprisingly opaque to many readers. The point here is not to reassert this rather obvious limitation to political communication, though it is not unimportant, and as was discussed in Chapter 4, is not rendered less influential by the proliferation of digital and other news sources. More fundamental, however, is the part this most evident feature of the political communication landscape plays in the wider role of the media in limiting the capacity of their audiences to exercise fully the potential of citizenship. In maintaining the boundaries between legitimate and illegitimate dissent, the media are effectively containing the possibilities of the political imagination. The labelling and framing of particular forms and characteristics of dissent as either acceptable or not, have an important ideological function in setting limits to the political imaginary. The media are, thus, an apparatus for the management of dissent, forging and cumulatively defining a consensus that is powerfully bounded rhetorically and politically, and which thus renders the capacity to seek understanding and information beyond the normal limits of mainstream media a necessity for informed citizenship.

6

So what? Communications, inequality and citizenship

Throughout this book, the insistent purpose has been to uncover how inequalities make communications, both to and from citizens, reinforcements of those inequalities, as gaps in knowledge, information and voice become embedded in the contours of social division. The reasons for this are threefold. First, basic inequalities in resources, income and wealth are large and widening, a phenomenon mainly illustrated in previous chapters by data from what is probably one of the more extreme cases among the industrialised countries, the United Kingdom, but which is more widely evident. Secondly, the sources of information in the 'mainstream' media about public affairs and civic life are demonstrably and persistently inadequate, in many fields disseminating a partial or even misleading characterisation of one or other feature of the social landscape. Thirdly, the capacity to complement or even contrast this diet with active information-seeking of one kind or another is itself subject to the constraints of resource inequality, since information and knowledge are so often, and increasingly, purchasable commodities inequitably accessible to different population groups. The startling, rapid and powerful impact of digitalisation and online information-seeking and 'transmission' have exacerbated rather than mitigated these trends. These changes have made dissent both muted and manageable, the public and widespread dissemination of marginal or challenging ideas being subject to the same pressures of resource constraint and inequities of power.

All of this has important implications for our understanding of citizenship and democracy, since the very notion of citizenship carries with it the presumption of being informed, and having the capacity to voice, effectively and broadly, the conclusions derived from being informed. This would be of profound significance at any time, but it could be argued that a concatenation of very substantial social and global matters makes the ability to know and communicate the lessons of such knowledge of unprecedented importance.

The need to know - a world of risk and uncertainty

In the 1980s, sociologists developed the notion of a 'risk society', a formulation intended to capture some of the essential features of 'late modernity', notably the widening awareness of environmental damage, but also reflecting a growing recognition of changes, many with troubling as well as positive aspects, in everything from the way we relate to each other, to work, leisure, travel and such fundamental features of modern life as power and inequality. In this context societies, it was argued, were becoming more 'reflexive', and focused on the problems and obstacles being constructed for the future by the very processes of modernisation (Beck, 1992; Giddens, 1991). The need to know, to inform the capacity for active citizenship as part of this reflexivity, is made even more acute by the fundamental, perhaps existential, changes facing the populations of the planet's nations, rich and poor alike. Decades of relative prosperity and progress (much of it fuelled by unprecedented technological advance, or at least change) are succeeded by growing evidence of large-scale challenges. Five such global nightmares haunt the dreams and visions of political thought among many in the second quarter of the twenty-first century. These are rapidly widening inequalities, both within and between nations; climate change, more and more frequently labelled, tellingly, as the climate 'crisis'; surging rates of cross-national population movements, whether induced by civil war or by economic (often climate-change driven) necessity; the deepening crisis of democratic institutions, with parliaments, parties and representative bodies receiving diminishing engagement; and finally what might be termed the death of the civic, embracing, among other things, a significant shift in power and control from the statutory to the private, or from state to corporate. A brief explanation highlights the information needs engendered by each of these.

The scale and acceleration of inequality have been discussed in Chapter 2. Keeping such data up to date merely confirms the continuing gaps between rich and poor, and the extent of the widening gulf between opposite ends of the spectrum of incomes and wealth. In surveying these movements globally, Bourguignon has detailed how some reassuring data on the slightly diminishing inequalities *between* nations, difficult to applaud though they are, with daily accounts of mass disease, premature deaths, widespread starvation and subsistence survival, from much of the world, arriving in the glossy media of the richer countries, nonetheless also points to the awkward inconsistency that sees these possible glimmers of hope balanced by evidence of growing inequality *within* nations (Bourguignon, 2015). Many of the examples in the present book are drawn from data about the United Kingdom, though recognising that in recent years the country has become something of an extreme case even within this wider dismal array. In 2023, research at a London university found that the UK's richest fifty families had more wealth than the entire poorest half of the population and that the gap between the richest and the rest was accelerating: the ratio of wealth between the richest and average was three times higher in 2023 than in 1989, with the aggregate wealth of a rich individual in 2023 being 18,000 times that of the average (Tippet and Wildauer, 2023). The prognosis of the research was, not surprisingly, salutary; arguing that at present rates of change, the wealth of the richest 200 families would be larger than the entire GDP of the United Kingdom by 2035.

In most richer countries internal wealth inequality has by and large increased since the 1980's (De Zwart, 2019). These trends are tracked, insofar as data allows, by the annual UN Social Report, which, in its most recent version, notes that 'more than two-thirds of the world's population today live in countries where inequality has grown, and inequality is rising again even in some of the countries that have seen inequality decline in recent decades...' (UN Dept. of Economic and Social Affairs, 2023). In the USA the Gini coefficient, measuring inequality of incomes, actually increased slightly between 2007 and 2016. The arrival of Donald Trump as President led to significant tax cuts for the rich, and the country remains among the more unequal in the 'western world'. Between 1970 and 2020 median low household income in the USA rose by 45% while that of high-income households rose by 69% (World Economic Forum, 2022).

Arguably (and with less and less contestation) the dominant anxiety of any horizon-scanning adult in the first half of the twenty-first century, is about climate change, or its increasingly common encapsulation in the more obviously disquieting phrase 'climate crisis'. The appetite for fossil fuels and deforestation, resulting in anthropogenic global warming due to the rapid rise in carbon dioxide emissions, has created increasingly and tragically frequent consequences impossible to ignore. 'Extreme' events have become the commonplace of front pages. Severe heatwaves in Europe in 2022 were found to have caused 61,000 deaths (Ballester et al., 2023). The following year more records tumbled. In 2023 an unusually warm winter in many countries was followed by the world's hottest day on record in June. Unprecedented rainfall in California, ice storms in Texas, cyclones in Madagascar and Malawi, terrifyingly record high temperatures in much of Asia and southern Europe, torrential rain and floods in India, wildfires in Canada and tropical storms in the Atlantic became the recurrent stuff of weather reporting in the first half of 2023 alone. In the Antarctic, sea ice continued to disappear, reaching its lowest-ever recorded level by February. In the summer southern Europe scorched – in Athens, the Acropolis was closed to tourists because of the extreme heat risks and Rhodes saw mass evacuations of tourists from the spread of forest fires. In 2024, flash floods killed over 200 people in Spain and the country announced official national days of mourning, after a summer in which the south-eastern United States experienced unprecedentedly devastating hurricanes. It was little wonder that the UN Secretary-General spoke with unusual and intense apprehension in a June 2023 press conference, declaring that 'current policies are taking the world to a 2.8 degree temperature rise by the end of the century. That spells catastrophe...We are hurtling towards disaster, eyes wide open – with far too many willing to bet it all on wishful thinking, unproven technologies and silver bullet solutions' (Guterres, 2023). His wistful addendum that 'we must consider this as a moment of hope' (ibid.) seemed, despite its optimistic language, prompted by and in anticipation of little action or response. After all, the extent to which we have already passed or may be about to pass, irreversible 'tipping points' in the degradation of the environment, is a matter of intense scientific debate and much gloom (IPCC, 2023; Willcock, et al., 2023). As discussed in Chapter 3, environmental matters have had considerable exposure in the mainstream media, but the information and knowledge readily available without the active pursuit of more, remain significantly susceptible to the outpourings of vested interests and the exigencies of news reporting (Supran et al., 2023; Harbisher, 2023; Freedland, 2023; Cottle, 2023).

The deep anxieties about climate change, of course, embrace far more than weather extremes, to include also the impact of global warming on biodiversity, and in turn on broader eco-systems (Kolbert, 2014). While, not least in the USA, scepticism about human-made climate change remains obstinately high despite overwhelming scientific consensus to the contrary, the fossil fuel companies spend vast sums on persuading public opinion of the continued need for oil and gas extraction and of the imperfections, as they see it, of statements about the climate crisis (Freedland, op.cit).

The movement of people from one country to another has, of course, always been a feature of human experience. But the scale of such migration, and the severity and consequences of 'forced migration', with large numbers driven by civil war, occupation or the privations bequeathed by climate change and its impact on subsistence living and agriculture, have accelerated vastly in recent times. The political consequences are briefly described below. The UN estimated that in 2017 alone the world population of forcibly displaced people was larger than the population of the United Kingdom, with about 44,000 people a day being displaced from their homes; by the end of 2022, the organisation calculated, 108.4 million people worldwide were forcibly displaced as a result of persecution, conflict, violence, human rights violations and events 'seriously disturbing public order', an increase of 19 million people compared to the end of 2021 (UNHCR, 2023; Palattiyil et al., 2022). While the media are still dominated by the northern hemisphere, the overwhelming majority of displacement occurs in the 'global south', resulting in inevitable, and perhaps disproportionate, attention being given to refugees and asylum seekers (two readily confusable and contestable terms) arriving in Europe. Establishing the facts and deeper explanatory causes of migration, not to mention the political and social implications of the complexities of asylum-seeking, refugee status, and so-called 'economic migration', is a daunting task in a minefield of rapid change, mythology, anxiety and misrepresentation (Mattelart, 2019).

The fourth of the challenges for the citizen seeking actively, and with adequate information, to fulfil their role, is exemplified in the widespread reduction in the perceived efficacy and impor-tance of traditional political institutions. The most commonly identified indicator of this is the simple act of voting, expressing periodically a demand for a change of representation, or perhaps for continuity. In Europe, voter turn-out in elections for the European Parliament declined steadily from the aggregate 62% recorded in 1979 to 49.5% in 1999, and to 43% in 2024, though with an uncharacteristic upturn to 51% in 2019 (Hosli et al., 2022). In national elections in most countries, recent decades have demonstrated a steady, sometimes dramatic, fall in election turn-out figures. Table 6.1 shows data from a number of countries illustrating this trend. Of course, there are particular local circumstances in many cases explaining these figures. They are unashamedly selective, exclude a few countries where no such trend is evident (Denmark and India, for example, are exceptions among these countries), and are for parliamentary elections, although in some countries presidential elections may be more significant. The table also excludes countries (such as Australia, Belgium or Brazil) where voting is mandatory. The trend, nonetheless, is undeniable: active if minimal involvement in parliamentary affairs through the act of voting is generally far less prevalent now than in the relatively recent past.

The decline of traditional democratic institutions, whether indexed by membership of political parties or voting, has been much discussed and analysed, and it is not the intention

Table 6.1 Voter turn-out in a number of countries in recent decades

| Country | Voter turn-out (%) | | | |
	Year	%	Year	%
Austria	1949	96.8	2019	75.6
Cameroon	1960	69.6	2020	43.8
Canada	1958	90.6	2021	62.3
Colombia	1958	68.9	2022	47.4
Croatia	1992	75.6	2020	46.9
Cuba	1986	97.7	2023	77.9
Czech Republic	1992	84.7	2021	65.4
Denmark	1950	81.9	2022	84.2
Finland	1962	85.1	2023	68.5
France	1956	82.7	2017	48.7
Germany	1976	90.8	2021	76.6
India	1962	61.2	2019	67.4
Indonesia	1977	90.6	2019	72.6
Iran	1996	77.2	2020	42.3
Iraq	2005	79.6	2021	43.5
Ireland	1954	76.4	2020	62.8
Israel	1965	85.9	2022	70.6
Italy	1994	86.1	2022	63.8
Japan	1980	74.6	2021	56.0
Mongolia	1992	95.6	2020	73.6
Morocco	1970	85.3	2021	50.9
Namibia	1989	97.0	2019	60.4
Netherlands	1981	87.0	2021	78.7
New Zealand	1981	91.4	2020	82.2
Nigeria	2003	49.3	2019	32.1
Norway	1965	85.4	2021	77.2
Poland	1985	78.9	2019	61.7
Portugal	1980	85.4	2022	58.0
Russia	1995	64.7	2021	51.6
Slovakia	1990	96.3	2020	65.8
Slovenia	1992	85.9	2022	71.0
South Africa	1994	86.9	2019	66.1
Sweden	1982	91.4	2022	84.2
United Kingdom	1951	81.9	2024	60.1
United States	1968	89.7	2020	70.8

Source: Adapted from International IDEA (2023).

here to enter this debate (see Burton and Tunnicliffe, 2022; for a discussion in the context of the United Kingdom). However, the decline of democratic institutions places further pressure on the active search for information required for participatory citizenship. Not merely involvement in such minimal tasks as voting, but trust in the capacity of institutions to perform their required tasks, is also in decline. The Edelman 'trust barometer', a regular survey on this and related matters, conducted most recently in 28 countries, shows that what the authors describe as a 'cycle of mistrust' is evident in all these countries, though their attempts to suggest the data show greater trust in business than in governments is perhaps less persuasive than the data showing a decline in trust in governments, and indeed in the media (Edelman Trust Institute, 2023).

One other consequence of such political disaffection with mainstream institutions may be a growing shift towards a more populist style of political action and support. Partly fuelled by the continuing transfer of power from civic to corporate sectors, partly by widening inequalities fostering a sense of fear and abandonment among those 'left behind', the vote for 'Brexit' in the United Kingdom in 2016, the election of Donald Trump to the USA presidency in 2017 and in 2024, and the rapid rise (though equally dramatic subsidence) of Boris Johnson in the UK, might each be seen as harbingers of this trend. The populist surge has been evident more widely throughout Europe, and had been so since the entry into the government of Jörg Haider's far-right party in Austria in 2000. The subsequent rise of, for example, Le Pen (father and daughter) in France, Meloni in Italy, the Vox party in Spain, the Golden Dawn movement in Greece, the AfD in Germany, Chega in Portugal, Geert Wilders in the Netherlands, Austria's far-right Freedom party (FPÖ), and far-right advances even in Sweden and Finland, all seemed to reflect a growing tide of far-right populism across the continent, much of it driven by mythology about 'nationalism' and invective, anecdote and rumour about immigration. In the 2024 elections to the EU parliament, far-right parties made large gains in many European countries. Le Pen's National Rally received a third of the votes in France, the AfD in Germany increased its 2019 share from 11% to 14%, while in Austria, the far-right Freedom party came top, with over 25% of the vote, and went on to attract nearly 29% of the vote in the 2024 Austrian legislative election. The explanation for radical political shifts is always complex, but the central role of disinformation, 'social media', and under-informed partial citizenship, unquestionably has formed part of this disquieting narrative.

The fifth 'grand challenge' confronting informed citizenship might be loosely termed the decline of the civic, that is to say, a diminishing awareness of or support for the collective or publicly endorsed and provided aspects of social and political life. It has been a truism of much modern sociology to regard the individuation of adult life in complex industrial societies as a growing norm. Raymond Williams memorably captured this in his discussions of 'mobile privatisation', focused especially on communications technology and transport, but embracing much else in the nature of contemporary experience (McGuigan, 2013). In his early classic study of American social life, social psychologist David Riesman identified the 'atomised' individuals living in a 'lonely crowd' in modern life, though the diagnosis may have not been intended to have the pejorative implications redolent in his title (Riesman, 1950). Over half a century later Sherry Turkle suggested that the internet and its various uses were resulting in us living 'alone together', fostering illusions of intimacy through second-hand social life, but eroding more fundamental connections (Turkle, 2012).

David Putnam captured much of this concern in an influential study of the daily lives of American adults published at the turn of the century, in which he lamented the collapse of community life, iconically indicated for him by the rise of bowling as a pastime, but the corollary collapse of bowling leagues and other signifiers of the collective (Putnam, 2001). Again technology, especially the mass media (and subsequently, in later writers' accounts, the internet), is seen as crucial in this trend, though earlier technologies were equally complicit – the telephone, for example facilitating distant rather than intimate contact. Generally, he voices doubts about the collective accomplishments of computer-mediated communication, because of the digital divide, the decline of trust and goodwill, the social divisiveness of online 'communities', which he terms 'cyberbalkanisation', and the drive to passive, individualised entertainment and commerce (ibid, Ch. 9). As newspaper reading has diminished, its replacement, initially by television, reduces civic engagement (ibid.: Ch. 13). Later reflection by Putnam arrives at the conclusion that, more generally, 'social capital' has been eroded (Putnam and Feldstein, 2003).

Running as a thread through all these characterisations of the 'decline of the civic' is the promising, yet too frequently disappointing, impact of new communications technologies. Behind that view lies the evidence of differentiated awareness of necessary information, and unequal access to the means to engage or share the 'collective' – in simpler terms the 'digital divide'. Three broad concepts that seek to capture the nature of collective life are examined briefly here, to show how the inequalities inherent in access to and command of communications profoundly shape social participation and activity.

The (divided) public sphere

The notion of the 'public sphere' is derived from, and most closely associated with, the work of the German philosopher and sociologist Jürgen Habermas. His book introducing and explaining the concept first appeared in German in 1962, though it became much more widely influential after its translation into English in 1989 (Habermas, 1989). The work, and its central concept, have profoundly influenced the study of media and communication, the latter being a central concern in Habermas's sociological theorising (Habermas, 1984), though its scope and embrace are very much wider. At root the concept is historical, identifying the bourgeois public sphere 'above all as the sphere of private people come together as a public...to engage [public authorities] in a debate over the general rules governing relations in the basically privatised but publicly relevant sphere of commodity exchange and social labour' (Habermas, 1989: 27). In between the private realm of civil society and the family and the public authority vested in the state, the public sphere was the space in which collective public reflection and debate were possible, emerging from the discursive sharing of people's experiences in the world of letters or institutions such as the coffee houses and salons of eighteenth century Europe. The political consequence was profound: 'through the vehicle of public opinion it put the state in touch with the needs of society' (ibid.: 31.).

The implications of this historical narrative for the role of media and communications in democracy are extensive. Though the communicative essentials envisaged by Habermas in this later phase are readily vulnerable to being seen as idealised – the ideal public sphere features communication that is reasoned, rational, inclusive, interactive and open – the ideal itself becomes a set of criteria against which to assess contemporary reality. For Habermas, not least influenced by writers such as Adorno and Horkheimer, or more generally the 'Frankfurt School', the growth and dominance of consumer capitalism has resulted in the 'refeudalisation' of the public sphere, as the crushing success of media corporations and the growth and power of advertising and public relations serve not just to distort, but to reverse, the expansion of the 'public sphere'.

This 'refeudalisation' thus characterises the modern era. We have moved from a 'culture-debating' to a 'culture-consuming' society. Advertising and public relations not only dominate the political economy of the society people inhabit, but suffuse the political communications they confront; the state treats its citizens as consumers, and it too 'competes for publicity' (Habermas, 1989: 195). The decline in the potency and virtue of the public sphere is much lamented by Habermas. By the time the internet is becoming widespread, he is wary not just of the rise of media conglomerates and corporate empires, but of the fragmentation of mass audiences into online special interest groups (Habermas, 2006: 412). The media are central to political communication, but utterly absorbed into the corporate power of the empires run by men like Silvio Berlusconi and Rupert Murdoch, so that the 'power structure of the public sphere may well distort the dynamics of mass communication and interfere with the normative requirement that relevant issues, required information and appropriate contributions be mobilised' (ibid.: 418). The transformation of the public sphere is inevitable given the all-powerful advance of consumer capitalism. However, while the integration of political information into commercial power structures is recognised, little is made of the variable capacity in such a system for informed citizenship, although cultural exclusion and social deprivation are noted as two key causes of diminished input by citizens into the political system (ibid.: 421).

Neckel takes this development one stage further, suggesting that refeudalisation involves renewed, even enhanced, privileges for the wealthy, complemented by exclusion for those of lesser means. As a result 'the public sphere regresses to a form that displays similar features to those typical of pre-modern social orders' (Neckel, 2020: 472). Widening and 'historically unprecedented' levels of inequality reinforce this process in the digital era, as 'the political citizen is replaced by the media consumer who actively participates in their own elimination as a *citoyen* through the 'like'-economy of social networks and the affect-laden communication of the internet' (ibid.: 472). The growth and widespread use of 'social media' have, as discussed earlier in this book, encouraged much optimistic and occasionally romanticised commentary about the potency of the new media for citizen journalism and bottom-up communication. For some this would represent a stage beyond the transformation of the public sphere described by Habermas, though, as Staab and Thiel note, 'digitalisation adds new aspects to the dangers of mass media democracy, such as unequal access to discursive power...' (Staab and Thiel, 2022: 132). Habermas is acutely aware of this double-edged potential in the digital media, in that 'social media also foster a further advance towards the commodification of lifeworld contexts' (Habermas, 2022: 163). His focus on electoral politics, however, means a particular concern with the rise of 'fake news' and the possible implications of diminished 'professional mediation' with growing scepticism about journalism and the rise of 'citizen journalism', but a much lesser concern with the consequences of unequal access to commodified information and to the means to give voice.

The public sphere, whether a historically complex description of a real social order or a set of communicative ideals prescribing the criteria by which an effective and normatively acceptable democracy might be evaluated, is dependent in any adequate account on the possibility of relatively egalitarian access to the means of participation in the public sphere, whether passively or actively. The commodification of communications goods and services in societies of wide, and widening, gulfs in wealth and income, is an inherent brake on the development of such a public sphere. In short, the public sphere is truncated and distorted in direct consequence of and proportion to levels of inequality.

Hegemony and the quest for information

A second concept hugely influential in social analysis and relevant here is that of hegemony. The concept was most substantially developed in the work of the Italian theorist and political activist Antonio Gramsci. Gramsci, at one time a leading figure in the Italian Communist Party, was prominent as a writer, teacher, and organiser in the workers' unions and socialist politics of Turin, and spent the last eleven years of his life, between 1926 and 1937, in prison, where he produced extensive writings on the politics of his time and locality, and on political theory. His central concept of hegemony describes the way that dominance is maintained through the ability of dominant classes to go beyond physical restraint to control the very thoughts and ideas of the time, in effect making prevailing ideas the 'common sense' of widespread and internalised understanding, and so rendering alternative and critical formulations quite literally 'unthinkable' (Gramsci, 2005; Fonseca, 2016). The concept became increasingly influential in the 1980s in considerations of the role of communications media, though not without reservations about its application (Gitlin, 1980; Moore, 1998).

The significance of this notion here is the power of ideas disseminated through the media to coalesce around a finite number of taken-for-granted assumptions, whose particularity requires access to alternative ideas to be questioned or even rendered disputable. Such interrogation necessitates, not just the diverse cacophony of messages found on 'social media', but the means to seek and obtain a range of diverse interpretations, accounts and source material; in other words, it requires reasonably egalitarian access to diverse information resources. Perhaps the abiding question for political sociology facing the detached observer, or possibly even more so the committed and engaged, is how, in advanced industrial societies displaying large and consequential inequalities, those benefitting least from the social order willingly accept and even acclaim it. The concept of hegemony invites consideration of much more than economic constraint or physical coercion, to identify consent, or more potently the willing acceptance, internalisation, and enthusiastic endorsement of an inegalitarian social order, as 'normal' or inevitable. Stuart Hall, an influential and creative interpreter of Gramsci's ideas, especially as they applied to late twentieth century Britain, was insistent that hegemony is always rooted in the economy, but nonetheless embraces the moral, intellectual, and ideological aspects of power suffusing a whole 'historical bloc' (Hall, 2021).

Perhaps the most enduring and pervasive set of ideas 'suffusing a whole historic bloc' in recent times is that of 'neo-liberalism'. The term is variably used and defined. Indeed one economist, despairing of achieving a viable and agreed definition, begins a book-length discussion of the dominance of economists' thought on contemporary politics with the self-denying ordinance that, having identified neo-liberalism as a label for our 'present way of thinking', he would thereafter 'avoid the word because most people never use it, and those who do cannot agree on its meaning' (Aldred, 2019: 3). Nevertheless a number of unspoken yet powerful axioms appear and reappear in any discussion of the term, notably the primacy of free markets, the important, indeed essential, role of large corporations, and the need to limit the scale, scope and cost of public services. For Andrew Gamble neo-liberalism is a dominant ideology 'whose dictums were once again being expressed as common sense', these being 'small state, sound money and free markets' (Gamble, 2019: 984). Colin Crouch regards the principle tenets of neo-liberalism as its faith in the price mechanism and its preference for oligopolistic corporations over 'interference' by government (Crouch, 2011: 17).

While its axioms and influence are characterised by some as the result of considered effort (Hill describes the work of some commentators who discern a 'deliberate campaign'), the presumptions loosely embraced by the label 'neo-liberalism' are strongly associated with the powerfully expressed and effectively implemented thoughts and theories of rightward shifting governments in the western industrial countries of recent decades, most obviously in Margaret Thatcher's Britain and Ronald Reagan's United States (Hill, 1998: 69; Phillips, 1996). For many writers the longevity and hegemonic embrace of many of the presumptions and axioms of neo-liberal economic thinking require explanation. They may, of course, as Davis suggests, be the result of persistent and energetic promotion and dissemination, being coupled with advertising, branding and promotional culture (Davis, 2013: 197). Gamble suggests four reasons for the enduring dispersion of neo-liberal ideas in the dominant cultures of contemporary capitalist societies, including the retreat of the state to being a guarantor of last resort rather than actively interventionist, the rise to dominance of US interests underpinned by neo-liberal thinking, the absence of any business interest pushing for a different approach, and the parallel absence of any political voicing or representation of an alternative set of policies (Gamble, 2019: 989–91). As he concludes, 'Most important of all it is expressed as a form of common sense derived from the lived experience citizens have of being buyers and sellers and market agents' (ibid.: 992).

The communications dimension to this hegemonic success is crucial. In routine appraisal of economic matters in the news, it is a common experience to be told the reaction of 'the markets' (or, perhaps, in the United Kingdom, 'the City'), with approval being a sign of unproblematic good news, and turbulence or resistance a clear signal of something untoward. In other words, the 'accredited witnesses' required to provide context for economic policy take for granted the role of disinterested arbiter offered by the partisan voices of neo-liberal action and centres of power. Bourdieu and Wacquant describe this as a 'planetary vulgate', loosely labelled by them as 'NewLiberalSpeak': 'undiscussed presuppositions' which amount to 'mental colonisation' (Bourdieu and Wacquant, 2001). This idea is developed and extended by Chakravartty and Schiller who describe what they label 'neo-liberal newspeak', massively extended through the news media and economic education, so that 'The dominant repetition of neo-liberal normative assumptions contrasting the negative pole of the state and the public against the positive pole of the free market and the individual became increasingly part of the common sense across most of the media...' (Chakravartty and Schiller, 2010: 677). Whether the result of concerted and forceful 'cultural imperialism' (as suggested by Bourdieu and Wacquant), or especially the fruit of efforts by economic journalism and corporate promotion, the neo-liberal ideology becomes embedded as common sense beyond which any alternative is, almost literally, unthinkable. Almost in despair the UK right-wing newspaper *Daily Mail* asked in an editorial in 2023, 'What happened to small-state, low tax Conservatism. Rewarding endeavour, personal responsibility and work ethic?' (leader, 25 January 2023).

A telling and prominent illustration of this hegemonic framing of debate appeared in public discussion and news coverage of the financial crises of 2008-9. In a careful and detailed examination of the production, content and reception of news about this period in the United Kingdom, Berry points to the comparative absence of even Keynesian interpretations of events available to mass audiences, and that in consideration of bailouts to banks, the notion of public banking and the necessity of public assistance for private banks was virtually unquestioned – 'there was no alternative' (Berry, 2019: 260, 272). This is corroborated by Kay and Salter (2014), who analyse BBC coverage of this period and conclude that it discursively normalised neo-liberal economics, not necessarily as desirable, but certainly as inevitable.

More broadly, as neo-liberalism became so pervasive, 'the contours of economic news narrowed...Meanwhile financialisation created a new core nexus of dominant news sources centred on a small group of political and financial elites who defined the economy in narrow and financialised terms' (ibid: 185). In a wider perspective, the presumptions and axioms of neo-liberalism become increasingly and unquestioningly applied to other social sectors. Examining the north American situation Oreskes and Conway see the presumptions of market dominance and the associated tenets of neo-liberalism as a 'big myth' (Oreskes and Conway, 2023). As Crouch observes, 'one of the main achievements of the neo-liberal political project is to place more or less all institutions in society – universities, hospitals, charities, as well as governments –under an obligation to behave as though they were business corporations' (Crouch, 2011: 167). This is, he concludes, an 'ideological triumph' (ibid.: 166). The very widespread dominance and success of variants of the neo-liberal hegemony has been extensively charted, and the details of the politics and ideological activities behind this are not examined here (see Robertson, 2010; Centeno and Cohen, 2012; Overbeek, 1992). But what Crouch describes in his book's title as 'the strange non-death of neo-liberalism' is a profound example of the substance of hegemony, and the importance and difficulty of breaking from it to seek alternative or contrary explanations of economic and political events and processes.

The comprehensive limitation of possibilities constrained by the hegemony of a dominant ideology bears a clear similarity in this account to the notion of the 'Overton window'. This somewhat nebulous, but frequently used, idea, describes the range of political options and policies conventionally regarded as possible, likely to command widespread support, or even conceivable, in any given period, and is often used in comment on the practical realities of political action in any particular place or time. The phrase emerged from the work of an American political scientist of the late twentieth century, Joseph Overton, though has been much developed by others since then (Mackinac Center, 2019). Like neo-liberalism or other pretenders to the throne of hegemony, any given set or range of ideas whose success results in wholesale saturation of a population's understanding of the limits of desirable, or more fundamentally, possible action, is the result very often of concerted and powerful action by interest groups and beneficiaries of the ideology in question, as the earlier discussion of lobbying in this book makes clear.

However characterised, the ideological ubiquity of hegemonic ideas creates, and becomes, a 'common sense' understanding of how political and social processes work, and how they might be understood and responded to, that effectively and profoundly prevents the active search for knowledge or dissent that might otherwise enrich public debate. Their very suffocating ubiquity renders the search for alternative or supplementary understanding not merely difficult but apparently unnecessary.

The search for the informed citizen

The central argument in this book is that inequalities truncate and obstruct citizenship in the digital age. This follows from any notion of citizenship that regards it as more than simply passive 'membership' of a political entity, most commonly a nation-state, but one that entails at least the possibility of active involvement in securing the rights, and fulfilling the duties, of a citizen. As Held formulates the question of the citizen: 'does he or she *also* have the capacities (the material and cultural resources) to choose between different courses of action in practice?' (Held, 1991: 21).

If we look at any definition of 'citizenship' it includes or presupposes the capacity to be, or to become, appropriately informed. As T.H. Marshall's classic analysis points out, the emergence of the civil rights underpinning of citizenship 'did not confer a right, but it recognised a capacity' (Marshall and Bottomore, 1992: 13). His seminal lectures (originally published in 1950) insist on both the positive and negative role of communications in citizenship. On what is termed in the present text as 'voice', he notes that 'the right to freedom of speech has little real substance if...you have...no means of making yourself heard' (ibid.: 21). The vast literature propelled by Marshall's work often points to this other side of the coin. The persistence, and even widening, of inequality, has direct consequences for the active citizen seeking to acquire (and that often means to purchase) the information necessary for the performance of duties and insistence on rights. What Saunders terms 'mediating institutions' (for example neighbourhood, church, voluntary associations, family), have in varying ways been undermined, leaving the citizen dependent on personal circumstances and resources for the assertion of citizenship rights (Saunders, 1993: 79).

The central concept here is that of the 'informed citizen'. Such a paragon would be an active seeker of information relevant to citizenship, have a good understanding of the political processes and events entailed, and of the ways these need to be viewed and read critically and quizzically when obtained indirectly, mainly from the mass media. This informed citizen, duly armed with critically assessed and fully considered information, could then become active effectively in civic life and public debate. This worthy would, in reality, be something of a boorish snob, an unlikely and no doubt improbable combination of sage and exemplar: someone to avoid in the pub. He or she and their like might populate the perfect democracy, but in truth exist beyond everyday reality even if providing the delusionary self-image treasured by a few. Nonetheless, the ideal type embodied in this array of attributes foregrounds the importance of accessible and diverse information.

The central concern of this book is how inequality obstructs this ideal state. Two further problems merit brief attention: the rise of 'fake news', and the spread and impact of 'unreason'.

The notion of 'fake news', as described in Chapter 4, achieved widespread currency due to its recurrent invocation by Donald Trump as an accusation against his detractors. The obvious equation of the phrase simply with news he found unappealing or hostile was finally recognised – in his rhetoric 'fake news' was news he did not like (Lind, 2018). But the term had wider application, sufficient to mobilise a full UK parliamentary enquiry, which concluded that the problem had become magnified by the growth of new technologies and 'social media', requiring greater transparency, and more substantial reigning in and regulation of the power of big tech companies (House of Commons, 2019). Many have usefully distinguished between misinformation, containing discernibly false material, and disinformation, containing material deliberately designed to deceive, for example for political ends. Wolf notes the huge increase in both as a consequence of the 'fundamental economics of information in the new age: collecting information remains costly, but dissemination is costless' (Wolf, 2023: 210). In a thoughtful overview, Zelizer underlines the extensive scepticism accruing to all journalism in the wake of the growth of 'fake news'. As she points out, public understanding of current events is degraded by what she terms the 'Anglo-American imaginary' in the wake of Trump (and indeed in the UK, Brexit), one of whose legacies is to 'have created two separate news empires peddling true and fake news as neighbours and a disinterested and disenfranchised public that is profoundly angry and distrustful of the very tools and expertise of all institutions, including journalism' (Zelizer, 2018: 146).

Of course 'fake news', as we have seen, is far from new, nor solely the consequence of 'social media'. Archetypal was the 'Zinoviev letter', published by the *Daily Mail* just before the 1924 UK general election, and whose veracity and impact were discussed in Chapter 4. History is replete with examples of what we would now label 'fake news'. In the mid-1700s at the height of the Jacobite rebellion, seditious printers circulated news that King George II was ill. The then Attorney-General said that 'publication of such false news of his Majesty has a tendency to disquiet the minds of his subjects'. In 1835 the *New York Sun* published stories of the discovery of life on the moon – eventually acknowledged by the paper as a hoax, while in 1897 the *New York Times* reported that Mark Twain was 'dying in poverty in London'. Famously, Twain commented sourly that the report was 'an exaggeration'.

The notion of 'fake news' inevitably posits its opposite – genuine news, a concept disarming a century of research establishing that news and the practice of journalism are social constructs, with human decisions about selection, priority, emphasis or interpretation unavoidable in the manufacture of news. Fear of fakery, and the hope that it can be deterred or confronted, have led to the rise of a substantial armoury broadly covered by the term 'fact-checking'. The fact-checking industry has its roots in the earnest and often invaluable efforts of individual news organisations to help their users interpret, or at least to treat sceptically, the more obviously outlandish or contentious claims they come across. In turn, this has even produced fact-checking organisations, such as 'Full Fact' in the United Kingdom, or Factcheck.org in the USA, and one step further, an umbrella organisation in the form of the International Fact Checking Network.

The idea that there is a sensible, credible, and verifiable account of social and public affairs is a seductive one and lies behind the recurrent calls for 'moderate' and 'objective' journalism, a debate far too complex to engage with here. However, the second problem alluded to here, that of 'unreason', is rooted in much larger, if more diffuse, assumptions about the tenor and currents of public debate. The charge implicit in this term is that the 'enlightenment project', rooted in the methodologies and veracities of science, and based on the clear presentation and rational evaluation of confirmable evidence, has been important in political discourse in modern times, but is also ever more threatened by disappearance under the onslaught of opposed ways of thinking. The result, as Taverne puts it, is that 'irrationality is on the rise in western society, and public opinion is increasingly dominated by unreflecting prejudice and unwillingness to engage with factual evidence' (Taverne, 2005). One consequence is to amplify scepticism about what are plainly, in his view at least, objectively desirable ends, for example, globalisation and capitalism. It is easy, in the writings of authors like this, to see how the leap is made from palpably unlikely tales about the fictional reconstruction of the moon landings, or of sightings of Elvis in South America, to suggest unreason leads to distrust of what are, actually, clearly contentious accounts. For Damian Thompson this betrays 'intellectual sloppiness', to be protected against by the certainty that 'despite the privatisation of knowledge, caused by the explosion of intellectual choice, Western society still has such a thing as the public domain' (Thompson, 2008: 126). But the diagnosis remains: 'Credulous thinking is spreading through society as fast and silently as a virus, and no one has a clue how long the epidemic will last' (ibid: 117). Thompson is not alone in locating the roots of this development in the political economy of recent times. Wheen describes the paradigms of the 1990s, in a book describing 'How Mumbo-Jumbo Conquered the World', as made possible by the privatisations of the Thatcher-Reagan regimes and their successors (Wheen, 2004: 274). The generalised sarcasm of Jonathan Swift in the eighteenth century, that 'Falsehood flies, and truth comes limping after it', is now given a historic specificity, but leaves unanswered the possible form of citizenly response.

Two ways to resolve this problem that have been strongly promoted and frequently developed are what has come to be termed 'deliberative democracy', and various versions of the enshrined and basic 'right to know'. Each warrants a brief explanation. At its most fundamental, deliberative democracy is, in Stephen Coleman's view, 'the missing element of contemporary democracy' (Coleman, 2017: 33). In most versions of deliberative democracy discussed in recent years, the common thread is to posit the democratic effectiveness and authenticity of delegating, or at least deriving the arguments for, decision-making to small, representative sections of the population who are given the opportunity to debate and consider relevant material before arriving at consensual recommendations about policy or action. This clearly goes beyond the simple right to vote and is built on many of the same foundations of critical rationality as discussed earlier in Habermas' notion of the public sphere.

Innumerable studies or trials of deliberative democracy have taken place in many countries. Inevitably, difficulties emerge in the practicalities and presumptions built into the process. Less powerful or influential sections of the population can find themselves overrun or under-heard if in unduly heterogeneous gatherings, leading some to suggest that such inequities can be diminished by allowing groups to meet in 'enclaves' of greater internal homogeneity (Karpowitz et al., 2009). Even if such inequities are engrained and unavoidable, more optimistic reviews suggest they may be relatively minor (Kennedy et al., 2021). Survey studies of the operation of deliberative democracy in Germany emphasise how, for it to be effective, important pre-requisites are inclusivity (engagement should be widespread and egalitarian), both political diversity and pluralism, and people's mutual understanding of others' views (Schmitt-Beck, 2022). The gendered dimension of inequitable ability to take part in or be permitted appropriate hearing or attention is an important dimension of these reservations (for an example of an initiative designed to forestall this see an Irish study in Harris et al., 2020).

Underlying all such appreciations and studies of deliberation as a better basis for democratic involvement is a presumption (or requirement) for participants to engage with the process equitably and fairly. This is achieved, where possible, through the provision to all participants of the information they need to consider and discuss relevant issues, and by the usual methodologies of representative involvement. Much deliberative democracy work is undertaken online, which, of course, ensures the process is embedded in existing inequities of access and ownership of online capacity. It also, of necessity, while actively distributing and providing relevant material for debate and consideration, cannot overcome pre-existing inegalitarian information and knowledge arising from the fundamental social structures of resource inequity. The ideal articulated in accounts of deliberative democracy has to be founded in the presumption, or requirement, that participants, however, selected or represented, and in whatever way their deliberations are rationally translated into citizen demands, arise from some degree of equitable access to necessary information. The structures of inequality, in other words, limit the possibilities of deliberation.

Wider than the many initiatives and experiments in deliberative democracy lie claims and aspirations to 'the right to know'. Understood as a fundamental human right, akin to clean water, food, health and political freedom, the concept is difficult to contest but unhelpfully vague in practice. It is invoked in the political declarations and charters of many countries, often in slightly limited circumstances such as the openness of information about environmental standards. However it is not insignificant that the United Nations, in addressing attempts to restrict access to the internet, affirmed in 2016 that 'the same rights that people have offline must also be protected online' (United Nations, 2016). This document, a revision to a 2012 declaration by the UN, is explicit about affirming a human rights approach in expanding access to the internet. The thinking is propelled by concern about state control or differential access and skills in the 'many forms of digital divides', but nevertheless sets out unambiguously that access to and freedom of information are basic human rights. It is a theme the United Nations has recurrently pursued. In 2022, the Secretary-General of the UN, Antonio Guterres, reminded the Security Council that 'communications is not a side issue or an afterthought' (United Nations, 2022).

Not surprisingly campaigners have sought to extend this, for example, in some countries, calling for a 'digital bill of rights', though frequently focused explicitly on internet regulation. In promoting this argument Drakopoulou and colleagues note that many users of Facebook and the like are scarcely aware that they are accessing the internet (Drakopoulou et al., 2016). Local initiatives on digital inclusion often make reference to this wider feature of information rights. Andy Burnham, the mayor of Greater Manchester in the United Kingdom, for example, writes bluntly that 'the time has come where we need to see digital connectivity as a basic human right' (Burnham, 2021). Serious insistence on a right to know immediately raises questions of how this might be achieved, or indeed what information should or should not be available, and how. Clearly, if taken seriously as a basis for policy, it would require ensuring that any information likely to be of relevance and use to the active citizen seeking to become an informed one, was not restricted either by classification nor, just as importantly, by the inaccessibility of that information to citizens without the resources necessary to obtain it.

Awareness of the digital divide(s) has driven innumerable initiatives in many countries and communities to overcome the apparent problem. In France, for example, a 'National Plan for Digital Inclusion' was launched in 2018. Aimed especially at the transformation of French businesses it also sought 'digital inclusion' for at least a third of the French population in the ensuing ten years. Particular attention was given to the need for re-training of those ill-equipped to cope with online information-seeking. In Germany, a 'Digital Strategy' was initiated in 2022, though the focus was the pressing need for greater digitalisation in the security realm. In the USA a programme supported by *Mastercard* aspires to a 'digital economy for all' by 2030, though its target is as much international as parochial (Digital Planet, 2024). Many initiatives seek to assist those in the population without the necessary skills to become better trained and less wary of online information-seeking. In the United Kingdom, the 'Good Things Foundation' pours considerable energy and expertise into such concerns, in seeking to create and sustain a 'national digital inclusion network' (www.goodthingsfoundation.org). Many charities, collectively operating under the umbrella of 'the Digital Poverty Alliance', have drawn attention to the problem, and in response, the company BT said it would offer 2,500 poorer households free devices and connectivity (Digital Poverty Alliance, 2023). Perhaps the grandest and most elaborate of such schemes appeared under the collective name of the 'Edison Alliance', (the name derives neatly from the carefully crafted phrase 'essential digital infrastructure and services network'). This was constructed by companies like Verizon, Mastercard, and Google organising together, and emerged from debates at the Davos Economic World Forum, seeking nothing less than to 'to enhance the lives of 1 billion people by 2025 through affordable and accessible digital solutions' (World Economic Forum, 2024). Their motives were doubtless selfless.

Two fundamental difficulties arise in the conceptualisation of such initiatives, forceful, helpful and effective though many most certainly are. The first is in the inevitable leaning towards a 'blaming the victim' presumption built into their objectives. If people do not avail themselves of information, especially online, it must be because of their obstinate unwillingness to do so, or their enduring lack of skills in using the facilities available to them. This has often in the past, and it must be said, still, underpinned many initiatives of the European Union (Golding, 2007). The information cornucopia exploded by the widespread and rapidly evolving digital world runs too far ahead of the competence of many of its potential beneficiaries, runs the argument, so the answer, it is presumed, is to educate those too misguided or insufficiently skilled to make best use of the materials available to them. The second difficulty is not unrelated to this line of thought. It arises from what might be termed 'the hardware myth', the gap between need and potential being filled by distributing to those apparently on the wrong side of the digital divide the necessary equipment (smartphones, tablets, personal computers) to enable them to participate online. This drove many of the initiatives supported during the educational hiatus and 'lockdowns' imposed by coronavirus disease 2019 (COVID-19), for example, as discussed earlier in this book. Again, the efforts involved and the benefits of such work should not be lightly dismissed, but as Thornham and colleagues have illustrated in research in one city in the United Kingdom, the result, as they neatly put it, can be 'online life without offline capital' (Thornham et al., 2017: 1801). Providing computers or phones to people without the means to use them (whether through lack of resources to feed pay-as-you-go fees, or inability to afford subscriptions or recurrent expenses) can be frustrating and unproductive, and at root does not address the fundamental problem.

So, what is that fundamental problem? Writers in the field of social policy have made very clear the necessary distinction between poverty and inequality, none more so than one of the leading theoreticians and researchers in that field, the late Peter Townsend. In his definition of poverty, however, lies the nub of the problem. He argues that people are in poverty 'when they lack the resources to obtain the types of diet, participate in the activities, and have the living conditions and amenities which are customary or are widely encouraged and approved, in the societies to which they belong' (Townsend, 1979: 31). In other words it is impossible to be a citizen, a full member of society, without the means to acquire and use the resources enabling the fulfilment of this role as is socially expected and required. Inequality means some have more of such resources than others, and citizenship in a society with substantial inequalities is denied to the less favoured. Not only the act of voting, but engagement with social process in any form that makes demands of its users, whether applying for a passport, reading up before writing a letter to the local councillor, registering for unemployment benefits, seeking work, or preparing for a daunting night at the local pub quiz, all increasingly demarcate the information rich from the information poor, and make up 'living conditions that are customary, or at least widely encouraged or approved'. In a phrase, it is inequality not communications that is determinant. The capacity to be fully engaged with and equitably participate in the society in which one lives requires at the very least the potential to seek, acquire, and where appropriate, disseminate information.

In that view of how society should function lies the presumption, and indeed necessity, of informed citizenship, whose equitable and widespread potential, as this book has argued, is itself in doubt. As capitalism has matured it has evolved progressively distinctive characteristics, including globalisation, problematic public finances, frequent stagnation, a transfer of power towards capital ownership, itself increasingly concentrated and corporate, and, most significantly the redistribution of wealth and income towards wealthier elites with concomitant widening inequalities. As Piketty has demonstrated, these trends are endemic to a market economy, as returns on capital exceed growth in income and output, with what he discerns as 'potentially terrifying' consequences for the long-term dynamics of wealth distribution (Piketty, 2014: 571). In turn, those consequences are regarded as inimical to the stability of democratic order. This fragility is viewed from one perspective, expressed by Martin Wolf, as likely if unchecked to 'corrode a democratic polity' (Wolf, 2023: 91). More apocalyptically, and from a more fundamentally radical perspective, Wolfgang Streeck sees the same trends as casting doubt on the longer-term viability of a capitalist economy (Streeck, 2016: 52). The presumed essential association of capitalism with democracy is far from inevitable, and indeed likely to be inherently contradictory. If democracy assumes and requires informed citizenship, the inequalities exacerbated by contemporary capitalism may themselves erode the democratic process.

Communications inequality is, then, at the core of understanding democracy in capitalist society, and is rooted in the problem of inequality more generally. The flow and value of communications by or to people are determined in breadth and volume by ineqitable resources. If the problem, and it is a problem, of communications and inequality is to be confronted, it can only be so by starting with the fundamental impediments and unfairness of inequality. Communications policy is social policy, and citizenship embracing all members of a society is impossible without the inequalities of communications rights, access, resources and capacity being related to the wider question of what Townsend characterises as 'the hierarchical and highly unequal distribution of resources' (ibid., 922). The problem of communications is first and foremost the problem of inequality.

Bibliography

Abbate, J. (1999) *Inventing the Internet.* Cambridge, MA: MIT Press.

Abd Hadi, Z. and McBride, N. (2000) 'The Commercialisation of Public Sector Information within UK Government Departments', *International Journal of Public Sector Management*, 13(7), pp. 552–570.

Abey, J. (2022) *Bridging the Digital Divide: Tackling Digital Inequality in a Post–pandemic World.* London: Fabian Society. Available at: https://digitalpovertyalliance.org/research_directiory/ridging-the-divide-tackling-digital-inequality-in-a-post-pandemic-world/ (Accessed: 27 June 2022).

AccessNow. (2021). *KeepItOn update: Who Is Shutting Down the Internet in 2021?* New York: AccessNow. https://www.accessnow.org/who-is-shutting-down-the-internet-in-2021/ (Accessed: 15 October 2021).

ActionAid (2021) *Mission Recovery: How Big Tech's Tax Bill Could Kickstart a Fairer Economy.* Johannesburg. Available at: https://actionaid.org/sites/default/files/publications/Mission%20Recovery_ActionAid%20Tax%20Report%202021.pdf (Accessed: 6 October 2021).

Adams, S. B. (2017) 'Arc of Empire: The Federal Telegraph Company, the U.S. Navy, and the Beginnings of Silicon Valley', *Business History Review*, 91(2), pp. 329–359.

Advani, A., Bangham, G. and Leslie, J. (2021) 'The UK's Wealth Distribution and Characteristics of High–Wealth Households', *Journal of Applied Public Economics*, 42(3–4), pp. 397–430.

Aldred, J. (2019) *Licence to Be Bad: How Economics Corrupted Us.* London: Allen Lane.

Al–Jenaibi, B. (2016) 'The Twitter Revolution in the Gulf Countries'', *Journal of Creative Communications*, 11(1), pp. 61–83.

Alkiviadou, N. (2019) 'Hate Speech on Social Media Networks: Towards a Regulatory Framework?', *Information and Communications Technology Law*, 28(1), pp. 19–35.

Alliance for Affordable Internet (2020) *2020 Affordability Report.* Available at: https://a4ai.org/affordability-report/report/2020/ (Accessed: 16 March 2021).

Allmann, K. (2021) *UK Digital Poverty Evidence: Interim Review.* London: Digital Poverty Alliance. Available at: https://digitalpovertyalliance.org/wp-content/uploads/2021/11/UK-Digital-Poverty-Evidence-Interim-Review-v1.016182.pdf (Accessed: 27 June 2022).

Almeida, V. (2015) 'Inequality and Redistribution in the Aftermath of the 2007–2008 Crisis: The US Case', *BSI Economics*,. Available at: http://www.bsi-economics.org/545-inequality-and-redistribution-in-the-aftermath-of-the-2007-2008-crisis-the-us-case (Accessed: 15 March 2022).

Anderson Jr., R. D. (1998) 'The Place of the Media in Popular Democracy', *Critical Review*, 12(4), pp. 481–500.

Antonelli, C. (2003) 'The Digital Divide: Understanding the Economics of New Information and Communication Technology in the Global Economy', *Information Economics and Policy*, 15(2), pp. 173–200.

Aral, S. (2020) *The Hype Machine: How Social Media Disrupts Our Elections, Our Economy, and Our Health – And How We Must Adapt.* New York: Harper Collins.

Aristotle (2016) *Aristotle's Politics: Writings from the Complete Works: Politics, Economics, Constitution of Athens*. Princeton University Press. Available at: https://www-jstor-org.libproxy.ncl.ac.uk/stable/j.ctv8pzdm7 (Accessed: 4 August 2022).

Arrtz, L. and Kamalipour, Y. R. (eds.) (2003) *The Globalization of Corporate Media Hegemony*. New York: State University of New York Press.

Arterton, F. C. (1987) *Teledemocracy: Can Technology Protect Democracy?* Newbury Park, CA: SAGE.

Atkinson, A. B. (2015) *Inequality: What Can Be Done?* Cambridge, MA and London: Harvard University Press.

Attewell, P. (2001) 'The First and Second Digital Divides', *Sociology of Education*, 74(3), pp. 252–259.

Ballester, J., Quijal-Zamorano, M., Méndez Turrubiates, R. F., Pegenaute, F., Herrmann, F. R., Robine, J. M. and Achebak, H. (2023) 'Heat-Related Mortality in Europe During the Summer of 2022,' *Nature Medicine*, 29, Available at: https://doi.org/10.1038/s41591-023-02419-z (Accessed: 19 January 2024).

Banks, J. (2010) 'Regulating Hate Speech Online', *International Review of Law, Computers & Technology*, 24(3), pp. 233–239.

Baran, N. (1998) 'The Privatization of Telecommunication', in McChesney, R., Meisken Wood, E. and Bellamy Foster, J. (eds.) *Capitalism and the Information Age*. New York: Monthly Review Press, pp. 123–133.

Barassi, V. (2017) *Activism on the Web: Everyday Struggles against Digital Capitalism*. London: Routledge.

Barclay, S., Barnett, S., Moore, M. and Townend, J. (2022) *Local News Deserts in the UK*. London: Charitable Journalism Project. Available at: https://publicbenefitnews.files.wordpress.com/2022/06/local-news-deserts-in-the-uk.pdf (Accessed: 30 June 2022).

Barnett, S. (2016) 'How our Mainstream Media Failed Democracy,' in Jackson, D., Thorsen, E. and Wring, D. (eds.) *EU Referendum Analysis 2016: Media, Voters and the Campaihn* (p. 47). Bournemouth: Bournemouth University.

Barrons, G. (2012) 'Examining the Use of Social Media in the 2011 Egyptian Revolution', *Contemporary Arab Affairs*, 5(1), pp. 54–67.

Bartels, L. M. (2016) *Unequal Democracy: The Political Economy of the New Gilded Age*. 2nd. edn. Princeton, NJ: Princeton University Press.

Bartlett, J. (2015) *The Dark Net*. London: Windmill Books.

Bartlett, J. (2018) *The People vs. Tech*. London: Ebury Press.

Barwise, P. and Watkins, L. (2018) 'The Evolution of Digital Dominance: How and Why We Got to GAFA,' in M. Moore and D. Tambini (eds.) *Digital Dominance: The Power of Google, Amazon, Facebook, and Apple*. Oxford: Oxford University Press, pp. 21–49.

Bauer, J. M., Berne, M. and Maitland, C. F. (2002) 'Internet Access in the European Union and in the United States', *Telematics and Informatics*, 19(2), pp. 117–137.

Beam, M. A., Hmielowski, J. D. and Hutchens, M. J. (2018) 'Democratic Digital Inequalities: Threat and Opportunity in Online Citizenship from Motivation and Ability', *American Behavioral Scientist*, 62(8), pp. 1079–1096.

Beck, U. (1992) *Risk Society: Towards a New Modernity*. London: SAGE.

Bennett, G. (2018) *The Zinoviev Letter: The Conspiracy that Never Dies*. Oxford: Oxford University Press.

Berners-Lee, T. (2010) 'Long Live The Web' *Scientific American*, 303(6), pp. 80–85.

Berridge, V. and Starns, P. (2005) 'The 'Invisible Industrialist' and Public Health: The Rise and Fall of 'Safer Smoking' in the 1970s,' in V. Berridge and K. Loughlin (eds.) *Medicine, the Market and the Mass Media*. London and New York: Routledge, pp. 172–191.

Berry, M. (2016a) 'No alternative to austerity: How the BBC broadcast news reported the deficit debate,' *Media Culture & Society*, 38(6), pp. 844–863.

Berry, M. (2016b) 'The UK Press and the Deficit Debate,' *Sociology*, 50(3), pp. 542–559.

Berry, M. (2019) *The Media, the Public and the Great Financial Crisis*. London: Palgrave Macmillan.

Birch, M. (2012) *Mediating Mental Health: Contexts, Debates and Analysis*. London: Ashgate.

Blackall, M. (2021) '"Transformational": Yorkshire Firm Cleans up Donated Laptops for Pupils at Home', *The Guardian*, 4 March 2021. Available at: https://www.theguardian.com/world/20 21/mar/04/transformational-yorkshire-firm-cleans-up-donated-laptops-for-pupils-at-home (Accessed: 5 March 2021).

Blain, N. and Hutchinson, D. (eds.) (2016). *Scotland's Referendum and the Media: National and International Perspectives*. Edinburgh: Edinburgh University Press.

Blakeley, G. (2020) 'The Big Tech Monopolies and the State', in Panitch, L. and Albo, G. (eds.) *Beyond Digital Capitalism: New Ways of Living*. London: Merlin Press, pp. 100–111.

Blumler, J. G. and Coleman, S. (2001) *Realising Democracy Online: A Civic Commons in Cyberspace*. London.

Bourdieu, P. and Wacquant, L. (2001) 'NewLiberalSpeak', *Radical Philosophy*, (105), pp. 2–5.

Bourguignon, F. (2015) *The Globalization of Inequality*. Princeton and Oxford: Princeton University Press.

Bovens, M. (2002) 'Information Rights: Citizenship in the Information Society', *The Journal of Political Philosophy*, 10(3), pp. 317–341.

Boyce, T. (2007). *Health, Risk and News: The MMR Vaccine and the Media* New York and Bern: Peter Lang.

Boykoff, J. (2006) 'Framing Dissent: Mass-Media Coverage of the Global Justice Movement', *New Political Science*, 28(2), pp. 201–228.

Boykoff, M. T. (2008) 'Media and Scientific Communication: a Case of Climate Change', *Communicating Environmental Geoscience*, 305, pp. 11–18.

Boykoff, M. T. (2011) *Who Speaks for the Climate? Making Sense of Media Reporting on Climate Change*. Cambridge and New York: Cambridge University Press.

Boyle, M. I., McCluskey, M. R., McLeod, D. M. and Stein, S. E. (2005) 'Newspapers and Protest: An Examination of Protest Coverage from 1960–1999', *Journalism & Mass Communication Quarterly*, 82(3), pp. 638–653.

Briant, E., Watson, N. and Philo, G. (2013) 'Reporting Disability in the Age of Austerity', *Disability & Society*, 28(6), pp. 874–889.

Brown, R. H., Barram, D. J. and Irving, L. (1995) *Falling through the Net: A Survey of the "Have Nots" in Rural and Urban America*. Washington. Available at: https://www.ntia.doc.gov/ntiahome/ fallingthru.html (Accessed: 30 March 2021).

Bruns, A., Highfield, T. and Burgess, J. (2013) 'The Arab Spring and Social Media Audiences: English and Arabic Twitter Users and Their Networks', *American Behavioral Scientist*, 57(7), pp. 871–898.

Büchi, M., Festic, N. and Latzer, M. (2018) 'How Social Well–Being Is Affected by Digital Inequalities', *International Journal of Communication*, 12, pp. 3686–3706.

Bukhari, J. (2017) 'Wall Street Spent $2 Billion Trying to Influence the 2016 Election', *Fortune*, March 8. Available at: https://fortune.com/2017/03/08/wall-street-2016-election-spending/ (Accessed: 14 April 2022).

Burnham, A. (2021) *Digital Inclusion as a Basic Human Right*. Available at: https://www.goodthin gsfoundation.org/what-we-do/news/digital-inclusion-as-a-basic-human-right/ (Accessed: 20 August 2021).

Burton, M. and Tunnicliffe, R. (2022) *Membership of Political Parties in Great Britain*. London: House of Commons Library.

Cabero-Almenara, J., Torres-Barzabal, L. and Hermosilla-Rodriguez, J. (2019) 'ICT and the Creation of Digital Citizenship', *Education in the Knowledge Society*, 20(22).

Cairncross, F. (1997) *The Death of Distance: How the Communications Revolution Will Change Our Lives*. London: Orion Business Books.

Cairncross, F. (2019) *The Cairncross Review: A Sustainable Future for Journalism*. London: Available at: https://assets.publishing.service.gov.uk/government/uploads/system/uploads/attachme nt_data/file/779882/021919_DCMS_Cairncross_Review_.pdf (Accessed: 1 November 2021).

Campus, D. (2010). 'Mediatization and Personification of politicians in France and Italy: The Case of Berlusconi and Sarkozy', *International Journal of Press/Politics*, 16(1), pp. 215–235.

Capgemini (2021) *2021 World Wealth Report*. Available at: https://worldwealthreport.com/ wp-content/uploads/sites/7/2021/07/World-Wealth-Report-2021.pdf (Accessed: 27 January 2022).

Carey, A. (1996) *Taking the Risk Out of Democracy: Corporate Propaganda versus Freedom and Liberty*. Champaign, IL: University of Illinois Press.

Carrington, D. (2022) 'Revealed: Oil Sector''s 'Staggering' $3bn-a-day Profits for Last 50 Years', *Guardian*, 21 July. Available at: https://www.theguardian.com/environment/2022/jul/21/ revealed-oil-sectors-staggering-profits-last-50-years (Accessed: 21 November 2022).

Carter Wood, J. (2016) 'Crime News and the Press', in Knepper, P. and Johansen, A. (eds.) *The Oxford Handbook of the History of Crime and Criminal Justice*. Oxford: Oxford University Press, pp. 301–319.

Castells, M. (2015) *Networks of Outrage and Hope: Social Movements in the Internet Age*. 2nd edn. Cambridge: Polity Press.

Castells, M. (2015). *Networks of Outrage and Hope: Social Movements in the Internet Age*. 2nd edn. Cambridge: Polity Press.

Cave, T. and Rowell, A. (2015) *A Quiet Word: Lobbying, Crony Capitalism, and Broken Politics in Britain*. London: Vintage Books.

Centeno, M. A. and Cohen, J. N. (2012) 'The Arc of Neoliberalism', *Annual Review of Sociology*, 38, pp. 317–340.

Center for Educational Research and Innovation (2000) *Learning to Bridge the Digital Divide*. Paris: Organisation for Economic Co–operation and Development.

Chadwick, A. (2006) *Internet Politics: States, Citizens, and New Communications Technologies*. New York and Oxford: Oxford University Press.

Chakravarrty, P. and Schiller, D. (2010) 'Neoliberal Newspeak and Digital Capitalism in Crisis', *Intenational Journal of Communication*, (4), pp. 670–692.

Chan, J. M. and Lee, C.-C. (1984) 'The Journalistic Paradigm of Civil Protests: A Case Study of Hong Kong', in A. Arno and W. Dissanayake (eds.) *The News Media in National and International Conflict*. Boulder, CO: Westview Press, pp. 183–202.

Chancel, L., Piketty, T., Saez, E. and Zucman, G. (2022) *World Inequality Report 2022*. Paris and Los Angeles: UNDP.

Chartered Institute of Public Finance and Accountancy (CIPFA) (2019) 'Decade of Austerity Sees 30% Drop in Library Spending',. Available at: https://www.cipfa.org/about-cipfa/press-office/latest-press-releases/decade-of-austerity-sees-30-drop-in-library-spending (Accessed: 6 December 2019).

Chartered Institute of Public Finance and Accountancy (CIPFA) (2020) 'Spend on British Libraries Drops by Nearly £20m',. Available at: https://www.cipfa.org/about-cipfa/press-office/latest-press-releases/spend-on-british-libraries-drops-by-nearly-20m (Accessed: 2 November 2021).

Chayko, M. (2016) *Superconnected: The Internet, Digital Media, and Techno–Social Life*. Thousand Oaks, CA: Sage Publications.

Chibnall, S. (1977) *Law and Order News: An Analysis of Crime Reporting in the British Press*. London: Tavistock.

Child Poverty Action Group (CPAG) (2021) *Digital Exclusion during the Pandemic*. London: CPAG. Available at: https://cpag.org.uk/policy-and-campaigns/briefing/digital-exclusion-during-pandemic (Accessed: 15 January 2021).

Chouliaraki, L. (2000) 'Political Discourse in the News: Democratizing Responsibility or Aestheticizing Politics?', *Discourse & Society*, 11(3), pp. 293–314.

Citizens Advice (2021) *Broadband Must Be Made Affordable for Everyone*. Available at: https://www.citizensadvice.org.uk/Global/CitizensAdvice/Consumer%20publications/Broadband%20must%20be%20made%20affordable%20for%20everyone%20(3).pdf (Accessed: 26 November 2021).

Clarke, G. R. G. (2001) *Bridging the Digital Divide: How Enterprise Ownership and Foreign Competition Affect Internet Access in Eastern Europe and Central Asia*. Washington, D.C. Available at: http://econ.worldbank.org/resource.php?type=5

Clawson, R. A. and Trice, R. (2000). 'Poverty as We Know It: Media Portrayals of the Poor', *Public Opinion Quarterly*, 64(1), pp. 53–64.

Climate Investigation Center (2018). 'Trade Associations and the Public Relations Industry'. Available at: https://climateinvestigations.org/trade-association-pr-spending/ (Accessed: 11 November 2022).

Cohen, S. (1972). *Folk Devils and Moral Panics: The Creation of Mods and Rockers*. London: MacGibbon and Kee.

Coleman, S., Griffiths, B. and Simmons, E. (2002). *Digital Jury – The Final Verdict*. London: Broadcasting Standards Commission and Hansard Society

Coleman, S. (2017) *Can the Internet Strengthen Democracy?* Cambridge: Polity.

Commission of the European Communities. (2005). *eInclusion revisited: The Local Dimension of the Information Society: SEC(2005) 206*. Brussels: Commission of the European Communities. Available at: http://europa.eu.int/comm/employment_social/news/2005/feb/eincllocal_en.pdf

Compaine, B. M. (ed.) (2001) *The Digital Divide: Facing a Crisis or Creating a Myth?* Cambridge, MA: MIT Press.

Copeland, E. (2017) 'UK Think Tanks, Mapped'. Available at: http://eddiecopeland.me/map-uk-think-tanks/ (Accessed: 3 November 2021).

Corneo, G. (2006) 'Media Capture in a Democracy: The Role of Wealth Concentration', *Journal of Public Economics*, 90(1–2), pp. 37–58.

Corner, J. (1998). 'Television News and Economic Exposition', in N. T. Gavin (ed.) *The Economy, Media and Public Knowledge*. Leicester: Leicester University Press, pp. 53–70.

Costanza-Chock, S. (2012). 'Mic Check! Media Cultures and the Occupy Movment,' *Social Movement Studies*, 11(3–4), pp. 375–385.

Costello, M. and Hawdon, J. (2020). Hate Speech in Online Spaces,' in T. Holt and A. Bossler (eds.) *The Palgrave Handbook of International Cybercrime and Cyberdeviance*. London: Palgrave Macmillan.

Cottle, S. (2008) 'Reporting Demonstrations: the Changing Media Politics of Dissent', *Media, Culture & Society*, 30(6), pp. 853–872.

Couldry, N. (2010) *Why Voice Matters: Culture and Politics after Neoliberalism*. Los Angeles and London: Sage.

Credit Suisse (2016) *Global Wealth Report 2016*. Credit Suisse. Available at: http://publications.cre dit-suisse.com/tasks/render/file/index.cfm?fileid=AD783798-ED07-E8C2-4405996B5B02A 32E (Accessed: 24 November 2016).

Credit Suisse (2021) *Global Wealth Report 2021*. Credit Suisse. Available at: http://publications.cre dit-suisse.com/tasks/render/file/index.cfm?fileid=AD783798-ED07-E8C2-4405996B5B02A32E (Accessed: 18 January 2022).

Cribb, J., Waters, T., Wernham, T. and Xu, X. (2021) *Living Standards, Poverty and Inequality in the UK: 2021*. London: Institute for Fiscal Studies.

Cronin, A. M. (2018) *Public Relations Capitalism: Promotional Culture, Publics and Commercial Democracy*. Basingstoke: Palgrave Macmillan.

Cross, S. (2014). 'Mad and Bad Media: Populism and Pathology in the British Tabloids', *European Journal of Communication*, 29(2), pp. 204–217.

Crossley, T. and O'Dea, C. (2016) *The Distribution of Household Wealth in the UK*. Institute for Fiscal Studies. Available at: https://www.ifs.org.uk/publications/8239 (Accessed: 29 September 2017).

Crouch, C. (2011) *The Strange Non-death of Neo-Liberalism*. Cambridge and Malden, MA: Polity Press.

Crouch, C. (2016) *The Knowledge Corrupters: Hidden Consequences of the Financial Takeover of Public Life*. Cambridge: Polity.

Cunningham, P. (1992). 'Teachers' Professional Image and the Press 1950–1990', *History of education*, 21(1), pp. 37–56.

Curran, J. and Seaton, J. (1981). *Power Without Responsibility: The Press and Broadcasting in Britain*. London: Fontana.

Curran, J., Gaber, I. and Petley, J. (2019) *Culture Wars: The Media and the British Left*. 2nd. edn. London: Routledge.

Curran, J. (2002). *Media and Power*. London: Routledge.

Dabla-Norris, E., Kochhar, K., Ricka, F., Suphaphiphat, N. and Tsounta, E. (2015) *Causes and Consequences of Income Inequality: A Global Perspective*. Washington. Available at: http:// www.imf.org/external/pubs/ft/sdn/2015/sdn1513.pdf

Dahlberg, L. (2001) 'The Internet and Democratic Discourse', *Information, Communication & Society*, 4(4), pp. 615–633.

Dailey, R. and Wenger, D. H. (2016) 'Source Variety, Event Frequency, and Context in Newspaper Crime Reporting', *International Journal of Communication*, (10), pp. 1700–1720.

Daniels, J. (2009) *Cyber-Racism: White Supremacy and the New Attack on Civil Rights*. Plymouth: Rowman & Littlefield.

Davis, A. (2000) 'Public Relations, News Production and Changing Patterns of Source Access in the British National Media', *Media, Culture & Society*, 22(1), pp. 39–59.

Davis, A. (2002) *Public Relations Democracy: Public Relations, Politics, and the Mass Media in Britain.* Manchester: Manchester University Press.

Davies, N. (2008) *Flat Earth News*. London: Chatto & Windus.

Davis, A. (2011) 'Mediation, Financialization, and the Global Financial Crisis', in Winseck, D. and Jin, D. Y. (eds.) *The Political Economies of Media: The Transformation of the Global Media Industries*. London: Bloomsbury, pp. 241–254.

Davis, A. (2013) *Promotional Cultures*. Cambridge: Polity Press.

De Benedictis, S., Allen, K. and Jensen, T. (2017). 'Portraying Poverty: The Economics and Ethics of Factual Welfare Television,' *Cultural Sociology*, 11(3), pp. 337–358.

De Zwart, P. (2019). 'The Global History of Inequality,' *International Review of Social History*, 64(2), pp. 309–323.

Deacon, D. and Golding, P. (1994) *Taxation and Representation: The Media, Political Communication and the Poll Tax*. Luton: John Libbey.

Dean, M. (2012) *Democracy under Attack: How the Media Distort Policy and Politics*. Bristol: Policy Press.

Delestre, I., Kopczuk, W., Miller, H. and Smith, K. (2022) *Top Income Inequality and Tax Policy*. London: Institute for Fiscal Studies. Available at: https://ifs.org.uk/inequality/top-income-inequality-and-tax-policy/ (Accessed: 7 April 2022).

Department for Work and Pensions (2024) *Households below Average Income: An Analysis of the UK Income Distribution: FYE 1995 to FYE 2023*. London: HMSO. Available at: https://www.gov.uk/government/statistics/households-below-average-income-for-financial-years-ending-1995-to-2023/households-below-average-income-an-analysis-of-the-uk-income-distribution-fye-1995-to-fye-2023 (Accessed: 22 March 2024).

Devereux, E. (1998). *Devils and Angels: Television, Ideology and the Coverage of Poverty*. Luton: University of Luton Press.

Devlin, H. (2023) 'Surge in Number of People in Hospital with Nutrient Deficiencies, NHS Figures Show', *Guardian*, 21 December. Available at: https://www.theguardian.com/uk-news/2023/dec/21/surge-in-number-of-people-in-hospital-with-nutrient-deficiencies-nhs-figures-show (Accessed: 22 December 2023).

Di Cicco, D. T. (2010) 'The Public Nuisance Paradigm: Changes in Mass Media Coverage of Political Protest Since the 1960s', *Journalism & Mass Communication Quarterly*, 87(1), pp. 135–153.

Diamond, L. (2010) 'Liberation Technology,' *Journal of Democracy*, 21(3), pp. 69–83.

Digital Planet (2024) *Imagining a Digital Economy for All*. Available at: https://digitalplanet.tufts.edu/idea2030/ (Accessed: 5 March 2024).

Digital Poverty Alliance. (2023) *UK Digital Poverty National Delivery Plan 2023*. DPA. Available at: https://digitalpovertyalliance.org/uk-national-delivery-plan-2023/ (Accessed: 5 March 2024).

Disability Rights UK. (2012) *Press Portrayal of Disabled People: A Rise in Hostility Fuelled by Austerity?* London: Disability Rights UK. Available at: https://www.disabilityrightsuk.org/about-us/press-office/press-and-media-2012/press-portrayal-disabled-people-rise-hostility-fuelled (Accessed: 16 June 2018).

Doering, C. (2021) 'Where the Dollars Go: Lobbying a Big Business for Large Food and Beverage CPGs', *FoodDive*, Available at: https://www.fooddive.com/news/where-the-dollars-go-lobbying-a-big-business-for-large-food-and-beverage-c/607982/?utm_source=Sailthru&utm_medium=email&utm_campaign=Issue:%202021-12-06%20Food%20Dive%20Newsletter%205Bissue:38423%5D&utm_term=Food%20Dive (Accessed: 4 August 2022).

Dogs of the Dow (2021) 'Largest Companies by Market Cap Today (TOP 50 LIST)',. Available at: https://www.dogsofthedow.com/largest-companies-by-market-cap.htm (Accessed: 11 October 2021).

Dolan, K. A. and Peterson–Withorn, C. (2022) *Forbes World's Billionaires List 2022: The Richest in 2022*. New York: Forbes. Available at: https://www.forbes.com/billionaires/ (Accessed: 11 January 2023).

Dorling, D. (2014) *Inequality and the 1%*. London: Verso.

Doyle, G. (2006) 'Financial News Journalism: A post-Enron Analysis of Approaches towards Economic and Financial News Production in the UK,' *Journalism*, 7(4), pp. 433–452.

Drakopolou, S., Grossman, W. and Moore, P. (2016) 'The Campaign for Digital Citizenship', *Soundings*, (62), pp. 107–120.

Drutman, L. (2015) *The Business of America Is Lobbying: How Corporations Became Politicized and Politics Became More Corporate*. New York: Oxford University Press.

Duffin, E. (2022) '*Total Lobbying Spending in the United States from 1998 to 2021*', Statista,. Available at: https://www.statista.com/statistics/257337/total-lobbying-spending-in-the-us/ #professional (Accessed: April 14 2022).

Dulong de Rosnay, M. and Stalder, F. (2020) 'Digital Commons', *Internet Policy Review*, 9(4). Available at: https://doi.org/10.14763/2020.4.1530 (Accessed: 10 October 2021).

Edelman Trust Institute. (2023) *2023 Edelman Trust Barometer*. Washington: Edelman Trust Institute. Available at: https://www.edelman.com/sites/g/files/aatuss191/files/2023-03/ 2023%20Edelman%20Trust%20Barometer%20Global%20Report%20FINAL.pdf (Accessed: 14 July 2023).

Edwards, L. (2018) 'Public Relations, Voice and Recognition: a Case Study', *Media, Culture & Society*, 40(3), pp. 317–332.

Eggers, D. (2014). *The Circle*. London and New York: Penguin.

Elmer, G. (2019) 'Prospecting Facebook: the Limits of the Economy of Attention', *Media, Culture & Society*, 41(3), pp. 332–346.

emarketer (2017) *US Total Media Ad Spend Share by Media, 2014–2020*. Available at: https://www. emarketer.com/Chart/US-Total-Media-Ad-Spending-Share-by-Media-2014-2020-of-total/ 186513 (Accessed: 26 September 2017).

Equality Trust (2022) *Inequality from the Top Down: Billionaire Britain 2022*. Croydon: Equality Trust. Available at: https://equalitytrust.org.uk/sites/default/files/BillionaireBritain2022 _hires.pdf (Accessed: 21 December 2022).

Eubanks, V. (2017). *Automating Inequality: How High-Tech Tools Profile, Police and Punish the Poor*. New York: St. Martin's Press.

Euromedia Research Group. (2022). *Euromedia Ownership Monitor Report 2022*. Salzburg: Available at: https://media-ownership.eu/findings/2022-assessments/report/ (Accessed: 21 December 2022).

European Commission Information Society Directorate General. (2002) *eGovernment: From Policy to Practice*. Brussels: European Commission Directorate F. Available at: https://digital-strategy .ec.europa.eu/en/policies/egovernment.

European Commission (2002) *e-Europe: An Information Society for All*. Available at: https://eur-lex.europa.eu/EN/legal-content/summary/eeurope-an-information-society-for-all.html

European Commission (2003) *Towards a Knowledge-Based Europe: The European Union and the Information Society*. Available at: https://op.europa.eu/en/publication-detail/-/publication/ 3a0f5454-1c91-46a6-aed1-fd3ca5dd8c64/language-en

European Commission (2016) *Standard Eurobarometer 83: Public Opinion in the European Union.* Brussels: European Commission. Available at: https://www.bing.com/images/search?q=euro pean+commission.+2016+standard+eurobarometer+83+public+opinion+in+the+european+ union&qpvt=European+Commission.+(2016)+Standard+Eurobarometer+83%3a+Public+Op inion+in+the+European+Union&form=IGRE&first=1 (Accessed: 20 January 2017).

European Parliament (2018) *Report on Media Pluralism and Media Freedom in the European Union.* Brussels: European Parliament Available at: https://www.europarl.europa.eu/doceo/ document/TA-8-2018-0204_EN.pdf (Accessed: 23 December 2022).

Evans, R. (2019) 'Half of England Is Owned by Less Than 1% of the Population', *Guardian.* Available at: https://www.theguardian.com/money/2019/apr/17/who–owns–england –thousand–secret–landowners–author (Accessed: 27 January 2022).

Fair Tax Mark (2021) *The Silicon Six and Their $100 Billion Global Tax Gap.* Available at: https:// fairtaxmark.net/silicon-six-end-the-decade-with-100-billion-tax-shortfall/ (Accessed: 14 October 2021).

Fenton, N. (2016) *Digital, Political, Radical.* Cambridge: Polity Press.

Finances Online (2021) '*74 Amazon Statistics You Must Know: 2020/2021 Market Share Analysis & Data*',. Available at: https://financesonline.com/amazon-statistics/#:~:text=By%202019%2C %20Amazon%E2%80%99s%20share%20of%20the%20total%20US,13.7%25%20of%20the %20worldwide%20online%20retail%20market%20sales. (Accessed: 13 October 2021).

Finn, C. E. (1986) 'The Rationale for the American Withdrawal,' *Comparative Education Review*, 30(1), pp. 140–147.

Fonseca, M. (2016) *Gramsci's Critique of Civil Society: Towards a New Concept of Hegemony.* London: Routledge.

Forbes (2021) '*World's Billionaires List: The Richest in 2021*',. Available at: https://www.forbes. com/billionaires/ (Accessed: 16 November 2021).

Fox, J. and Moreland, J. J. (2015) 'The Dark Side of Social Networking Sites: An Exploration of the Relational and Psychological Stressors Associated with Facebook Use and Affordances', *Computers in Human Behavior*, (45), pp. 168–176.

Frank, R. H. and Cook, P. J. (2010) *The Winner-Take-All Society: Why the Few at the Top Get So Much More Than the Rest of Us.* New York: Virgin Books.

Freedland, J. (2023) 'As Heat Records Break, the Climate Movement Has the Right Answers – but the Words Are All Wrong', *The Guardian*, 14 July. Available at: https://www.theguardian.com/ commentisfree/2023/jul/14/big-oil-climate-crisis-fossil-fuel-public (Accessed: 16 July 2023).

Freedman, D. (2002) 'A 'Technological Idiot'? Raymond Williams and Communications Technology', *Information, Communication & Society*, 5(3), pp. 425–442.

Freudenburg, W. R. and Muselli, V. (2010) 'Global Warming Estimates, Media Expectations, and the Asymmetry of Scientific Challenge', *Global Environmental Change–Human and Policy Dimensions*, 20(3), pp. 483–491.

Fuchs, C. (2009) 'The Role of Income Inequality in a Multivariate Cross–National Analysis of the Digital Divide', *Social Science Computer Review*, 27(1), pp. 41–58.

Fuchs, C. (2021) 'The Digital Commons and the Digital Public Sphere: How to Advance Digital Democracy Today', *Westminster Papers in Communication and Culture*, 16(1), pp. 9–26.

Full Story Media. (2018) 'The Decline of UK Journalism', (and what it means for your business) [Press release]. Available at: https://fullstorymedia.co.uk/2018/06/29/the-decline-of-uk-journ alism-and-what-it-means-for-your-business/

Gaber, I. (2016) 'Bending Over Backwards: The BBC and the Referendum Campaign', in D. Jackson, E. Thorsen and D. Wring (eds.), *EU Referendum Analysis 2016: Media Voters and the Campaign*. Bournemouth: Political Studies Association, p. 54.

Gaber, I. (2019) 'All Change at the Top', in J. Curran, I. Gaber and J. Petley (Eds.), *Culture Wars: The British Media and the Left*. London: Routledge, pp. 218–239.

Gaby, S. and Caren, N. (2016) 'The Rise of Inequality: How Social Movements Shape Discursive Fields', *Mobilisation: International Quarterly*, 21(4), pp. 413–429.

Gamble, A. (2019) 'Why Is Neo–Liberalism So Resilient?', *Critical Sociology*, 45(7–8), pp. 983–994.

Ganesh, S. and Stohl, C. (2013) 'From Wall Street to Wellington: Protests in an Era of Digital Ubiquity', *Communication Monographs*, 80(4), pp. 425–451.

Gangadharan, S. P. (2015) 'The Downside of Digital Inclusion: Expectations and Experiences of Privacy and Surveillance Among Marginal Internet Users', *New Media and Society*, 19(4), pp. 597–615.

Garland, R. (2017) 'Between Mediatisation and Politicisation: The Changing Role and Position of Whitehall Press Officers in the Age of Political Spin', *Public Relations Inquiry*, 6(2), pp. 171–189.

Garland, R. (2018) 'The Unseen Power of Creative News Management in Government: The Marginalisation of UK Government Press Officers between 1997 and 2015', *Journal of Communication Management*, 22(4), pp. 416–431.

Garnham, N. (1986) 'The Media and the Public Sphere', in Golding, P., Murdock, G. and Schlesinger, P. (eds.) *Communicating Politics: Mass Communications and the Political Process*. Leicester: Leicester University Press, pp. 37–53.

Garside, J. (2015) 'Recession Rich: Britain's Wealthiest Double Net Worth since Crisis', *The Guardian*, 26 April.(Accessed: 15 March 2022).

Gates, B. (1995) *The Road Ahead*. London: Viking.

Gayle, D. (2021) 'Facebook Aware of Instagram's Harmful Effect on Teenage Girls, Leak Reveals', *Guardian*, 14 September 2021. Available at: https://www.theguardian.com/technology/2021/sep/14/facebook-aware-instagram-harmful-effect-teenage-girls-leak-reveals (Accessed: 14 September 2021).

Gelles–Watnick, R. (2024) *Americans' Use of Mobile Technology and Home Broadband*. Pew Research Center. Available at: https://www.pewresearch.org/internet/2024/01/31/americans-use-of-mobile-technology-and-home-broadband/ (Accessed: 19 March 2024).

Geoghegan, P. (2020) *Democracy for Sale: Dark Money and Dirty Politics*. London: Head of Zeus.

Georgieva, K. (2024) *The Economic Possibilities for my Grandchildren*. Available at: https://www.imf.org/en/News/Articles/2024/03/08/sp031424-kings-college-cambridge-kristalina-georgieva (Accessed: March 15 2024).

Gerbaudo, P. (2018) 'Social Media and Populism: An Elective Affinity?', *Media, Culture & Society*, 40(5), pp. 745–753.

Giddens, A. (1991) *The Consequences of Modernity*. Oxford: Polity.

Gilens, M. (2014) *Affluence and Influence: Economic Inequality and Political Power in America*. Princeton, NJ: Princeton University Press.

Gillespie, A. and Robins, K. (1989) 'Geographical Inequalities: The Spatial Bias of the New Communication Technologies', *Journal of Communication*, 39(3), pp. 7–18.

Giroux, H. A. (2015) 'Totalitarian Paranoia in the Post-Orwellian Surveillance State', *Cultural studies*, 29(2), pp. 108–140.

Gitlin, T. (1980) *The Whole World Is Watching: Mass Media in the Making and Unmaking of the New Left*. Berkeley: University of California Press.

Gitlin, T. (2012) *Occupy Nation: The Roots, the Spirit, and the Promise of Occupy Wall Street*. New York: Harper Collins.

Glenza, J. (2019) 'Revealed: the Free–Market Groups Helping the Tobacco Industry', *The Guardian*, 23 January 2019. Available at: https://www.theguardian.com/business/ng–int eractive/2019/jan/23/free–market-thinktanks-tobacco-industry (Accessed: 28 July 2022).

Gohdes, A. R. (2020) 'Repression Technology: Internet Accessibility and State Violence,' *American Journal of Political Science*, 64(3), pp. 488–503.

Goldacre, B. (2008). *Bad Science*. London: Fourth Estate.

Goldacre, B. (2009) *Bad Science*. London: Fourth Estate.

Golding, P. and Elliott, P. (1979) *Making the News*. London: Longman.

Golding, P. and Harris, P. (eds.) (1997) *Beyond Cultural Imperialism: Globalization, Communication & the New International Order*. London, Thousand Oaks, New Delhi: SAGE.

Golding, P. and Middleton, S. (1982) *Images of Welfare: Press and Public Attitudes to Poverty*. Oxford: Martin Robertson.

Golding, P. and Murdock, G. (1978) 'Theories of Communication and Theories of Society', *Communication Research* 5(3), pp. 339–356.

Golding, P. and Murdock, G. (2023). 'The Political Economy of Contemporary Journalism and the Crisis of Public Knowledge', in S. Allan (ed.) *The Routledge Companion to News and Journalism*. 2nd edn. London: Routledge, pp. 36–45.

Golding, P. (1994) 'Telling Stories: Sociology, Journalism and the Informed Citizen', *European Journal of Communication*, 9(4), pp. 461–484.

Golding, P. (2000) 'Forthcoming Features: Information and Communications Technologies and the Sociology of the Future', *Sociology*, 34(1), pp. 165–184.

Golding, P. (2007) 'Eurocrats, Technocrats, and Democrats: Competing Ideologies in the European Information Society', *European Societies*, 9(5), pp. 719–734.

Golding, P. (2017) 'Citizen Detriment: Communications, Inequality, and Social Order', *International Journal of Communication*, 11. Available at: http://ijoc.org/index.php/ijoc (Accessed: 28 September 2017).

Goldstein, R. A. (2011) 'Imaging the Frame: Media Representations of Teachers, Their Unions, NCLB, and Education Reform', *Educational Policy*, 25(4), pp. 543–576.

Gonzales, A. (2015) 'The Contemporary US Digital Divide: From Initial Access to Technology Maintenance', *Information, communication & society*, 19(2), pp. 234–248.

Good Things Foundation (2023) *Public Sector Pioneers: Reusing IT Equipment to Bridge the Digital Divide*. Good Things Foundation. Available at: https://www.goodthingsfoundation.org/ insights/public-sector-pioneers-reusing-it-equipment-to-bridge-the-digital-divide/?utm_so urce=Good+Things+Foundation+Newsletter&utm_campaign=def0590b16-EMAIL_CA MPAIGN_2019_04_05_08_12_COPY_01&utm_medium=email&utm_term=0_874c1db cc0-def0590b16-110169635 (Accessed: 30 November 2023).

Gore, A. (1994) *Information Superhighways Speech*. Available at: http://vlib.iue.it/history/internet/ algorespeech.html (Accessed: 14 November 2019).

Gottlieb, J. (2015) 'Protest News Framing Cycle: How the *New York Times* Covered Occupy Wall Street', *International Journal of Communication*, 9, pp. 231–253.

Graber, D. (1976) *Verbal Behaviour and Politics*. Urbana, Il: University of Illinois Press.

Gramsci, A. (2005) *Selections from the Prison Notebooks*. London Lawrence & Wishart.

Green, F. (2020) *Schoolwork in Lockdown: New Evidence on the Epidemic of Educational Poverty* (LLAKES Research paper 67). London: Centre for Learning and Life Chances in Knowledge Economies and Societies (LLAKES) Available at: https://www.llakes.ac.uk/wp-content/uploads/2021/03/RP-67-Francis-Green-Research-Paper-combined-file.pdf (Accessed: 20 November 2020).

Greenstein, S. (2015) *How the Internet Became Commercial: Innovation, Privatization, and the Birth of a New Network*. Princeton and Oxford: Princeton University Press.

Gregoriou, C., & Paterson, L. L. (2017) '"Reservoir of Rage Swamps Wall St" the Linguistic Construction and Evaluation of Occupy in International Print Media', *Journal of Language Aggression and Conflict*, 5(1), pp. 57–80.

Grimes, D. R. (2019) *The Irrational Ape: Why We Fall for Disinformation, Conspiracy Theory and Propaganda*. London and New York: Simon and Schuster.

Guccione, D. (2021) *The State of Cybersecurity*. Available at: https://www.csoonline.com/article/3249765/what-is-the-dark-web-how-to-access-it-and-what-youll-find.html (Accessed: 16 September 2021).

Gunkel, D. (2003) 'Second Thoughts: toward a Critique of the Digital Divide', *New Media & Society*, 5(4), pp. 499–522.

Guterres, A. (2023) 'Secretary-General's Press Conference - on Climate'. 15 June. New York: United Nations. Available at: https://www.un.org/sg/en/content/sg/press-encounter/2023-06-15/secretary-generals-press-conference-climate (Accessed: June 16 2023).

Guttman, A. (2022) *Public Relations in the U.S. – Statistics & Facts*. Washington. Available at: https://www.statista.com/topics/3521/public–relations/#topicHeader__wrapper (Accessed: 5 October 2022).

Habermas, J. (1984) *The Theory of Communicative Action*. London: Heinemann.

Habermas, J. (1989 [orig. 1962]) *The Structural Transformation of the Public Sphere*. Cambridge: Polity.

Habermas, J. (2006) 'Political Communication in Media Society: Does Democracy Still Enjoy an Epistemic Dimension? The Impact of Normative Theory on Empirical Research', *Communication Theory*, 16(4), pp. 411–426.

Habermas, J. (2022) 'Reflections and Hypotheses on a Further Structural Transformation of the Political Public Sphere', *Theory, Culture & Society*, 39(4), pp. 145–171.

Hall, S. (2003) 'New Labour's Double Shuffle', *Soundings*, 24, pp. 10–24.

Hall, S. (2017) 'Gramsci and Us'. Available at: https://www.versobooks.com/en-gb/blogs/news/2448-stuart-hall-gramsci-and-us (Accessed: 12 April 2023).

Hall, S. (2021). *The Hard Road to Renewal: Thatcherism and the Crisis of the Left*. London: Verso.

Hallin, D. (1992) 'Sound-bite news: TV Coverage of Elections 1968-1998', *Journal of Communication*, 42(2), pp. 5–24.

Halloran, J. D., Elliott, P., & Murdock, G. (1970). *Demonstrations and Communication: A Case Study*. Harmondsworth: Penguin.

Hamelink, C. (1997) 'MacBride with Hindsight,' in P. Golding and P. Harris (Eds.), *Beyond Cultural Imperialism*. London: SAGE, pp. 69–93.

Hammond, K. (2004) 'Monsters of Modernity: Frankenstein and Modern Environmentalism', *Cultural Geographies*, 11, pp. 181–198.

Hanlon, M. (2013) 'Reason and Unreason in Twenty–First Century Science', *European Review*, 21(S1), pp. S4–S8.

Hannington, W. (1938). *A Short History of the Unemployed*. London: Victor Gollancz.

Hansard Society (2016). *Audit of Political Engagement 13: The 2016 Report*. London: Hansard Society. Available at: https://assets.contentful.com/u1rlvvbs33ri/24aY1mkabGU0uEsoUO ekGW/06380afa29a63008e97fb41cdb8dcad0/Publication__Audit-of-Political-Engagement-13.pdf (Accessed: January 20, 2017).

Hansen, A. (2010). *Environment, Media and Communication*. Abingdon and New York: Routledge.

Hanusch, F., Banjac, S. and Maares, P. (2020) 'The Power of Commercial Influences: How Lifestyle Journalists Experience Pressure from Advertising and Public Relations', *Journalism Practice*, 14(9), pp. 1029–1046.

Harbisher, B. (ed.) (2023). *The Mediation of Sustainability: Development Goals, Social Movements, and Public Dissent*. London and New York: Rowman & Littlefield.

Hargittai, E. (2002) 'Second Level Digital Divide: Differences in People's Online Skills', *First Monday*, 7(4), pp. 1–14. Available at: http://firstmonday.org/article/view/942/864 (Accessed: 12 April 2022).

Harrabin, R., Coote, A. and Allen, J. (2003) *Health In the News: Risk, Reporting and Media Influence (1857174801)*. London. Available at: www.kingsfund.org.uk/publications (Accessed: 12 August 2010).

Harris, C., Farrell, D. M. and Brennan, M. (2020) 'Women's Voices in a Deliberative Assembly: An Analysis of Gender Rates of Participation in Ireland's Convention on the Constitution 2012–2014', *The British Journal of Politics & International Relations*, 23(1), pp. 175–193.

Harvard University (2022) *The Future of Media Project*. Cambridge, MA: University, H. Available at: https://projects.iq.harvard.edu/futureofmedia/us-media-index (Accessed: 27 November 2022).

Hayes, A. (2024). *Biggest Companies in the World by Market Cap*. https://www.investopedia.com/biggest-companies-in-the-world-by-market-cap-5212784 (Accessed 12 July 2024).

Held, D. (1991) 'Between State and Civil Society: Citizenship', in Andrews, G. (ed.) *Citizenship*. London: Lawrence & Wishart, pp. 19–36.

Hellawell, S. (2001) *Beyond Access: ICT and Social Inclusion*. London: Fabian Society.

Helsper, E. J. and Reisdorf, B. C. (2017) 'The emergence of a "digital underclass" in Great Britain and Sweden: Changing Reasons for Digital Exclusion,' *New Media & Society*, 19(8), pp. 1253–1270.

Helsper, E. J. (2021) *The Digital Disconnect: The Social Causes and Consequences of Digital Inequalities*. London: SAGE.

Henry, N., Vasil, S. and Witt, A. (2021) 'Digital Citizenship in a Global Society: a Feminist Approach', *Feminist Media Studies*, 22(8), pp. 1972–1989.

High Pay Centre (2024) *High Pay Hour 2024*. London: Centre, H. P. Available at: https://highpay centre.org/high-pay-hour-2024/ (Accessed: 5 January 2024).

Hilbert, M. (2016) 'The Bad News Is that the Digital Access Divide Is Here to Stay: Domestically Installed Bandwidths Among 172 Countries for 1986–2014', *Telecommunications Policy*, 40(6), pp. 567–581.

Hill, D. (1998) 'Neo–liberalism and Hegemony Revisited', *Educational Philosophy and Theory*, 30(1), pp. 69–83.

Hindman, M. (2009) *The Myth of Digital Democracy*. Princeton, NJ: Princeton University Press.

Hintz, A., Dencik, L. and Wahl–Jorgensen, K. (2019) *Digital Citizenship in a Datafied Society*. Cambridge: Polity Press.

Hirsch, D. (2024) '*The UK's Inadequate and Unfair Safety Net*', Abrdn Financial Fairness Trust. Aberdeen. Available at: https://www.financialfairness.org.uk/docs?editionId=c9f66338-7c19-4ee8-8634-b0f800c19dc6 (Accessed: 31 January 2024).

Hirschman, A. O. (1970) *Exit, Voice, and Loyalty: Responses to Decline in Firms, Organizations, and States*. Cambridge, Mass.: Harvard University Press.

HoldtheFrontPage (2021) *Hyperlocal Publications*. Available at: https://www.holdthefrontpage. co.uk/directory/hyperlocal-publications/ (Accessed: 10 November 2021).

Hosli, M. O., Kantorowicz, J., Nagtzaam, M. A. M. and Haas, M. I. (2022) *Turnout in European Parliament Elections 1979–2019*, European Politics and Society. https://doi.org/10.1080/237 45118.2022.2137918

House of Commons Education Committee (2020) *Oral Evidence: The Impact of Covid–19 on Education and Children's Services, June 3rd. 2020. HC 254*. Available at: https://committees. parliament.uk/oralevidence/441/html/ (Accessed: 18 June 2020).

House of Commons Public Administration Select Committee (2008) *Lobbying: Access and Influence in Whitehall. HC 36–1*. London. Available at: http:// www.publications.parliament.uk/pa/cm200809/cmselect/cmpubadm/36/36i.pdf (Accessed: January 18 2017).

House of Commons. (2000) *Select Committee on Health Minutes of Evidence*. London: HMSO. Available at: https://publications.parliament.uk/pa/cm199900/cmselect/cmhealth/27/001 2001.htm (Accessed: 10 November 2022).

House of Commons (2019) *Disinformation and 'fake News': Final Report of Digital, Culture, Media and Sport Committee. HC 1791*. London. Available at: https://publications.parliament.uk/pa/ cm201719/cmselect/cmcumeds/1791/1791.pdf (Accessed: 11 October 2021).

House of Lords Communications and Digital Committee (2023) *Digital Exclusion*. London: House of Lords. Available at: https://publications.parliament.uk/pa/ld5803/ldselect/ldcomm/219/ 21902.htm (Accessed: 29 June 2023).

I Daniel Blake (2016). Film, Directed by Ken Loach.

Ibis World. (2022). *Public Relations Firms Industry in the US - Market Research Report*. New York: Ibis World. Available at: https://www.ibisworld.com/united-states/market-research-reports/ public-relations-firms-industry/ (Accessed: 5 October 2022).

InfluenceMap (2020) 'Climate Change and Digital Advertising: Climate Science Disinformation in Facebook Advertising',. Available at: https://influencemap.org/report/Climate-Change-and-Digital-Advertising-86222daed29c6f49ab2da76b0df15f76# (Accessed: 30 September 2021).

Ingham, F. (2021) *'PR Industry Roars Back' – 2021 PRCA UK Census*. Available at: https://www. prca.org.uk/PR-industry-roars-back-2021-PRCA-UK-Census (Accessed: 4 October 2022).

International IDEA (2023) *The Global State of Democracy Initiative*. Available at: https://idea.int/ democracytracker/searchable–archive (Accessed: 12 July 2023).

International Telecommunication Union (ITU) (2021) *Measuring Digital Development: Facts and Figures 2021*. Geneva: ITU. Available at: https://www.itu.int/en/ITU-D/Statistics/Documents/ facts/FactsFigures2021.pdf (Accessed: 14 January 2022).

IPCC (Intergovernmental Panel on Climate Change) (2023) *AR6 Synthesis Report: Climate Change 2023*. Switzerland IPCC. Available at: https://www.ipcc.ch/report/sixth-assessment-report-cycle/ (Accessed: June 15 2023).

Irwin, S. (2018) 'Lay Perceptions of Inequality and Social Structure', *Sociology*, 52(2), pp. 211–227.

Isin, E. and Ruppert, E. (2015) *Being Digital Citizens*. New York: Rowman & Littlefield International.

ITEA (Information Technology for European Advancement) (2002) *Building the Digital Future*. Available at: https://itea4.org/media/itea-previews-the-digital-future-symposium-review-award-winners-panel-discussion.html

Jacques, P. J., Dunlap, R. E. and Freeman, M. (2008) 'The Organisation of Denial: Conservative Think Tanks and Environmental Scepticism', *Environmental Politics*, 17(3), pp. 349–385.

Jeanneny, J.–N. (2007) *Google and the Myth of Universal Knowledge*. Chicago: University of Chicago Press.

Jewkes, Y. (2015) *Media and Crime*. 3rd edn. London: SAGE.

Jigsaw Research (2022) *News Consumption in the UK: 2022*. London: ofcom. Available at: https://www.ofcom.org.uk/__data/assets/pdf_file/0027/241947/News-Consumption-in-the-UK-2022-report.pdf (Accessed: 19 December 2022).

Kagami, M. and Tsuji, M. (2002) *Digital Divide or Digital Jump: Beyond 'IT' Revolution*. Tokyo: Institute of Developing Economies Japan External Trade Organization.

Kale, S. (2020) '"You Can't Pay Cash Here": How Our New Cashless Society Harms the Most Vulnerable', *The Guardian*, 24 June 2020. Available at: https://www.theguardian.com/money/2020/jun/24/you-cant-pay-cash-here-how-cashless-society-harms-most-vulnerable (Accessed: 25 June 2020).

Karpowitz, C. F, Raphael, C. and Hammond, A. S. (2009) 'Deliberative Democracy and Inequality: Two Cheers for Enclave Deliberation Among the Disempowered', *Politics & Society*, 37(4), pp. 576–615.

Kavada, A. (2015) 'Creating the Collective: Social Media, the Occupy Movement, and its Constitution as a Collective Actor', *Information, Communication & Society*, 18(8), pp. 872–886.

Kay, J. B. and Salter, L. (2014) 'Framing the Cuts: An analysis of the BBC's Discursive Framing of the ConDem Cuts Agenda', *Journalism*, 15(6), pp. 754–772.

Keen, A. (2015) *The Internet Is Not the Answer*. London: Atlantic Books.

Kim, S.-H. and Willis, L. A. (2007) 'Talking about Obesity: News Framing of Who Is Responsible for Causing and Fixing the Problem', *Journal of Health Communication*, 12(4), 359–376.

Kirkpatrick, D. (2011) *The Facebook Effect*. London: Virgin Books.

Klikauer, T. (2021) *Media Capitalism: Hegemony in the Age of Mass Deception*. London: Palgrave Macmillan.

Knowles, S., Phillips, G. and Lidberg, J. (2015) 'Reporting the Global Financial Crisis: A Longitudinal Tri–nation Study of Mainstream Financial Journalism', *Journalism Studies*, pp. 1–19.

Kolbert, E. (2014). *The Sixth Extinction: An Unnatural History*. London: Bloomsbury Publishing.

Korupp, S. E. and Szydlik, M. (2005) 'Causes and Trends of the Digital Divide', *European Sociological Review*, 21(4), pp. 409–422.

Kroll, G. (2001). 'The "Silent Springs" of Rachel Carson: Mass Media and the Origins of Modern Environmentalism. *Public Understanding of Science*, (10), pp. 403–420.

Kyriakidou, M. and Osuna, J. J. O. (2017) 'The Indignados Protests in the Spanish and Greek Press: Beyond the 'protest Paradigm'?', *European Journal of Communication*, 32(5), pp. 457–472.

Labio-Bernal, A. (2018) 'Anti-Communism and the Mainstream Online Press in Spain: Criticism of Podemos as a Strategy of a Two-Party System in Crisis,' in J. Pedro-Carañana, D. Broudy, and J. Klaehn (eds.) *The Propaganda Model Today: Filtering Perception and Awarenes*. London: University of Westminster Press, pp. 125–141.

Lakhani, N. (2023) 'Record Number of Fossil Fuel Lobbyists Get Access to Cop28 Climate Talks', *The Guardian*, 6 December. Available at: https://www.theguardian.com/environment/2023/dec/05/record-number-of-fossil-fuel-lobbyists-get-access-to-cop28-climate-talks (Accessed: 6 December 2023).

Lamare, A. (2017) *Billionaires Who Own the Media in the United States*. Available at: https://www.celebritynetworth.com/articles/billionaire-news/billionaires-media-united-states/ (Accessed: 11 January 2023).

Larsen, C. A., & Dejgaard, T. E. (2013). The Institutional Logic of the Poor and Welfare Recipients: A comparative study of British, Swedish and Danish Newspapers. *Journal of European Social Policy*, 23(3), pp. 287–299.

Legg, H. (2022) 'Who Owns the News in the US? New Analysis Reveals Top Owners and Publishers', *PressGazette: Future of Media*, 30 September. Available at: https://pressgazette.co.uk/comment-analysis/who-owns-us-news/ (Accessed: 25 November 2022).

Leguina, A. and Downey, J. (2021) 'Getting Things Done: Inequalities, Internet Use and Everyday Life', *New Media & Society*, 23(7), pp. 1824–1849.

Leishman, F., & Mason, P. (2003) *Policing and the Media: Facts, Fictions and Factions*. Devon: Willan Publishing.

Lens, V. (2002) 'Welfare Reform, Personal Narratives and the Media: How Welfare Recipients and Journalists Frame the Welfare Debate', *Journal of Poverty*, 6(2), pp. 1–20.

Lester, L. (2010) *Media and Environment*. Cambridge: Polity Press.

Lewis, J. and Cushion, S. (2019) 'Think Tanks, Television News and Impartiality: The Ideological Balance of Sources in BBC Programming', *Journalism Studies*, 20(4), pp. 480–499.

Lewis, J., Wahl–Jorgensen, K. and Inthorn, S. (2004) 'Images of Citizenship on Television News: Constructing a Passive Public', *Journalism Studies*, 5(2), pp. 153–164.

Lewis, C. (1992) 'Making Sense of Common Sense: A Framework for Tracking Hegemony', *Critical Studies in Mass Communication*, 9(3), pp. 277–292.

Lin, J., & Phillips, S. (2014). 'Media Coverage of Capital Murder: Exceptions Sustain the Rule', *Justice Quarterly*, 31(5), pp. 934–959.

Lind, D. (2018) 'President Donald Trump Finally Admits that "Fake News" Just Means News He Doesn't like', *Vox*, May 9. Available at: https://www.vox.com/policy-and-politics/2018/5/9/17335306/trump-tweet-twitter-latest-fake-news-credentials (Accessed: 30 September 2021).

Lishchuk, R. (2021) 'How Large Would Tech Companies Be if They Were Countries?', *Mackeeper blog*,. Available at: https://mackeeper.com/blog/tech-giants-as-countries/ (Accessed: 7 October 2021).

Lloyd, J. and Toogood, L. (2015) *Journalism and PR: News Media and Public Relations in the Digital Age*. London: I. B. Tauris.

Loader, B. B. and Mercea, D. (eds.) (2015) *Social Media and Democracy: Innovations in Participatory Politics*. London: Routledge.

Lockard, J. (1997) 'Progressive Politics, Electronic Individualism, and the Myth of Virtual Community', in D. Porter (ed.) *Internet Culture*. New York and London: Routledge, pp. 219–231.

Logan, N. (2014) 'Corporate Voice and Ideology: An Alternate Approach to Understanding Public Relations History', *Public Relations Review*, 40(4), pp. 661–668.

Loughborough Centre for Research in Media and Culture. (2015). *Media Coverage of the 2015 Campaign (Report 5)*. Loughborough: Loughborough University. https://blog.lboro.ac.uk/crcc/general-election/media-coverage-of-the-2015-campaign-report-5/ (Accessed January 20 2017).

Loughborough Centre for Research in Media and Culture. (2024). *Media Coverage of the 2024 Campaign (Report 5)*. Loughborough: Loughborough University. https://www.lboro.ac.uk/news-events/general-election/report-5-2024/#section-4 (Accessed: July 12 2024).

Lucas, R. (2020). 'The Surveillance Business', *New Left Review*, 121, pp. 132–141.

Lugo-Ocando, J. (2014) *Blaming the Victim: How Global Journalism Fails Those in Poverty*. London: Pluto Press.

Lugo-Ocando, J. (2017) *Crime Statistics in the News: Journalism, Numbers and Social Deviation*. London: Palgrave.

Lutz, C. (2019) 'Digital Inequalities in the Age of Artificial Intelligence and Big Data', *Human Behavior & Emerging Technologies*, 1(2), pp. 141–148.

Lynch, K. (2022) 'WingX: Bizjet Flights Reached New Records in 2021', *AIN Monthly*, 6 January 2022. Available at: https://www.ainonline.com/aviation-news/business-aviation/2022-01-06/wingx-bizjet-flights-reached-new-records-2021 (Accessed: January 7 2022).

MacBride, S. (1980) *Many Voices, One World*. London, New York and Paris: Kogan Page/UNESCO.

Mackinac Center (2019) *The Overton Window*. Michigan. Available at: https://www.mackinac.org/overtonwindow (Accessed: 15 December 2023).

Macnamara, J. (2013) 'Beyond Voice: Audience–Making and the Work and Architecture of Listening as New Media Literacies', *Continuum: Journal of Media & Cultural Studies–*, 27(1), pp. 160–175.

MacRaild, D. M. (2008) 'The Jarrow Crusade: Protest and Legend.', *Labour History Review*, 73(1), pp. 167–180.

Manning, P. (2013) 'Financial Journalism, News Sources and the Banking Crisis', *Journalism*, 14(2), pp. 173–189.

Manokha, I. (2018) 'Surveillance, Panopticism, and Self-Discipline in the Digital Age', *Surveillance & Society*, 16(2), pp. 219–237.

Marshall, T. H. and Bottomore, T. (1992) *Citizenship and Social Class*. London: Pluto Press.

Mason, P. (ed.) (2003) *Criminal Visions: Media Representations of Crime and Justice*. Devon: Willan Publishing.

Mattelart, T., Papathanassopoulos, S. and Trappel, J. (2019) 'Information and News Inequalities', in Trappel, J. (ed.) *Digital Media Inequalities: Policies against Divides, Distrust and Discrimination*. Gothenburg: Nordicom, pp. 215–228.

McAlone, N. (2016) *Cable TV Price Increases Have Beaten Inflation Every Single Year for 20 Years*. Washington. Available at: https://uk.finance.yahoo.com/news/cable-tv-price-increases-beaten-174859415.html?guccounter=1&guce_referrer=aHR0cHM6Ly93d3cuYmluZy5jb20v&guce_referrer_sig=AQAAAG_nDGIAtvsgiCePExVHMdw1utYxZqkiYQesitBQGswd-EQf8wHCCQl7GBRTYpHOEemLKBoXV7WZEbqAmIolqxTiu9xHzkaiVsOOCeNR7g-0kHloYdrOBfMZ2bVdR4JfIuemeAa8dsQQl-mdPkQXTOcd5mxf_Q8MZCbVjZMeBpGS (Accessed: 8 November 2021).

McChesney, R. (2013). *Digital Disconnect: How Capitalism is turning the Internet against Democracy*. New York: The New Press.

McComas, K. and Shanahan, J. (1999) 'Telling Stories about Global Climate Change', *Communication Research*, 26(1), pp. 30–57.

McGarty, C., Thomas, E. and Bliuc, A. (2014) 'New Technologies, New Identities, and the Growth of Mass Opposition in the Arab Spring', *Political Psychology*, 35(6), pp. 725–740.

McGinty, E. E., Kennedy-Hendricks, A., Choksy, S. and Barry, C. L. (2016). 'Trends in News Media Coverage of Mental Illness in the United States: 1995–2014,' *Health Affairs*, 35(6), pp. 1121–1129.

McGuigan, J. (2013) 'Mobile Privatisation and the Neoliberal Self', *Key Words: A Journal of Cultural Materialism*, (11), pp. 75–89.

McKibben, B. (2020). 'When "Creatives" Turn Destructive: Image-Makers and the Climate Crisis', *The New Yorker*, 21 November 2020. Available at: https://www.newyorker.com/news/daily-comment/when-creatives-turn-destructive-image-makers-and-the-climate-crisis (Accessed: 21 June 2024).

McQuail, D. (2013). *Journalism and Society*. London and Thousand Oaks, CA: SAGE.

Media Matters (2017) *How Broadcast Networks Covered Climate Change in 2016*. Available at: https://www.mediamatters.org/donald-trump/how-broadcast-networks-covered-climate-change-2016 (Accessed: 16 February 2024).

Media Reform Coalition (2021) *Who Owns the UK Media?* London. Available at: https://www.mediareform.org.uk/wp–content/uploads/2021/03/Who–Owns–the–UK–Media_final2.pdf (Accessed: 22 December 2022).

Mediatique (2018) *Overview of Recent Dynamics in the UK Press Market*. London. Available at: https://secure.toolkitfiles.co.uk/clients/19826/sitedata/Reports/Press–report–for–DCMS.pdf (Accessed: 5 November 2021).

Merton, R. K. (1968) 'The Matthew Effect in Science: The Reward and Communication Systems of Science Are Considered', *Science*, 159(3810), pp. 56–63.

Milanovic, B. (2016) *Global Inequality: A New Approach for the Age of Globalization*. Cambridge, MA: Harvard University Press.

Miller, D. and Dinan, W. (2000) 'The Rise of the PR Industry in Britain, 1979–98', *European Journal of Communication*, 15(1), pp. 5–35.

Miller, D. and Dinan, W. (2008) *A Century of Spin: How Public Relations Became the Cutting Edge of Corporate Power*. London: Pluto Press.

Milmo, D. (2021) 'YouTube to Remove Misinformation Videos about All Vaccines', *Guardian*, 29 September 2021. Available at: https://www.theguardian.com/technology/2021/sep/29/youtube-to-remove-misinformation-videos-about-all-vaccines (Accessed: 30 September 2021).

Milne, K. (2005) *Manufacturing Dissent: Single–Issue Protest, the Public and the Press (1841801410)*. London. Available at: http://www.demos.co.uk/catalogue/manufacturingdissentbook/

Moore, M. and Tambini, D. (eds.) (2018) *Digital Dominance: The Power of Google, Amazon, Facebook, and Apple*. Oxford: Oxford University Press.

Moore, R. C. (1998) 'Hegemony, Agency, and Dialectical Tension in Ellul's Technological Society,' *Journal of Communication*, 48(3), pp. 129–144.

Moran, M. and Litwak, M. (2021) *The Industry Agenda: Big Tech*. Washington: The Revolving Door Project. Available at: https://therevolvingdoorproject.org/the-industry-agenda-big-tech/ (Accessed: 16 December 2022).

Morozov, E. (2011) *The Net Delusion: How Not to Liberate the World*. Harmondsworth: Penguin.

Morrison, J. (2018). *Scroungers: Moral Panics and Media Myths*. London: Zed Books.

Morse, S. (2016) 'They can Read all about It: An Analysis of Global Newspaper Reporting of Genetically Modified Crop Varieties between 1996 and 2013', *Outlook on Agriculture*, 45(1), pp. 7–17.

Morus, I. R. (2001) '"The Nervous System of Britain": Space, Time and the Electric Telegraph in the Victorian Age', *The British Journal for the History of Science*, 33(4), pp. 455–475.

Mosco, V. (2017) *Becoming Digital: Towards a Post–Internet Society*. Bingley, UK: Emerald Publishing.

Mossberger, K. (2008) 'Toward Digital Citizenship: Addressing Inequality in the Information Age', in Chadwick, A. and Howard, P. N. (eds.) *Routledge Handbook of Internet Politics*. London: Routledge.

Mufson, S. (2022) More than 450 scientists call on PR and ad firms to cut their ties with fossil fuel clients. *Washington Post*, 19 January 2022. Available at: https://www.washingtonpost.com/climate-environment/2022/01/19/pr-firms-fossil-fuels-climate/ (Accessed: 15 November 2022).

Murdock, G. and Golding, P. (1974) 'For a Political Economy of the Mass Media', in R. Miliband and J. Saville (eds.) *The Socialist Register 1973*. London: Merlin Press, pp. 205–234.

Murdock, G. and Golding, P. (1989) 'Information Poverty and Political Inequality – Citizenship in the Age of Privatized Communications', *Journal of Communication*, 39(3), pp. 180–195.

Murdock, G. and Golding, P. (1991) 'Culture, Communications, and Political Economy', In J. Curran and M. Gurevitch (eds.), *Mass Media and Society*. London: Edward Arnold, pp. 15–32.

Murdock, G. and Golding, P. (2004) 'Dismantling the Digital Divide: Rethinking the Dynamics of Participation and Exclusion', in Calabrese, A. and Sparks, C. (eds.) *Toward a Political Economy of Culture: Capitalism and Communication in the Twenty-First Century*. Oxford: Rowman and Littlefield.

Murdock, G., Brevini, B. and Ward, M. (2025). *News Corp: Empire of Influence*. London: Routledge.

Nathanson, C. A. (1999) 'Social Movements as Catalysts for Policy Change: The Case of Smoking and Guns', *Journal of Health Politics and Law*, 24(3), pp. 421–88.

National Center for Education Statistics. (2018) *Education Expenditures by Country*. National Center for Education Statistics. Available at: https://nces.ed.gov/programs/coe/indicator_cmd.asp, ac

National Foundation for Educational Research (NFER). (2020) *Pupil Engagement in Remote Learning*. London: National Foundation for Educational Research. Available at: https://www.nfer.ac.uk/schools-responses-to-covid-19-pupil-engagement-in-remote-learning/ (Accessed: October 5 2023).

National Telecommunications and Information Administration (1995) *Falling through the Net I: A Survey of the 'have–Nots' in Rural and Urban America*. Washington. (Accessed: 4 March 2021).

National Telecommunications and Information Administration (1998) *Falling through the Net II: New Data on the Digital Divide*. Washington. Available at: https://www.ntia.doc.gov/report/1998/falling-through-net-ii-new-data-digital-divide (Accessed: 4 March 2021).

National Telecommunications and Information Administration (1999) *Falling through the Net III: Defining the Digital Divide*. Washington. https://www.ntia.gov/report/1999/falling-through-net-defining-digital-divide (Accessed: 4 March 2021).

National Telecommunications and Information Administration (2000) *Falling through the Net IV: Towards Digital Inclusion*. Washington. https://www.ntia.gov/report/2000/falling-through-net-toward-digital-inclusion (Accessed: 4 March 2021).

Neate, R. (2017) 'More Than a Million People Join Ranks of Very Wealthy after Stock Markets Boom', *The Guardian*, 28 September. Available at: https://www.theguardian.com/business/2017/sep/28/more-than-a-million-people-join-ranks-of-very-wealthy-after-stock-markets-boom

Neate, R. (2020) ''Billionaires' Worth Rises to $10.2 Trillion amid Covid Crisis', *The Guardian*, 7 October.(Accessed: 7 October 2020).

Neckel, S. (2020) 'The Refeudalization of Modern Capitalism', *Journal of Sociology*, 56(3), pp. 472–486.

Negrine, R. (2016) *Politics and the Mass Media in Britain.* (2nd. ed.). London: Routledge.

Negroponte, N. (1995) *Being Digital.* London: Hodder & Stoughton.

Neubauer, R. (2011) 'Manufacturing Junk: Think Tanks, Climate Denial, and Neoliberal Hegemony', *Australian Journal of Communication*, 38(3), pp. 65–88.

Nielsen, R. K. (2016) 'Introduction: The Uncertain Future of Local Journalism', in Nielsen, R. K. (ed.) *Local Journalism: The Decline of Newspapers and the Rise of Digital Media.* London and New York: I. B. Tauris, pp. 1–30.

Niranjan, A. (2023) 'Heatwave Last Summer Killed 61,000 People in Europe, Research Finds', *Guardian*, 10 July. Available at: https://www.theguardian.com/environment/2023/jul/10/heatwave-last-summer-killed-61000-people-in-europe-research-finds?CMP=Share_iOSApp_Other (Accessed: 10 July 2023).

Norstat (2019) *PR and Communications Census 2019.* Available at: https://www.prca.org.uk/sites/default/files/PRCA_PR_Census_2019_v9-8-pdf%20%285%29.pdf (Accessed: 3 November 2021).

O'Hara, K. and Stevens, D. (2006) *Inequality.Com: Power, Poverty and the Digital Divide.* Oxford: Oneworld Publications.

Obesity Health Alliance (2021) 'Unhealthy Food and Drink Marketing on TV and Online and Childhood Obesity: The Evidence',. Available at: https://obesityhealthalliance.org.uk/wp-content/uploads/2021/06/TV-and-digital-marketing-briefing-June21.pdf (Accessed: 4 August 2022).

OECD (2021) *Lobbying in the 21st Century: Transparency, Integrity and Access.* Available at: https://www.oecd-ilibrary.org/sites/c6d8eff8-en/1/3/1/index.html?itemId=/content/publication/c6d8eff8-en&_csp_=381daa981c42f6b279b070444f653f78&itemIGO=oecd&itemContentType=book (Accessed: 29 November 2022).

Ofcom (2020a) *Online Nation: 2020 Summary Report.* London. Available at: https://www.ofcom.org.uk/__data/assets/pdf_file/0028/196408/online-nation-2020-summary.pdf

Ofcom (2020b) *Covid-19 News and Information: Summary of Views about Misinformation.* London: Ofcom. Available at: https://www.ofcom.org.uk/__data/assets/pdf_file/0017/203318/covid-19-news-consumption-week-twenty-five-misinformation-deep-dive.pdf (Accessed: 11 June 2020).

Ofcom (2021a) *One in Three Video–Sharing Users Find Hate Speech.* Available at: https://www.ofcom.org.uk/about-ofcom/latest/features-and-news/one-in-three-video-sharing-users-find-hate-speech (Accessed: 20 September 2021).

Ofcom (2021b) *Affordability of Communications Services.* London. Available at: https://www.ofcom.org.uk/phones-telecoms-and-internet/information-for-industry/policy/affordability-of-communications-services (Accessed: 25 August 2021).

Ofcom (2021c) *News Consumption in the UK: 2021, Overview of Research Findings.* London: Ofcom.

Ofcom (2021d) *Online Nation: 2021 Report.* London: Ofcom. Available at: https://www.ofcom.org.uk/__data/assets/pdf_file/0028/196408/online-nation-2020-summary.pdf (Accessed: 2 February 2022).

Ofcom (2024) *Communications Affordability Tracker.* London: ofcom. Available at: https://www.ofcom.org.uk/research-and-data/multi-sector-research/affordability-tracker (Accessed: 27 February 2024).

Office for National Statistics (2019) *Internet Users, UK: 2019.* London. Available at: https://www.ons.gov.uk/businessindustryandtrade/itandinternetindustry/bulletins/internetusers/2019 (Accessed: 24 June 2020).

Office for National Statistics (2021a) *Household Income Inequality, UK: Financial Year Ending 2020.* London. Available at: https://www.ons.gov.uk/peoplepopulationandcommunity/personal andhouseholdfinances/incomeandwealth/bulletins/householdincomeinequalityfinancial/ financialyearending2020 (Accessed: 2 December 2021).

Office for National Statistics (2021b) *Average Household Income, UK: Financial Year 2020.* London. Available at: https://www.ons.gov.uk/peoplepopulationandcommunity/personaland householdfinances/incomeandwealth/bulletins/householddisposableincomeandinequality/ financialyear2020 (Accessed: November 5 2021).

Office for National Statistics (ONS) (2022) *Family Spending in the UK: April 2020 to March 2021.* London. Available at: https://www.ons.gov.uk/peoplepopulationandcommunity/personala ndhouseholdfinances/expenditure/bulletins/familyspendingintheuk/april2020tomarch2021 #family-spending-data (Accessed: 21 July 2022).

Open Secrets. (2024). *Lobbying Data Summary.* https://www.opensecrets.org/federal-lobbying (Accessed: 25 July 2024).

Oreskes, N. and Conway, E. M. (2012) *Merchants of Doubt: How a Handful of Scientists Obscured the Truth on Issues from Tobacco Smoke to Global Warming.* New York and London: Bloomsbury.

Oreskes, N. and Conway, E. M. (2023a) 'Out of Business', *RSA Journal*, (2), pp. 31–33.

Oreskes, N. and Conway, E. M. (2023b) *The Big Myth.* New York: Bloomsbury Publishing.

Overbeek, H. (ed.) (1992) *Restructuring Hegemony in the Global Political Economy.* London and New York: Routledge.

Oxfam (2023) *Survival of the Richest: How We Must Tax the Super–rich Now to Fight Inequality.* Oxford: Oxfam. Available at: https://www.oxfam.org/en/research/survival–richest (Accessed: 17 January 2023).

Oxfam (2024) *Inequality Inc.* Oxford: Oxfam. Available at: https://oxfamilibrary.openrepository. com/bitstream/handle/10546/621583/bp-inequality-inc-150124-summ-en.pdf;jsessionid= 23854B2D04EF4D494EB3CAEB737C373C?sequence=30 (Accessed: 15 January 2024).

Palattiyil, G., Sidhva, D., Derr, A. S. and Macgowan, M. (2021) 'Global Trends in Forced Migration: Policy, Practice and Research Imperatives for Social Work', *International Social Work*, 65(6), pp. 1111–1129.

Park, R. (1941) 'News and the Power of the Press', *American Journal of Sociology*, 47, pp. 1–11.

Parvin, P. (2022) 'Hidden in Plain Sight: How Lobby Organisations Undermine Democracy', in Bennett, M., Brouwer, H. and Claassen, R. (eds.) *Wealth and Power.* London: Routledge, pp. 229–251.

Paterson, L. L., Coffey-Glover, L. and Peplow, D. (2016). 'Negotiating Stance within Discourses of Class: Reactions to Benefits Street', *Discourse & Society*, 27(2), pp. 195–214.

Perry, M. (2002) 'The Jarrow Crusade's Return: The 'New Labour Party' of Jarrow and Ellen Wilkinson, MP', *Northern History*, 39(2), pp. 265–278.

Perry, M. (2005) *The Jarrow Crusade: Protest and Legend.* Sunderland: Sunderland University Press.

Peston, R. (2008) *Who Runs Britain: How the Super-rich Are Changing Our Lives.* London: Hodder & Stoughton.

Petersen, A. (2005). 'The Metaphors of Risk: Biotechnology in the News', *Health, Risk & Society*, 7(3), pp. 203–208.

Peterson, A., Wahlstrom, M. and Wennerhag, M. (2015) 'European Anti-Austerity Protests - Beyond "Old" and "New" Social Movements?' *Acta Sociologica*, 58(4), pp. 293–310.

Pettigrew, M., & MacLure, M. (1997). 'The press, public Knowledge and the Grant-Maintained Schools Policy,' *British Journal of Educational Studies*, 45(4), pp. 392–405. Accessed 16 July 2018

Pew Research Center (2021) *U.S. Newsroom Employment Has Fallen 26% since 2008*. Washington. Available at: https://www.pewresearch.org/fact-tank/2021/07/13/u-s-newsroom-employment-has-fallen-26-since-2008/ (Accessed: 3 November 2021).

Pfeffer, F. T. and Waitkus, N. (2021) 'Comparing Child Wealth Inequality across Countries', *The Russell Sage Foundation Journal of the Social Sciences*, 7(3), pp. 28–49.

Phillips, L. (1996). 'Rhetoric and the Spread of the Discourse of Thatcherism', *Discourse & Society*, 7(2), pp. 209–241.

Philo, G. (ed.) (1996) *Media and Mental Distress*. Harlow: Longman.

Pickard, T. (1982) *Jarrow March*. London: Allison & Busby.

Piketty, T. (2014) *Capital in the Twenty–First Century*. Cambridge, MA and London: Belknap Press of Harvard University Press.

Piketty, T. (2021) 'Brahmin Left versus Merchant Right: Rising Inequality and the Changing Structure of Political Conflict in France, the United States and the United Kingdon, 1948–2020', in Gethin, A., Martínez-Toledano, C. and Piketty, T. (eds.) *Political Cleavages and Social Inequalities: A Study of Fifty Democracies, 1948–2020*. Boston: Harvard University Press, pp. 85–135.

Ponsford, D. (2016) *Former Daily Editor Says up to 80 Per cent of UK Local Newspaper Journalism Jobs Have Gone since 2006*. Available at: http://www.pressgazette.co.uk/former-daily-editor-says-up-to-80-per-cent-of-uk-local-newspaper-journalism-jobs-have-gone-since-2006/ (Accessed: 17 January 2017).

Popiel, P. (2018) 'The Tech Lobby: Tracing the Contours of New Media Elite Lobbying Power', *Communication Culture & Critique*, 11(4), pp. 566–585.

Porter, A. (2010) 'David Cameron Warns Lobbying Is Next Political Scandal', Daily Telegraph, 8 February. Available at: http://www.telegraph.co.uk/news/election-2010/7189466/David-Cameron-warns-lobbying-is-next-political-scandal.html

PRCA (Public Relations and Communications Association) (2021) *PR and Communications Census 2021 | UK*. London: PRCA.

PRovoke Media (2019) *Global Top 250 PR Agency Ranking 2019*. Available at: https://www.provokemedia.com/ranking-and-data/global-pr-agency-rankings/2019-pr-agency-rankings/top-250 (Accessed: 3 November 2021).

Public Relations and Communications Association (2021) *PR and Communications Census 2021*. London: PRCA. Available at: https://news.prca.org.uk/pr-industry-showing-signs-of-strong-recovery-2021-prca-uk-census/ (Accessed: 14 April 2022).

Purdue, A. W. (1982a) 'Jarrow Politics, 1885–1914 – the Challenge to Liberal Hegemony', *Northern History*, 18, pp. 182–198.

Purdue, A. W. (1982b) 'The Myth of the Jarrow March', *New Society*, 61(1025), pp. 50–51.

Putnam, R. D. (2001) *Bowling Alone: The Collapse and Revival of American Community*. New York: Touchstone Books.

Puttnam, R. D. and Feldstein, L. M. (2003) *Better Together: Restoring the American Community*. New York: Simon and Schuster.

Quist, P. and Auble, D. (2022) *Layers of Lobbying: Federal and State Lobbying Trends in Spending, Representation and Messaging*. Washington, DC: Open Secrets. Available at: https://www.opensecrets.org/news/reports/layers-of-lobbying/ (Accessed: 22 July 2022).

Ragnedda, M. and Muschert, G. W. (eds.) (2018) *Theorizing Digital Divides*. Abingdon and New York: Routledge.

Ragnedda, M. (2017) *The Third Digital Divide: A Weberian Approach to Digital Inequalities*. London and New York: Routledge.

Ralph, A. and Wilson, H. (2017) 'Big Business Spends £25m on Lobbying Politicians,' *The Times*, 15 April 2017. Available at: https://www.thetimes.co.uk/article/big-business-spends-25m-on-lobbying-politicians-2b2bjsjmx (Accessed: 27 November 2022).

Rancière, J. (2004) *The Philosopher and His Poor*. Durham: Duke University Press.

Redden, J. (2014) *The Mediation of Poverty: The News, New Media, and Politics*. Boulder, CO: Rowman and Littlefield.

Reuters Institute (2021) *Reuters Institute Digital News Report 2021*. Reuters Institute. Available at: https://reutersinstitute.politics.ox.ac.uk/digital-news-report/2021 (Accessed: 16 August 2021).

Riesman, D. (1950) *The Lonely Crowd: A Study of the Changing American Character*. New Haven and London: Yale University Press.

Roach, C. (1997) 'The Western World and the NWICO: United they Stand?', in P. Golding and P. Harris (eds.), *Beyond Cultural Imperialism*. London: SAGE, pp. 94–116.

Robertson, J. W. (2010) 'The Last Days of Free Market Hegemony? UK TV News Coverage of Economic Issues in spring 2008', *Media, Culture & Society*, 32(3), pp. 517–529.

Robinson, J. P. and Martin, S. (2010) 'IT Use and Declining Social Capital? More Cold Water from the General Social Survey (GSS) and the American Time-Use Survey (ATUS),' *Social Science Computer review*, 28(1), pp. 45–63.

Robinson, L., Cotten, S. R., Ono, H., Quan–Haase, A., Mesch, G., Chen, W., Schulz, J., Hale, T. M. and Stern, M. J. (2015) 'Digital Inequalities and Why They Matter', *Information, Communication & Society*, 18(5), pp. 569–582.

Robinson, T. (2009) *Jeff Bezos: Amazon.Com Architect*. Minnesota: Abdo Publishing Company.

Roszak, T. (1988) *The Cult of Information: The Folklore of Computers and the True Art of Thinking*. London: Paladin.

Rowbotham, J., Stevenson, K. and Pegg, S. (2013) *Crime News in Modern Britain: Press Reporting and Responsibility, 1820–2010*. Basingstoke and New York: Palgrave Macmillan.

Royal Commission on the Press 1961-1962. (1962) *Report*. Cmd. 1811. London: Her Majesty's Stationery Office.

Royal Commission on the Press (1949) *Royal Commission on the Press 1947–1949*. Cmd. 7700. London: HMSO.

Rule, S. (1989) 'Reagan Gets a Red Carpet from British', *The New York Times*, June 14. Available at: https://www.nytimes.com/1989/06/14/world/reagan-gets-a-red-carpet-from-british.html

Runciman, W. G. (1966) *Relative Deprivation and Social Justice: A Study of Attitudes to Social Inequality in Twentieth–Century England*. London: Routledge and Kegan Paul.

Rushe, D. (2022) 'Tax the Rich: These One Percenters Want People like Them to Pay Higher Taxes', *The Guardian*, 8 April. Available at: https://www.theguardian.com/us-news/2022/apr/08/patriotic-millionaires-one-percenters-pay-higher-taxes (Accessed: 8 April 2022).

Rushkoff, D. (2016) *Throwing Rocks at the Google Bus*. New York: Portfolio/Penguin.

Russell, A. (2001) 'The Zapatistas Online', *Gazette*, 63(5), pp. 399–413.

Salem, S. (2015) 'Creating Spaces for Dissent: The Role of Social Media in the 2011 Egyptian Revolution', in Trottier, D. and Fuchs, C. (eds.) *Social Media, Politics and the State: Protests,*

Revolutions, Riots, Crime and Policing in the Age of Facebook, Twitter and YouTube. London: Routledge, pp. 171–188.

Sanz Sabido, R. and Price, S. (2017). 'Anti-Austerity Protests, Brexit and Britishness in the News', in T. Papaioannou and S. Gupta (eds.), *Media Representations of Anti-Austerity Protests in the EU.* London: Routledge, pp. 143–161.

Saunders, P. (1993) 'Citizenship in a Liberal Society', in B. S. Turner (ed.) *Citizenship and Social Theory.* London: SAGE, pp. 57–90.

Schifferes, S. and Roberts, R. (eds.) (2015) *The Media and Financial Crisis: Comparative and Historical Perspectives.* London and New York: Routledge.

Schiffrin, A. (2015) 'The Press and the Financial Crisis: A Review of the Literature', *Sociology Compass*, 9(8), pp. 639–653.

Schiller, H. I. (1996) *Information Inequality: The Deepening Social Crisis in America.* New York and London: Routledge.

Schiller, D. (1999) *Information Capitalism.* Cambridge, MA: MIT Press.

Schmitt-Beck, R. (2022) 'Prerequisites of Deliberative Democracy: Inclusivity, Publicity, and Heterogeneity of German Citizens' Everyday Political Talk', *Studies in Communication and Media*, 11(1), pp. 7–72.

Schudson, M. (1996) 'The Informed Citizen in Historical Context', *Research in the Teaching of English*, 30(3), pp. 361–369.

Schütz, A. (1946) 'The Well–Informed Citizen: An Essay on the Social Distribution of Knowledge', *Social Research*, 13(4), pp. 463–478.

Seale, C. (2002) *Media & Health.* London: SAGE.

Sevignani, S. (2022) 'Digital Transformations and the Ideological Formation of the Public Sphere: Hegemonic, Populist or Popular Communication?', *Theory, Culture & Society*, 39(4), pp. 91–109.

Shahbaz, A. and Funk, A. (2021) *Freedom on the Net 2021.* Washington: House, F. Available at: https://freedomhouse.org/sites/default/files/2021–09/FOTN_2021_Complete_Booklet_09162 021_FINAL_UPDATED.pdf (Accessed: 14 October 2021).

Shahin, S., Zheng, P., Sturm, H. A. and Fadnis, D. (2016) 'Protesting the Paradigm: A Comparative Study of News Coverage of Protests in Brazil, China, and India', *International Journal of Press/Politics*, 21(2), pp. 143–164.

Sharma, R. (2021) '*The Billionaire Boom: How the Super–rich Soaked up Covid Cash*', Financial Times, May 14. Available at: https://www.ft.com/content/747a76dd-f018-4d0d-a9f3-4069bf2f5a93 (Accessed: 16 March 2022).

Sharman, D. (2018) 'UK Journalist Numbers Increase – But Experts Warn Industry Becoming "Londoncentric"', *Hold The Front Page*, 31 October 2018. Available at: https://www.holdthe frontpage.co.uk/2018/news/uk-journalist-numbers-increase-but-experts-warn-industry-beco ming-londoncentric/ (Accessed: 6 October 2022).

Shaxson, N. (2015) *Why Google Is Paying Just 2% Tax Rate in the UK.* London: Network, T. J. Available at: https://taxjustice.net/reports/why-google-is-paying-just-2-tax-rate-in-the-uk/ (Accessed: 6 October 2021).

Shrubsole, G. (2019) *Who Owns England?: How We Lost Our Green and Pleasant Land, and How to Take it Back.* London: William Collins.

Signorelli, N. (1993). *Mass Media Images and Impact on Health.* Westport, CN: Greenwood Press.

Simpson, F. (2020) 'Government Laptop Scheme A 'National Scandal' as 68,000 Devices Still Not Delivered', *Children and Young People Now,*. Available at: https://www.cypnow.co.uk/news/article/government-laptop-scheme-a-national-scandal-as-68-000-devices-still-not-delivered (Accessed: 17 June 2020).

Smith, D. C. (2002). 'Overcoming the Digital Divide', *Peace & Policy*, 7, pp. 40–43.

Smith, B. (2021) *Tools and Weapons: The Promise and the Peril of the Digital Age*. London: Hodder & Stoughton.

Solijonov, A. (2016) *Voter Turnout Trends Around the World*. International Institute for Democracy and Electoral Assistance. Available at: https://www.agora-parl.org/sites/default/files/voter-turnout-trends-around-the-world_0.pdf (Accessed: 16 August 2017).

Splichal, S. (2002) 'Rethinking Publicness: The Precedence of the Right to Communicate', *Javnost – The Public*, 9(3), pp. 83–105.

Srnicek, N. (2017) *Platform Capitalism*. Cambridge: Polity Press.

Staab, P. and Thiel, T. (2022) 'Social Media and the Digital Structural Transformation of the Public Sphere', *Theory, Culture & Society*, 39(4), pp. 129–143.

Standage, T. (1998) *The Victorial Internet*. London: Weidenfeld and Nicolson.

Starkman, D. (2015) *The Watchdog that Didn't Bark: The Financial Crisis and the Disappearance of Investigative Journalism*. New York and Chichester: Columbia University Press.

Statista (2017) 'Distribution of Advertising Spending in the United States from 2010 to 2020, by Media',. Available at: https://www.statista.com/statistics/272316/advertising-spending-share-in-the-us-by-media/ (Accessed: 9 August 2017).

Statista (2021) 'Facebook – Statistics & Facts'. Available at: https://www.statista.com/topics/751/facebook/ (Accessed: 7 October 2021).

Statista (2022a) *Leading Lobbying Industries in the United States in 2021, by Total Lobbying Spending*. Wsahington. Available at: https://www.statista.com/statistics/257364/top-lobbying-industries-in-the-us/ (Accessed: 24 November 2022).

Statista (2022b) *Total Lobbying Spending in the United States from 1998 to 2021*. Washington. Available at: https://www.statista.com/statistics/257337/total-lobbying-spending-in-the-us/ (Accessed: 24 November 2022).

Stiglitz, J. E. (2013) *The Price of Inequality*. London: Penguin.

Stiglitz, J. E. (2017) 'Towards a Taxonomy of Media Capture', in Schiffrin, A. (ed.) *In the Service of Power: Media Capture and the Threat to Democracy*. Washington: National Endowment for Democracy, pp. 9–17.

Stoll, C. (1995) *Silicon Snake Oil*. London: Macmillan.

Stone, B. (2013) *The Everything Store: Jeff Bezos and the Age of Amazon*. London: Transworld Digital.

Stone, E. (2021) *Digital Exclusion & Health Inequalities*. London: Good Things Foundation. Available at: https://www.goodthingsfoundation.org/insights/digital-exclusion-and-health-inequalities/ (Accessed: 27 August 2021).

Strassheim, J. (2023) 'Neo-liberalism and Post-truth: Expertise and the Market Model', *Theory, Culture & Society*, 40(6), pp. 107–124.

Streeck, W. (2016) *How Will Capitalism End?* London and New York: Verso.

Strover, S., Whitacre, B., Rhinesmith, C. and Schrubbe, A. (2020) 'The Digital Inclusion Role of Rural Libraries: Social Inequalities through Space and Place', *Media, Culture & Society*, 42(2), pp. 242–259.

Sussman, G. (1997) *Communication, Technology, and Politics in the Information Age.* Thousand Oaks, CA: SAGE.

Sutton Trust (2020) *Written Evidence to House of Commons Select Committe Inquiry into Impact of Covid-19.* London. Available at: https://committees.parliament.uk/writtenevidence/6379/pdf/ (Accessed: 18 June 2020).

Syvertsen, T. (2017). *Media Resistance – Protest, Dislike, Abstention.* Cham, Switzerland: Palgrave Macmillan.

Syvertsen, T. (2020) *Digital Detox: The Politics of Disconnecting.* Bingley: Emerald Publishing.

Tan, H. (2022) 'It's Not Just Jeff Bezos. Super Rich Around the World Are Snapping up Superyachts as Sales Hit a Record High Last Year', Business Insider. Available at: https://www.businessinsider.com/super-rich-snapping-up-superyachts-sales-up-80-percent-2022-2?r=US&IR=T (Accessed: 10 February 2022).

Tang, P. and Bussink, H. (2017) *EU Tax Revenue Loss from Google and Facebook.* Brussels. Available at: https://static.financieel–management.nl/documents/16690/EU–Tax–Revenue–Loss–from–Google–and–Facebook.pdf (Accessed: 7 October 2016).

Taverne, D. (2005) *The March of Unreason: Science, Democracy, and the New Fundamentalism.* Oxford: Oxford University Press.

Teach First (2021) '*Over a Third of Parents Have Children with No Exclusive Use of a Device to Work from Home*'. Available at: https://www.teachfirst.org.uk/press-release/ongoing-digital-divide (Accessed: 10 June 2021).

Therborn, G. (2021) Inequality and Democracy. *New Left Review* (129), pp. 5–26.

Thompson, D. (2008) *Counterknowledge: How We Surrendered to Conspiracy Theories, Quack Medicine, Bogus Science and Fake History.* London: Atlantic Books.

Thornham, H. and Gómez Cruz, E. (2016) '[Im]mobility in the Age of [im]mobile Phones: Young NEETs and Digital Practices', *New Media & Society*, 19(11), pp. 1794–1809.

Tippet, B. and Wildauer, R. (2023) *The Good Life at the Top: Analysing the Sunday Times Rich List 1989–2023.* London: University of Greenwich. Available at: https://gala.gre.ac.uk/id/eprint/42714/9/42714_TIPPET_The_good_life_at_the_top.pdf (Accessed: 11 June 2023).

Tobitt, C. (2020) '*UK Local Newspaper Closures: At Least 265 Titles Gone since 2005, but Pace of Decline Has Slowed*', PressGazette, 20 August. Available at: https://www.pressgazette.co.uk/uk-local-newspaper-closures-at-least-265-local-newspaper-titles-gone-since-2005-but-pace-of-decline-has-slowed/ (Accessed: 2 November 2020).

Toporowski, J. (1996) Beyond Banking: Financial Institutions and the Poor. In P. Golding (ed.) *Excluding the Poor* (pp. 55–69). London: Child Poverty Action Group.

Townsend, P. (1979) *Poverty in the United Kingdom.* Harmondsworth: Penguin Books.

Trades Union Congress. (2020) *Challenging Amazon Report: What can We Do about Amazon's Treatment of Its Workers?* London: Trades Union Congress Available at: https://www.tuc.org.uk/sites/default/files/2020-10/Challenging%20Amazon%20%28final%29.pdf (Accessed: 11 October 2021).

Transparency International UK (2015) *Accountable Influence: Bringing Lobbying Out of the Shadows.* London. Available at: https://www.transparency.org.uk/sites/default/files/pdf/publications/Accountable_Influence_Bringing_Lobbying_out_of_the_Shadows.pdf (Accessed: 24 November 2022).

Trappel, J. (2019a) 'Inequality, (New) Media and Communications', in Trappel, J. (ed.) *Digital Media Inequalities: Policies against Divides, Distrust and Discrimination.* Gothenburg: Nordicom, pp. 9–30.

Trappel, J. (ed.) (2019b) *Digital Media Inequalities: Policies against Divides, Distrust and Discrimination*. Gothenburg: Nordicom.

Treré, E., Natale, S., Keightley, E. and Punethambekar, A. (2020) 'The Limits and Boundaries of Digital Disconnection', *Media, Culture & Society*, 42(4), pp. 605–609.

Trivundza, I. T. and Brlek, S. S. (2017) 'Looking for Mr Hyde: The protest paradigm, violence and (de) legitimation of mass political protests', *International Journal of Media and Cultural Politics*, 13(1–2), pp. 131–148.

Trottier, D. and Fuchs, C. (eds.) (2015) *Social Media, Politics and the State. Protests, Revolutions, Riots, Crime and Policing in the Age of Facebook, Twitter and YouTube*. New York: Routledge.

Tully, J. (2009). 'A Victorian Ecological Disaster: Imperialism, the Telegraph, and Gutta-Percha', *Journal of World History*, 20(4), pp. 559–579.

Turkle, S. (2012) *Alone Together: Why We Expect More from Technology and Less from Each Other*. New York: Basic Books.

Turner, B. S. (ed.) (1993) *Citizenship and Social Theory*. London: Sage Publications.

U.S. Census Bureau (2023) *Current Population Survey, 2022 and 2023*. Washington. Available at: https://www.census.gov/content/dam/Census/library/visualizations/2022/demo/p60–276/figure3.pdf (Accessed: 15 March 2024).

UBS Global Family Office (2020) *Riding the Storm*. Zurich. Available at: https://www.ubs.com/content/dam/static/noindex/wealth-management/ubs-billionaires-report-2020-spread.pdf

UN Dept. of Economic and Social Affairs. (2023). *Leaving No One Behind in an Ageing World: World Social Report 2023*. New York: United Nations. Available at: https://www.un.org/development/desa/dspd/world-social-report/2023-2.html (Accessed: 4 July 2023).

UNHCR United Nations Refugee Agency (2023) *Global Trends Report 2022*. Geneva: UNHCR.Available at: https://www.unhcr.org/global-trends-report-2022 (Accessed: 15 June 2023).

United Nations (2016) *The Promotion, Protection and Enjoyment of Human Rights on the Internet (Oral Revisions)*. Geneva: UN. Available at: https://digitallibrary.un.org/record/731540 (Accessed: 8 November 2019).

United Nations (2022) *Guterres to Security Council: Access to Information a Human Right*. Available at: https://www.un.org/en/delegate/guterres-security-council-access-information-human-right#:~:text=Access%20to%20information%20is%20a%20human%20right%2C%20Secretary-General,death%2C%20and%20the%20difference%20between%20peace%20and%20war%E2%80%9D. (Accessed: 4 March 2024).

Uppal, C., Sartoretto, P. and Cheruiyet, D. (2019) 'The Case for Communication Rights: A Rights–Based Approach to Media Development', *Global Media and Communication*, 15(3), pp. 323–343.

Van Biezen, I., Mair, P. and Poguntke, T. (2012) 'Going, going, …Gone? The Decline of Party Membership in Contemporary Europe', *European Journal of Political Research*, 51(1), pp. 24–56.

Van Deursen, A. and Van Dijk, J. (2019) 'The First–Level Digital Divide Shifts from Inequalities in Physical Access to Inequalities in Material Access', *New Media & Society*, 21(2), pp. 354–375.

Van Dijck, J. (2013) *The Culture of Connectivity: A Critical History of Social Media*. Oxford: Oxford University Press.

Van Dijck, J. (2019) 'Governing Digital Societies: Private Platforms, Public Values', *Computer Law & Security Report*, 36.

Van Dijk, J. A. G. M. (2005) *The Deepening Divide: Inequality in the Information Society*. London: SAGE.

Verstraeten, H. (1996) 'The Media and the Transformation of the Public Sphere: A Contribution for a Critical Political Economy of the Public Sphere', *European Journal of Communication*, 11(3), pp. 347–.

Vogels, E. A. (2021) *Digital Divide Persists Even as Americans with Lower Incomes Make Gains in Tech Adoption*. Available at: https://www.pewresearch.org/short-reads/2021/06/22/digital-divide-persists-even-as-americans-with-lower-incomes-make-gains-in-tech-adoption/#:~:text=Abo ut%20four-in-ten%20adults%20with%20lower%20incomes%20do%20not,in%20househo lds%20earning%20%24100%2C000%20or%20more%20a%20year (Accessed: 16 March 2023).

Vogels, E. A. (2021) *The Extent of the U.S. Digital Divide in 2 Charts*. Available at: https://www. weforum.org/agenda/2021/06/digital-divide-persists-even-as-americans-with-lower-incomes-make-gains-in-tech-adoption/ (Accessed: 27 February 2024).

Wall Street Journal Staff (2021) 'Five Tech Giants Just Keep Growing', *Wall Street Journal*, 1 May. Available at: https://www.wsj.com/articles/five-tech-giants-just-keep-growing-11619841644 (Accessed: 11 October 2021).

Wall Street Journal (2021) 'The Facebook Files', *Wall Street Journal*, 6 October. Available at: https://www.wsj.com/articles/the–facebook–files–11631713039 (Accessed: 6 October 2021).

Wallace, J. and Erickson, J. (1993) *Hard Drive: Bill Gates and the Making of the Microsoft Empire*. New York: Harperbusiness.

Wallach, O. (2020) 'How Big Tech Makes Their Billions', *Visual Capitalist,*. Available at: https:// www.visualcapitalist.com/how-big-tech-makes-their-billions-2020/ (Accessed: 6 October 2021).

Wallach, O. (2021) 'The World's Tech Giants, Compared to the Size of Economies', *Visual Capitalist,*. Available at: https://www.visualcapitalist.com/the-tech-giants-worth-compared-economies-countries/ (Accessed: 27 September 2021).

Warburton, T. and Saunders, M. (1996) 'Representing Teachers' Professional Culture through Cartoons. *British Journal of Educational Studies*, 44(3), pp. 307–325.

Warf, B. (2010) 'The Digital Divide in the U.S. In the 21st Century', in Ferro, E. (ed.) *Handbook of Research on Overcoming Digital Divides Constructing an Equitable and Competitive Information Society*. Hershey, PA: IGI Global, pp. 112–130.

Waterson, J. (2020) 'One in Six Jobs to Go as BBC Cuts 450 Staff from Regional Programmes', *The Guardian*, 2 July. Available at: https://www.theguardian.com/media/2020/jul/02/local-tv-stars-to-go-as-bbc-cuts-450-staff-from-regional-programmes

Watts, G. (2022) 'COVID–19 and the Digital Divide in the UK', *Lancet Digital Health*, 2(8), pp. e395–396.

Weaver, D. A. and Scacco, J. M. (2013) 'Revisiting the Protest Paradigm: The Tea Party as Filtered through PrimeTime Cable News', *International Journal of Press/Politics*, 18(1), pp. 61–84.

Weiss-Blatt, N. (2021). *The Techlash and Tech Crisis Communication*. Bingley, UK: Emerald Publishing.

Wellcome Foundation. (2019) *Wellcome Global Monitor 2018*. London: Wellcome Foundation Available at: https://wellcome.ac.uk/reports/wellcome-global-monitor/2018 (Accessed: 19 June 2019).

Wheen, F. (2004) *How Mumbo–Jumbo Conquered the World*. London: Harper Perennial.

Wilhelm, A. G. (2000) *Democracy in the Digital Age: Challenges to Political Life in Cyberspace*. New York: Routledge.

Wilkins, L. (1964) *Social Deviance: Social Policy, Action and Research*. London: Tavistock.

Wilkinson, R. and Pickett, K. (2010) *The Spirit Level: Why Equality Is Better for Everyone*. Harmondsworth: Penguin.

Wilkinson, E. (1939) *The Town that Was Murdered: The Life Story of Jarrow*. London: Victor Gollancz.

Williams, G. (1998) 'Digital Dystopia', *Index on Censorship*, 4, pp. 186–192.

Wills, D. and Reeves, S. (2009) 'Facebook as a Political Weapon: Information in Social Networks', *British Politics*, 4(2), pp. 265–281.

Winseck, D. R. and Pike, R. M. (2007) *Communication and Empire: Media, Markets, and Globalization, 1860–1930*. Durham, NC: Duke University Press.

Winslow, L. (2017) '"Not exactly a Model of Good Hygiene": Theorizing an Aesthetic of Disgust in the Occupy Wall Street Movement', *Critical Studies in Media Communication*, 34(3), pp. 278–292.

Witte, J. C. and Mannon, S. E. (2010) *The Internet and Social Inequalities*. New York and Abingdon: Routledge.

Wolf, M. (2023) *The Crisis of Democratic Capitalism*. London: Allen Lane.

Wolfsfeld, G., Segev, E. and Sheafer, T. (2013) 'Social Media and the Arab Spring: Politics Comes First', *International Journal of Press/Politics*, 182(115–137).

Woodhouse, J. (2021) *Regulating Online Harms*. HC Library Report No. 8743. London: Library, H. o. C. Available at: https://researchbriefings.files.parliament.uk/documents/CBP-8743/CBP-8743.pdf (Accessed: 1 October 2021).

World Economic Forum (2022) *Household Income Distribution in the U.S. Washington*. Available at: https://www.weforum.org/agenda/2022/07/household-income-distribution-wealth-inequality-united-states/ (Accessed: 6 July 2023).

World Economic Forum (2024) *Edison Alliance – Impact Report*. Available at: https://www3.weforum.org/docs/WEF_EDISON_Alliance_Impact_Report_2024.pdf (Accessed: 5 March 2024).

World Health Organisation (2024) *Commercial Determinants of Noncommunicable Diseases in the WHO European Region*. Available at: https://www.who.int/europe/publications/i/item/9789289061162 (Accessed: 3 July 2024).

Xu, X. (2022) *Return of Bumper Pay Growth in Finance Fuels New Rise in Earnings Inequality*. Available at: https://ifs.org.uk/publications/16042 (Accessed: 4 May 2022).

Zelizer, B. (2018) 'Resetting Journalism in the Aftermath of Brexit and Trump', *European Journal of Communication*, 33(2), pp. 140–156.

Zillien, N. and Hargittai, E. (2009) 'Digital Distinction: Status–Specific Types of Internet Usage', *Social Science Quarterly*, 90(2), pp. 274–291.

Zittrain, J. (2008) *The Future of the Internet and How to Stop It*. London: Allen Lane.

Zuboff, S. (2019) *The Age of Surveillance Capitalism*. London: Profile Books.

Index